The

NEW

TEACHER'S

Almanack

A Complete Guide to Every Day of the School Year

Recipes • Games • Remarkable Tales • Riddles • Experiments

100s of UNIQUE IDEAS

and Suggestions of a most Practical Nature For the TEACHER

By Dara Newmarr

THE <u>NEW</u> TEACHER'S ALMANACK
Practical Ideas for Every Day
of the School Year

Dana Newmann

The Center for Applied Research in Education, Inc.

West Nyack, New York   10994

Many of the small woodcut illustrations within
are reproductions from the fine Dover Press
Pictorial Archives Series. This copyright-free
material comes primarily from *1800 Woodcuts by
Thomas Berwick and His School*, edited by Blanche
Cirker, 1962.

About the Author

A graduate of Mills College in Oakland, California, Dana Newmann has been an elementary teacher and reading specialist for more than 15 years. Her experience includes teaching in the public schools of Monterey and Carmel, California, and with the U.S. Army Dependents Group in Hanau, West Germany. In addition, she has served as the Reading Specialist for the New Mexico State Department of Education.

Ms. Newmann has also authored two other practical aids for teachers: *Individual Discovery Activity Cards* (The Center, 1974-75) and *The Teacher's Desk Companion* (Macmillan, 1979).

Ms. Newmann lives in Santa Fe, New Mexico, with her husband and daughter. She presently teaches at Little Earth School in Santa Fe.

a word of introduction

The original `Teacher's Almanack' has been called `The Fanny Farmer' of the classroom. I hope this new edition will prove to be just as helpful to you. Its format remains the same: historical notes and lively ideas for each of your teaching days!

This new edition is a direct descendant of Poor Richard's Almanac. Practicality is emphasized. I've tried to make `The New Teacher's Almanac' informative and provocative. There are lots of unusual scientific facts, word etymologies and historical anecdotes. Supplemental riddles and complete copy to facilitate construction of meaningful bulletin boards are often included. At the back of the book are recipes for art supplies and classroom cooking — a different recipe for each week of the school year! Your students can make beef jerky, hot cross buns, cottage cheese or George Washington's favorite cake! Metric measurement equivalents are included. What a natural and enjoyable way to learn geography, math — and good nutrition!

Kids love to write letters and get materials and ~~ers in response. In this new edition you'll find some 150 addresses each of which I have personally contacted. (Of course, with time, some of these addresses could change. You may want to send an advance post-card to an address to be certain of its validity before giving it to a student to use. It's an idea.)

In 'The New Teacher's Almanack' I've included biographic material on many women and men who are historical figures. I have used a controlled vocabulary when writing these biographies so that they may be read aloud to your class to help in the practice of listening skills, or you can duplicate them for the students to read individually.

I hope you'll find this 'New Teacher's Almanac' as much fun to use as I've had in compiling it. And I'd wish that the following pages help the 1980s to be the most rewarding decade of teaching that you've ever had!

Dana Newmann

Early almanacs were always slightly unpolished. You were conscious of the fact that they were hand made. Well, 'The Teacher's Almanack' was also written and printed by fallible humans and so if you use the original 'Almanack,' please note the following: Page 34 Leaf Skeleton instructions do not work as stated. Delete these four paragraphs. (Thanks to Mrs. Susan M. Sheffert of Normal, Illinois.)

Page 66 Wet Chalk Drawings measurements should read. 1/8 cup sugar to each cup of water.

Page 99 Hanukkah Cookies require these ingredients: 3/4 cup butter, 1 cup sugar, 2 eggs, 2 1/2 cups flour, 1 tsp. baking powder, 2 tsp. vanilla, pinch of salt.

Page 131, second paragraph, should read: (see page 17).

Page 267 Delete asbestos as a modeling material as asbestos particles have been found hazardous to health.

I deeply regret any inconvenience that you may have experienced as a consequence of these errors.

D.N.

The person who makes no mistakes does not usually make anything... EJ Phelps

Table of Contents

Katowes Cake, Sesame-Seed Candies; Christmas music featuring orchestral instruments; holiday bulletin board; Christmas customs in 20 countries; Christmas room environment: stained glass window, pine cone wreath; Christmas reading suggestions; a listening activity with geometric shapes; Christmas art: easy star, paper snowmen, metallic balls, pasta snowflakes and stars, braided wreath; Advent calendars; quick n' easy gifts, gift wrapping ideas, and cards; December phys ed: Santa's pack, candy cane relay race; holiday parties.

January   162

Calendar of important dates; etymology and quotations; information and activities related to:

How to make a set of tangrams; calendar game; making an engraving in the classroom; how to make and play "Doublets"; individual inventory; non-competitive games; 110 riddles plus 24 "hard" ones; how to grow 28 common plants from seed; art: printmaking, rubbings, monoprints, linoleum block prints, felt-block printing, silkscreen prints; six quick games; recipe for snow ice cream.

February   195

Calendar of important dates; etymology and quotations; information and activities related to:

How to make a barometer; weather riddles; Valentine's bulletin boards; Valentine crossword puzzle; Valentine cards and party suggestions; codes and how to crack them; language arts activities: letter to the teacher, writing haiku, spelling; math memory questions; focus on the world's endangered species; parts of the orchestra; bubble-blowing; exploring geometric shapes; recipe for Hamentaschen.

class time capsule; environmental bulletin board; Attributes, a review game; writing activity featuring pets; how to trap and raise insects in the classroom; developing a Creative Corner.

June 320

Calendar of important dates; etymology and quotations; information and activities related to:

World Environment Day (327) • Freedom of the Press Day (328) • Birth of Jeanette Rankin (329) • Flag Day (320) • Father's Day (331) • Summer Solstice (332) • Birth of Anne Morrow Lindbergh (332) • Birth of Helen Keller (333)

Guidelines for the last weeks of school; activities with newspapers; bulletin board lettering suggestions; game of Presidents; wheel-of-fortune reading activity; how to set up a summer reading club; raising tadpoles in the classroom; directions for drying fruit; helpful hints for getting ready for NEXT Year!

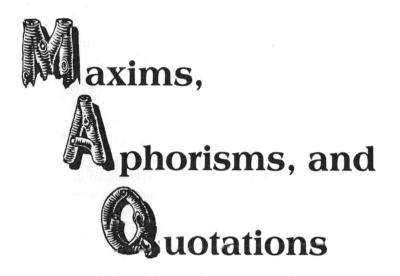

Maxims, Aphorisms, and Quotations

Relating to Teaching

The art of teaching is the art of assisting discovery.
—*Mark van Doren*

Wisdom is meaningless until your own experience has given it meaning.—*Bergen Evans*

Before beginning, prepare carefully.—*Cicero*

There are only two lasting bequests we can hope to give our children. One of these is roots; the other, wings.—*Hodding Carter*

The object of education is to prepare the young to educate themselves throughout their lives.—*Robert Hutchins*

Why in the world are salaries higher for administrators when the basic mission is teaching?—*Gov. Jerry Brown*

The first idea that the child must acquire, in order to be actively disciplined, is that of the difference between good and evil; and the task of the educator lies in seeing that the child does not confound good with immobility, and evil with activity . . . our aim is to discipline for activity, for work, for good; not for immobility, not for passivity, not for obedience.—*Maria Montessori*

I respect faith, but doubt is what gets you an education.
                                                        —*Wilson Mizner*

Native ability without education is a tree without fruit.
                                                        —*Aristippus*

I asked myself what I could do to make the day good for children and for myself. And my answer was: Look at the pressures which distort your life and do something positive about them.—*Anonymous educator*

In teaching it is the method and not the content that is the message—the drawing out, not the pumping in.—*Ashley Montagu*

I hear and I forget.
I see and I remember.
I do and I understand.
      —*Chinese proverb*

Children need love, especially when they do not deserve it.
                                                        —*Harold S. Hulbert*

If I can stop one heart from breaking, I shall not live in vain.
                                                        —*Emily Dickinson*

There is a destiny that makes us brothers, none goes his way alone. All that we send into the lives of others comes back into our own.
                                                        —*Edwin Markham*

Small opportunities are often the beginning of great enterprises.
—*Demosthenes*

If I try to be like him, who will be like me?—*Yiddish proverb*

We are all here for a spell, get all the good laughs you can.
—*Will Rogers*

Our plans miscarry because they have no aim. When a man does not know what harbor he is making for, no wind is the right wind.
—*Seneca*

There are three things extreamly hard: Steel, and a Diamond, and to Know Oneself.—*Olde English proverb*

When the well's dry, we know the worth of water.
—*Spanish proverb*

To be wronged is nothing unless you continue to remember it.
—*Confucius*

Forgiveness is the key to action and freedom.—*Hannah Arendt*

Remember, happiness doesn't depend upon who you are or what you have, it depends solely upon what you think—*Dale Carnegie*

Seven wealthy towns contend for Homer dead
Thro' which the living Homer begg'd his bread.
—*Greek*

Happy is he who knows the reasons for things.—*Virgil*

If not now, when?
If not by me, by whom?
—*The Talmud*

With money in your pocket you are wise and you are handsome and you sing well, too.—*Polish proverb*

Dwarves on the shoulders of giants see farther than the giants. themselves.—*Stella Didacus*

"The wisdom of nations lies in their proverbs which are brief and pithy. Collect and learn them. You have much in little; they save time speaking; and upon occasion may be the fullest and safest answers."

(Edifying quotations appear throughout The Teacher's Almanack. Any of these which are appropriate for your class can be clearly printed on

*large rectangles of paper or card stock and posted about the room. Fre-
quent changes will be especially effective in keeping the children's attention and interest.)*

A Very Short History of the Calendar
(including a description of the major Jewish holidays)

> *Thirty dayes hath November
> April, June, and September,
> February hath xxviii alone,
> And all the rest have xxxi.*
> —*Richard Grafton: 1562*

Early man kept track of time by counting the suns and darknesses,
by tying knots in ropes, making notches on sticks and, eventually, by
noticing the changes in the positions of the sun, moon and stars.

Most of the holidays are in some way related to divisions of time—
especially to the seasons. Primitive man celebrated the beginning of
each of the four seasons; those early holidays exist today in differing
forms throughout the world.

The Babylonians made the first calendar and based it on the moon,
counting twelve lunar months to a year. An extra month was added
about every four years to keep the seasons straight. The Greek, Semitic
and Egyptian peoples adopted the Babylonian calendar. Later the
Egyptians created a calendar that more nearly matched the seasons.
This lunar calendar is used today by the Mohammedans and the Jews.

Therefore, the exact dates of the Jewish holidays vary from year to
year. The Jewish calendar reckons from the year 3761 B.C., which is
traditionally given as the date of the Creation. (Although most of the
world now operates on a Gregorian calendar, which is a solar one, the
lunar calendar is still of some contemporary significance. Your Jewish
students celebrate holidays based on it.) The Jewish holidays include:
Rosh Hashana, Yom Kippur, Sukkoth, Hanukkah, Purim, Pesach and
Shabuoth. Each is noted in this book as it occurs during the school year.

In 46 B.C. Julius Caesar ordered a new calendar developed. This
Roman calendar made use of the Egyptian year and encompassed
365-1/4 days, every fourth year having 366 days. There were twelve
months in this calendar; Augustus and Julius Caesar each named one for
himself, each taking a day from February, making August and July
months having 31 days. (A complete historical description precedes
each month as it is covered in the almanack.)

In 1582, Pope Gregory XIII requested that the error in the old calendar be corrected; the resulting Leap Year system is still in use today. The Gregorian calendar also made January first New Year's Day.

English-speaking countries began using the Gregorian calendar in 1752 and moved the calendar up eleven days. China adopted this calendar in 1912, as Russia did in 1914, and it is the standard in use throughout the world today.

Calendars for the Classroom

Lower grades. Stretch white oilcloth over a two-foot-square piece of lightweight wood. Screw 35 hooks into the board through the oilcloth as shown below. Each month, use rubber cement to affix cut-out paper letters in an appropriate color to the oilcloth at the top of the calendar. Keep 31 tagboard cards, each bearing a large, clear number, at the side of the calendar. Place the calendar upright in the chalk tray of the chalkboard, and each morning, hang the card bearing that day's date on the appropriate hook.

Middle and upper grades. A big bright pocket calendar is made from felt. The detachable pockets with glued-on numerals can hold classroom reminders, an activity announcement, children's letters to the teacher, science notes or riddles of the day. The pockets are attached by metal snaps or Velcro strips and can be rearranged each month. This is also true of the felt letters that spell out the name of the month.

When presenting background information on each holiday, care should be taken to clearly distinguish between historic and legendary material. (Can the children?) It may be pointed out to the class that holi-

days are observed for specific reasons: to preserve a tradition, to mark a patriotic or religious event. (Can the children think of any other reasons?)

The use of holiday themes should not dominate a teaching program to the exclusion of other meaningful themes.

Be discriminating in your choice of the projects suggested here. Next year you can always try those projects which you were unable to fit into this year's schedule.

Allow the children to interpret these projects. In fact, different approaches to the same project should be encouraged whenever practical. Many times the children's variations will afford learning experiences that are especially fruitful.

Creating a Student-Designed Classroom

A youth who had begun to read geometry with Euclid, when he had learned the first proposition, inquired, "What do I get by learning these things?" So Euclid called a slave and said, "Give him threepence, since he must make a gain out of what he learns."
—*Euclid of Alexandria (ca. 4th century B.C.)*

Norman Douglas, English novelist, said, "If you want to see what children can do, you must stop giving them things." Why not provide your class with the construction materials° and see what kind of class-room environment *they* can create, what kind of answers *they* can devise.

First ask them, as a group, to come up with suggestions for kinds of work areas they'd like to have in their room; construction, quiet reading, science laboratory, art, hobby displays, whatever. These will, of course, vary with class-level and student interests. Then have each student sign up for work on the area which most interests her/him. These smaller groups will plan the area, decide what it needs, assign the units (cub-byholes, shelves, seating, supply shelves) to fill the needs of that area. Once the area design is completed, the students will then see how they can use the materials you have to offer and what materials (these are often most exciting) *they* may be able to scrounge at their homes or in their neighborhoods.

This is the kind of group-goal activity that keeps the classroom from becoming fragmented into 32 students working at 32 levels, some students ten stations behind the others. And it also is a legitimate learning exercise that really makes the classroom their territory, their "home" room.

Some Activities to Develop Creativity

1. *Looking at things in a new way.* Bring a few simple objects to class. Ask the children to imagine something else that resembles each object. There are no wrong answers, only mind-stretching fun. Then ask the students to think up some new, unusual use for each of the objects. Finally, reverse the approach and have a child describe how a common object (unnamed) might look to a person from another planet. Let the other kids suggest different objects that he/she may be thinking of.

°Here is a partial list of *free* materials you can acquire:

An overseas moving company will sometimes offer a huge, well-built packing crate to be used as a private study area or clubhouse, or a fiberboard drum for a rocket ship, a silo or a quiet place.

Fabric shops throw away the long tubes on which heavy goods are rolled, which make good storage tubes. Fabric remnants, odd buttons, spools, ribbon ends may also be available.

Appliance or department stores dispose of boxes and crates of all sizes. A variety of good sturdy boxes in different sizes and shapes will be most helpful.

Shoe stores offer shoe boxes that have myriad uses.

Ice cream stores, restaurants can be asked to save their empty three-gallon cardboard ice cream containers which can be used as cubbyholes, spatter paint screen forms or Kachina masks.

Soft drink companies often sell, at a nominal fee, wooden soft drink crates.

Phone or electric power companies offer large spools to be used as tables, desks, or construction elements.

Cleaning and laundry establishments and even laundromats will sometimes arrange to save unredeemed sheets for you (teepee, Arab tent, ghosts, curtains) or clothing (dramatics, role-playing, dress-up). Such an arrangement might also be made with an appliance repair shop, from which you may be able to acquire unclaimed (working or non-working) appliances.

2. *What is really impossible?* Ask the children to make lists of impossibilities, then have these shared with the class. Encourage the children to try to refute any of these impossibilities, using reasonable— if fantastic—arrangements. Or you may collect the long lists and have a student cull these in order to make a master list of impossibilities. Duplicate this list (or make a bulletin board display using it on the following day). Then ask the students to read it, and try to refute any they can. Handle this lightly; emphasize the humor inherent in such a project.

3. *Have each student imagine "a book that was written just for me."* How would it be unlike (better than) any book they've ever read? What would make it so special? What qualities would it have: humor, adventure, mystery, fantasy (horror)? Some students may want to develop this book into a reality.

4. *Let's think up some new critters.* You may start off by saying, "I've just invented a new 'critter' that keeps you up-to-date on world news. He has 2 TVs for eyes: one shows Europe and one shows the U.S. He has a ticker-tape tongue and you can listen to his earphones for weather reports." Encourage the children to come up with their own "critter creations." Each new animal should be praised for its particular merits and originality. A similar activity, using inventions or holidays, can be developed at another time.

5. *How many ways can we do it?* Suggest a simple problem to the class such as "Your dog is lost. How could you go about finding him?" Ask the students to think of a variety of ways of solving this problem, such as riding a bike downtown to look for him, calling the dog pound, advertising in the paper, and so on. Encourage them to come up with novel, if unlikely, methods for finding the animal. They may say things like "rent a helicopter or use a loud-speaker to broadcast your voice all over town," and then they might *really* take off with ideas like: "Build a huge fan. Put it by his doghouse. Put a juicy steak by the fan and let it send the smell all over the neighborhood," or "Have Snoopy fly his airplane on a reconnaissance mission," and so on.

(Many of the Creative Writing Self-Starters, page 287, might also be appropriate for use in oral language sessions to help develop the children's originality of thought.)

September

Warm September brings fruit,
Sportsmen then begin to shoot.

†† National Better Breakfast Month (Cereal Institute, 135 South LaSalle Street, Chicago, IL 60603)

†† Labor Day is the first Monday in September.

1   World War II began with Nazi Germany's invasion of Poland in 1939.

2   U.S. Treasury Department was established by Congress in 1789.

3   The Treaty of Paris, ending the American Revolutionary War, was signed in Paris in 1783.

4   Los Angeles, California was founded as El Pueblo de Nuestra Señora de la Reina de los Angeles de Porciancula in 1781.

    George Eastman patented the first roll-film camera and registered the name Kodak in 1888.

5   First U.S. gasoline pump was bought by Jake Gumper of Fort Wayne, Indiana in 1885.

6   Jane Addams, pioneer social worker, was born 1860, Cedarville, Illinois.

††   National Hispanic Heritage Week, by Presidential proclamation, beginning with the second Sunday of September

7   First use of the nickname "Uncle Sam" in *The Troy Post*, Troy, New York in 1813.

8   First permanent settlement of Europeans on the North American continent (St. Augustine, Florida) was headed by Spaniard Don Pedro Menendez de Avilés in 1565.

      On this day in 1664, Peter Stuyvesant surrendered the Province of New Netherlands and the City of New Amsterdam to the British, who changed its name to New York in honor of their leader, James, Duke of York and of Albany.

      On this day in 1974, President Gerald Ford granted former President Richard Nixon "a full, free and absolute" pardon for any crimes he may have committed when he was in Office.

9   On this day, the term "United States" became official. The Second Continental Congress ruled that the words "United Colonies" would be altered, for the future, to "The United States," 1776.

      Leo Tolstoy, writer, was born in Yasnaya Polyana, Russia in 1828.

      California Admission Day, commemorates the 31st state's entrance into the Union in 1850.

10   First defeat in history of an English squadron took place during the War of 1812 when U.S. Captain Oliver Perry defeated the British on Lake Erie in 1813.

11   On this day in 1609, Henry Hudson discovered Manhattan Island.

12   Elizabeth Barrett married Robert Browning on this day in 1846.

13   First national election authorized by U.S. Congress ("to be held the first Wednesday in January next, 1789").

14 On this day in 1741, the composer George Frederick Handel, having worked for 23 straight days, finished "The Messiah."

On this day in 1901, Vice President Theodore Roosevelt succeeded President William McKinley as our 26th U.S. President, as McKinley had died of the wound he received September 6, 1901.

15 William Howard Taft, 27th U.S. President, born in Cincinnati, Ohio in 1857.

On this day in 1935, the Nazis in Germany enacted the Nuremberg Laws depriving all Jews of their citizenship, reviving ghettos and proclaiming the Swastika as the national flag. A pogrom of violent racial and religious prosecution began.

16 On this day in 1620, the Pilgrims sailed on the Mayflower from Plymouth, England to the New World.

The town of Shawmut, Massachusetts, changed its name to Boston, on this day in 1630.

Cherokee Strip Day marks the opening of Oklahoma Territory to 100,000 settlers, who rushed into the Strip to claim shares in the 6,000,000 acres between Oklahoma and Kansas, 1893.

17 By Presidential proclamation Constitution Week, which includes this day, commemorates the Constitutional Convention's adoption of the U.S. Constitution (subject to ratification by the States) in 1787.

Today is Citizenship Day, which also commemorates the adoption of the Constitution.

William Carlos Williams, physician and poet, was born in Rutherford, New Jersey in 1883.

18 On this day in 1793, George Washington laid the cornerstone of the Capitol in Washington, D.C.

19 On this day in 1846, poet Elizabeth Barrett Browning left her father's house in London to join Robert Browning, her secret husband of one week.

On this day in 1863, Abraham Lincoln delivered his Gettysburg Address.

Vice President Chester A. Arthur succeeded President James A. Garfield as our 21st President when Garfield died after being wounded (by a disappointed office-seeker) in the Baltimore and Ohio Railroad Station on July 2, 1881.

Mickey Mouse was first seen in the Disney cartoon *Steamboat Willie* in New York City, 1928.

20 Portugese explorer Ferdinand Magellan, with five ships and 270 men, set sail (under the Spanish flag) on the first voyage round the world in 1519.

21 On this day in 1792 France abolished the monarchy, replacing it with the First Republic.

First successful gasoline-propelled motor car made in the United States was made by Frank Duryea, using his brother Charles' design. Frank drove the car through the streets of Springfield, Massachusetts in 1893.

United States Post Office was established in 1789.

President Lincoln issued The Emancipation Proclamation in 1862.

23 Autumnal Equinox. Fall begins on or about this day.

First commencement of the first college in America was held at Harvard College, Cambridge, Massachusetts, 1642.

The Lewis and Clark Expedition, after two years, four months and ten days, completed its exploration of the West and arrived back in St. Louis, Missouri in 1806. (They had travelled over 8,000 miles by boat, horse, and on foot.)

†† National Dog Week begins with the Sunday of the last full week of the month (National Dog Week, 111 E. Wacker Drive, Chicago, IL 60601).

24 F. Scott Fitzgerald, writer, was born in St. Paul, Minnesota in 1896.

25 On this day in 1789, Congress submitted 12 Constitutional Amendments to the States for ratification; 10 were ratified, and became the Bill of Rights.

William Faulkner, writer, was born in New Albany, Mississippi in 1897.

26 American Indian Day.

On this day in 1919, after making 40 speeches on behalf of the Treaty of Versailles, President Woodrow Wilson collapsed in his private train en route to Wichita, Kansas. He was taken back to the White House where he suffered the stroke that incapacitated him for months and from which he never recovered.

T. S. Eliot, poet-playwright, born in St. Louis, Missouri in 1888.

29 On this day in 1789, the United States established a Regular Army of 700 men.

30 Truman Capote, writer, was born in New Orleans, Louisiana in 1924.

Babe Ruth hit his 60th home run of the season for the New York Yankees, 1927.

After three futile attempts by phone to Mississippi Governor Barnett directing him to comply with a federal court order to admit a Black, James Meredith, to the University of Mississippi, President Kennedy sent National Guard and Army troops to Oxford, Mississippi, to restore order. A violent riot broke out as U.S. Marshals escorted Meredith on campus, 1962.

September

The early Roman calendar began with March, therefore September was its seventh month; *septem* = seven in Latin.

SEPTEMBER QUOTATIONS

What is an epigram?
A dwarfish whole.
Its body brevity, and wit its soul.
                    —Coleridge

†† I quote others only the better to express myself.—*Montaigne*

†† Labor Day: There are three rules for happiness in Industry; these three rules are: A self-selected task, a self-created plan for doing that task, and freedom to use the plan.—*Anonymous*

13 Voters quickly forget what a man says.—*Richard M. Nixon*

It makes no difference who you vote for—the two parties are really one party representing 4% of the people.—*Gore Vidal*

Bad officials are elected by good citizens who don't vote.—*George Jean Nathan.*

17 As soon as any man says of the affairs of state, "What does it matter to me?" the state may be given up as lost.—*J. J. Rousseau*

A silent majority and government by the people is incompatible.—*Tom Hayden*

Not all people in this world are ready for the democratic process!—*Barry Goldwater*

Our constitution protects aliens, drunks and U.S. Senators. There ought to be one day (just), when there is an open season on senators.—*Will Rogers*

21 As I would not be a slave, so I would not be a master. This expresses my idea of democracy.—*Abraham Lincoln*

26 The savage American was conquered and subdued at the expense of the instinctive and intuitive sympathy of the human soul. The fight was too brutal.—*D. H. Lawrence*

When asked by an anthropologist what the Indians called America before the white man came, an Indian answered simply, "Ours."—*Vine Deloria, Jr.*

SEPTEMBER EVENTS

● **Better Breakfast Month** [Entire month]

Good nutrition must become an integral part of classroom learning every week. It's a fact that lots of people don't eat breakfast, and another that you aren't in a position to monitor your students' eating patterns. But you can help the children become aware of the importance of good nutrition. In the classroom, you can emphasize the particular nutritive value of *each* food cooked there. The Nutritive Value of Foods (75¢) lists 615 foods and dishes, and breaks each down into nutritive values (water, food energy, protein, fat, fatty acids, carbohydrates, calcium, iron, vitamin A, Thiamine (B1), B complex, niacin, riboflavin (B2), ascorbic acid (C)). This book can be purchased from:

> The Superintendent of Documents
> U.S. Government Printing Office
> Washington, D.C. 20402

A very clear vitamin chart, including the functions of vitamins, their sources, history, and deficiency results, is free on request from

> Merck, Sharp & Dohme
> West Point, PA 19486

Teaching about the four food groups has always been less than exciting. But the U.S. Department of Agriculture, Office of Communication, offers four very cleverly designed nutrition sheets for the lower grades: "Fred the Horse Who Likes Bread," "Meet Molly Moo," "Mary Mutton and the Meat Group," and "Gussie Goose Introduces the Fruit and Vegetable Group." Short stories, puzzles and games clearly explain the food groups and their importance. These sheets can be duplicated and are free from the U.S. Government Printing Office (address given previously).

Free breakfast-time bookmarks and a little cartoon-illustrated booklet, "Why Do You Need Vitamin C?" are available from:

> The Department of Citrus
> Florida Citrus Commission
> Lakeland, FL 33802

You may request classroom quantities of these materials which are suitable for use with early and middle graders.

• *Labor Day*   [First Monday in September]

Etymology

The first Monday in September is observed as "Labor's holiday" in the United States. The word "labor" comes from the Latin *laborare*, which means "to be tired." This is the day on which the workers of America are honored.

• *First Roll-Film Camera Patented, 1888*   [4]

In 1884 George Eastman invented a machine that made photographic paper in long rolls. This made photography inexpensive and popularized the "Brownie" box camera.

The first actual photograph was taken in 1824 by Joseph Niepce in France.

Here is a source of inexpensive classroom cameras ($3.00 for a sample camera and film). Write, requesting information, to:

> Power Sales Company
> Box 113
> Willow Grove, PA 19090

Classroom cameras can be used in many ways. Kids can take photos to illustrate field trips (and later retell sequence of events for photo captions), natural science studies, or autobiographical illustrations.

Expanding-Photograph Art Project

Older students are often fascinated by these art forms. Have the kids cut out magazine close-up photos of faces or objects. These photos are then cut into long strips. These are glued onto a white sheet of paper leaving equal amounts of space between each strip. Every strip must be included.

This idea can be used on eye-catching bulletin board displays.

● *California Joined the Union, 1850* [9]

Etymology

California gets its name from a 16th century fairy tale: "Las Sergas de Esplandian." The heroine of this Spanish romance, Calafia, ruled over a fabled treasure island, California, and this name was probably applied to Lower California soon after its discovery in 1533!

● *National Hispanic Week* [Second Sunday in September]

It isn't possible, in five school days, to deal in depth with America's Hispanic heritage. But this week can afford the beginning of a year-long awareness of the many heritages of America's people.

A classroom chart, compiled by the students and based on the one below, can be started this week. Additions to the chart can be made throughout the year. These could emphasize the ethnic origins of class members or of groups of people who interest the individual children and have contributed to making our country "The Great Melting Pot."

The children make the illustrations for this chart, and it can remain posted all year.

Here are some ways in which the people of America have influenced each other.

A. Foods we get from:
   1. Native Americans—
        corn, squash, beans, chile, turkey
   2. Spaniards—
        fruit trees, spices, sugar, grains
   3. Mexicans—
        chocolate, tomatoes, peas, potatoes

B. Clothing we get from:
   1. Native Americans—
        turquoise and shell bead necklaces, moccasins,
        leather fringe
   2. Spaniards—
        laces, full skirts, cowboy-style clothing

    3. Mexicans—
        woven serapes, rebozos, juipils

C. Tools we get from:
    1. Native Americans—
        pottery, baskets, hanging loom, irrigation canal system
    2. Spaniards—
        guns, the wheel, work horses
    3. Mexicans—
        wooden ranching and farming tools

D. Architecture:
    1. Native Americans—
        adobe building bricks, vaulted horno ovens,
        apartment multi-dwelling buildings
    2. Spaniards—
        arches, iron grill work on windows and doors, patios,
        tiles, carved support posts, chimney construction
    3. Mexicans—
        viga roof beams, latilla cross lattice-work of ceilings

E. Words we get from:
    1. Native Americans—
        moccasins, skunk, wigwam, squaw, toboggan, raccoon,
    tomahawk, totem, bayou, caribou, chipmunk, hickory, hominy,
    moose, opposum
    2. Spaniards
        patio, canyon, bronco, sombrero, taco, mosquito, pronto,
    key, vigilante, tornado, sierra, cockroach, burro, buffalo, breeze,
    alligator

F. Life values° we get from:
    1. Native Americans—
        idea of an interdependence between all living things, art
    2. Spaniards—
        Catholicism, communal ownership, water rights,
        Spanish music, art, dance
    3. Mexicans—
        Mexican art, dance, music

°Of course, many other early Americans may also have had some of these life values!

Students could also trace on a world map the routes of the Spanish people to the New World, by way of Florida, New Mexico, California, and Arizona.

• *Constitution Week* [Includes September 17, Citizenship Day]

What was it like for the men who drew up our U.S. Constitution? During the time when our Constitution was being given its final form, there was a tense atmosphere among these delegates, one of absolute secrecy!

The delegates met in Philadelphia behind locked doors. They each swore never to divulge what took place within those locked rooms. No outsiders were admitted—and this included the press!

The Constitutional Convention was called for May 14, but it wasn't until September 12, with the proceedings still secret, that the Constitution was adopted when 39 delegates signed and 16 refused to sign.

When the Constitution was at last made public and offered to the states for ratification, only three states (Georgia, Delaware, and New Jersey) did so unanimously. Businessmen and landowners generally favored the document, but it drew strong criticism from great numbers of the people. John Adams, himself, admitted that he felt our Constitution "was extorted from the grinding necessity of a reluctant people."

"The Making of the Constitution" (ISBN–670–451746) is one of the American Jackdaws, a series of outstanding mini-courses in history (about $6 each) including, for example: Vikings, Women in Revolt, Volcanoes. You can receive a free "General Guide to the Use of Jackdaws in the Classroom" by writing

The Viking Press
625 Madison Avenue
New York, NY 10022

• *First Showing of Mickey Mouse Cartoons, 1928* [19]

Kids love to read comic books and it is a legitimate way to practice reading. Even if every word is not decoded, the comic book gives children practice in seeing sequential events, using contextual clues and finding the humor and drama in written words. You can get a collection of comic books for the classroom by picking them up at a flea market (5¢-20¢ each) or by running a newspaper want-ad that explains why you want the books (emphasize that you aren't interested in collector's issues, which are very valuable and expensive).

A "Funny Papers Learning Center" will require a stack of old funny papers, comic books, magazines, white drawing paper, newsprint, glue, scissors, felt tip pens, a big scrapbook (with clear plastic adhesive pages), and envelopes and writing paper. The manipulatives could include comic strips laminated with clear Contac paper and cut into squares. The children shuffle them and then lay them out in a correct sequence. (A square from the same strip of another date may be included so that the child lays out the strip in the right order and removes the one frame that doesn't belong.)

A big class scrapbook of cartoons and jokes could be developed to point out good and poor grammar, basic penmanship and spelling. These cartoons can be collected from printed sources and also created by the children.

Ask the class to think up some *Catch 22* sentences that point up good English and punctuation, each example illustrating a double-bind, such as:

- You can't do this until you show that you can do it carefully.
- *"Don't raise your voice!"* she yelled.
- "I-uh-d-d-don't feel n-n-nervous."
- "Stop bossing people around!"
- Correkt speling is reel important.

Suggest that three children form a syndicate: one member to furnish the ideas, one to draw up the episodes and one to write the dialogue. Such original comic strips could come out weekly or be posted at the Center as they are completed.

Furnish blank comic strips in which you've cut out the words from each character's balloon. Back cartoon with white paper and have the students fill in the talk.

Let the children decide by personal poll-taking what their favorite cartoon characters are. Then have them write stories in the first-person about their individual favorites.

On some sheets, mix up cartoon characters and ask them to write characteristic dialogue between them. For example, put together B.C. and Popeye or Blondie and Snoopy. This could lead to a lot of laughs.

The large paperback book *Paper Movie Machines: Mini-Movies to Make* (Bud Wentz, Troubador Press, 385 Fremont St., San Francisco, CA 94105 © 1975, $2.50) can easily be the core of a Cartoon Learning Center. It has 27 ready-to-go home movies!

(NOTE: Before using this book, delete the top two "black-face" cartoons on page 16. These reproductions of 19th century zoetrope strips are not appropriate for use in the classroom.)

The Eastman Company (Rochester, N.Y. 14650) offers a wood base zoetrope which is sturdy and well-crafted. Although it does cost $20, it may be a good investment for you as it will fascinate the students and facilitate use of their handmade zoetrope strips. It should also last for years!

Two Walt Disney educational comic books ("Mickey & Goofy Explore Energy" and "Mickey & Goofy Explore Energy Conservation") are free from:

> Exxon
> 1251 Avenue of the Americas
> New York, NY 10020

Interested students can write for a free copy of *Sprocket Man*, a comic book about bicycle safety available from:

> U.S. Consumer Product Safety Commission
> Washington, D.C. 20207

Students can also get a free comic book "The Amazing Story of Measurement" from:

> The Cooper Group
> P. O. Box 728
> Apex, NC 27502

● *First Voyage Round the World Began, 1519*   [20]

Etymology

Fernao de Magalhaes, a Portugese navigator, and his five ships, set sail on this day in 1519. The long hard journey was filled with bad luck. Water supplies ran low, food was infected with insects and on the very day that Magellan, as we call him, was to discover a passage, one of his ships turned and fled back to Europe.

Magellan kept going. At last, sailing west, he entered a huge calm body of water. After months of bad seas, Magellan's men were very happy to be on calm seas at last. Magellan called the ocean El Pacífico, the peaceful one!

It wasn't until the 1800s that seamen learned that the Pacific Ocean covers 1/3 of the earth—it is bigger than all the land on the planet put together. The edges of this ocean are often quiet and calm but much of it is filled with storms and huge waves. By the time we learned this everyone had grown accustomed to calling these often wild stormy seas: the *Pacific* Ocean.

FALL TO _

● *Autumnal Equinox*   [22 or 23]

Etymology

In the Middle Ages, five hundred years ago, the farmers spoke Latin and they had no calendars. The year was divided into periods for their work with the earth: planting time, tilling time, harvest time. One of their expressions, seed time, passed into the French language as "seison" and later came into English as the work *season.*

With the beginning of this new season, fall, discuss with the children the meaning of "equinox": equal night and day, twelve hours of night and twelve hours of day. The sun rises directly in the East and sets directly in the West; at the equator the sun is directly overhead at twelve o'clock noon. Discuss the cause of ensuing shorter days, the process and importance of hibernation, migration, and the possible reasons that this season is sometimes called "Indian Summer." Talk about deciduous and non-deciduous trees.

Fall Bulletin Boards

General suggestions. Remember that a bulletin board is a learning device to reward and encourage outstanding work; it is *not* a decoration. Try the incorporation of eye-catching titles, lead phrases, unusual textures, photographs and actual objects. Place (written) materials at children's eye-level. Ask yourself occasionally if the displays reflect the *current* interest of the children.

Here is a 100% Natural Fall Bulletin Board!

Display a collection of natural objects brought in by you and the children: (try not to have exact duplicates) cocoons, pressed leaves, bark, stones, seed pods, cones, dried grasses, feathers, different wood samples, seed pits, and nuts and dried rose hips. Eventually objects such as dog fur and egg shells may be contributed.

Clearly number and display on the board a dozen of these natural objects. Beside them post a sign:

"Here's a game to play by yourself or with a friend. There are lots of right answers. Try and name the natural object that is the smoothest, the oldest, the most useful to people, the one that's still alive, the one that people can eat. Which ones do you think might make a good dye for cloth? A bookmark? A tea? Building materials?"

Look in these magazines. Cut out some pictures that match some of these natural things. Put them in a pile here. (These pictures can later be mounted on cards and used in a Nature Mix and Match game. Be sure the magazines are ones which have lots of nature pictures in them.)

Fall Food Center

A permanent *Cooking Center* for your classroom can be used in the preparation of purely seasonal foods. It will also assure that your students have an exposure to good nutrition information.

To prepare for classroom cooking, first, identify any allergies students may have and any foods their parents do not wish them to eat. Keep a list of these in your lesson plan book so that you may refer to it when selecting recipes for classroom preparation. Go over a recipe orally with the class before its actual preparation. Individual students or a committee can be made responsible for organizing the utensils needed for each recipe. The center can store pans, lids, wooden spoons, measuring cups, spoons, plastic bowls, knives, hot plate, oven, spatulas, cookie sheets, potholders, aprons and towels. Ingredients can be donated by parents, but it's wise to have back-up ingredients to use in the event a student is unable to bring something as assigned. The use of honey in place of refined sugar and whole grain (unbleached) flour should be stressed.

A suggested list of seasonal recipes, organized by the school year, appears on pg. 345, but it's always good to capitalize on recipe ideas that come up in class! It's fun, occasionally, to have a parent come in and conduct a discussion-demonstration on his/her culinary specialty!

The Fall Food Center might have signs that say:

Now's your chance!

Vote here for the recipes *you'd* like to try this month:

Sweet Indian pudding (Just like the one served at the first Thanksgiving dinner!)

Slush Sno-Cones?

Spoon Bread?

Berry Jam?

Fruit Leather?

Vote here. Put your initials by the one *you'd* like to try. (Post nutritional breakdown of each of the foods and let the students check these to see which is the best deal in terms of vitamins, minerals and calories!)

Also, post the chart in Figure 1.

Refer to it often. Periodically supply duplicated sheets of this chart with certain info left out. Let the students fill in the blanks— eventually they'll be able to do it without referring to the chart.

Metric Conversion Chart*
Volume

tsp	teaspoons	5	milliliters	ml
Tbsp	tablespoons	15	milliliters	ml
fl oz	fluid ounces	30	milliliters	ml
c	cups	0.24	liters	l
pt	pints	0.47	liters	l
qt	quarts	0.95	liters	l
gal	gallons	3.8	liters	l
ft³	cubic feet	0.03	cubic meters	m³
yd³	cubic yards	0.76	cubic meters	m³

*From National Bureau of Standards Special Publication 365.

Temperature

°F   Fahrenheit   5/9   Celsius temperature °C
      temperature   (after
                    subtract-
                    ing 32)

Figure 1

Fall Language Arts:

Fall Science

This is a fine time of year for nature field trips. If you would like to know how to emphasize conservation, the interdependence of natural creatures and their adaption to their environment, The State of California Resource Agency offers a very good *Teacher's Guide (Part I) (Morro Bay, Los Ossos Oaks and Montana de Oro) Before and After the Field Trip* for $1.50. Write to:

> Department of Parks and Recreation
> P. O. Box 2390
> Sacramento, CA 95811.

[IT'S A FACT: Birds do not migrate in the fall in order to escape from the cold to a warmer climate. They migrate in order to eat, because their food supply disappears as the weather grows colder.]

Natural Dyes

Natural Dye Sources

Red: Bermuda onionskins, cherries

Pink: sassafras tea (sold at health food stores)

Yellow: onionskins, grass or leaves of pear, willow trees or marigold

Orange: sassafras roots, bark

Blue: chestnuts, red cabbage

Green: rhubarb leaves, morning glory blossoms

Caution: Rhubarb leaves are poisonous.

Purple: blackberries, elderberries

Brown: tea leaves, walnut shells

Black: black walnut leaves

(Rusty nails added to a dye will make the dye darker.)

Cut the plant into small pieces and place these in a pan. Add a little water (use pure water that has no minerals in it) and boil for 5-20 minutes depending on the color intensity wanted. Strain the dye through a piece of dampened cheesecloth (available at hardware stores) and pour contents into a glass jar. Add a tablespoon (15 ml) vinegar to each batch of dye *except* the onionskin dyes. Vinegar sets the color.

Children will enjoy experimenting with other plants and substances to invent their own natural dyes. Each student may produce his own dye chart with samples of the same yarn, fabric or paper dyed different colors and the dye source identified next to each sample. Kids can also experiment with decorative paper dying by folding a small piece of rice paper or newsprint and dipping the corners into colored dye and then refolding it and dipping it into another color of dye.

Autumn Art

Leaf and dried plant notes. These can be used when sending thank-you notes to the room mother, school secretary, or principal. Have the children collect small flowers, grasses, leaves, feathers and *thin* pieces of bark. Have the children cut 6" × 9" or 7" × 10" pieces of paper and fold them in half. (Scraps of good colored paper can be collected from art supply stores.) Clear Contac vinyl is sold by the yard at some hardware and dime stores. Cut the vinyl (with its backing attached) a little bigger than the unfolded note paper. Have the students remove backing from 1/2 the vinyl and smooth it onto the back of the notepaper. Then each child makes a little dried arrangement on the front of the notepaper. Holding the plants in place, they gradually pull off the rest of the vinyl backing and draw it smoothly over the arrangement. Any air pockets are pressed out and rough vinyl edges are trimmed off.

Sand-casting. Each child removes one side from a half-gallon waxed milk carton. The cartons are filled three-fourths full of sand.

Using a sprinkling or atomizer-spray bottle, the child dampens sand with water. Designs are then outlined in the sand with a small stick. Tablespoons are used to scoop out the sand within the confines of the design; a depth of two or three inches should be reached. Objects can be stamped firmly down into the dampened sand: (eucalyptus) seed pod or heavily veined leaf outlines are appropriate. After the impression is made, remove the object. If any decoration is to be added to the piece (small shells, colored glass, ceramic fragments, little stones, marbles, pieces of metal, and so on), these are pressed lightly *face down* in the sand.

In a plastic wastebasket the plaster of Paris is mixed (by the teacher) according to directions on the package. Using a plastic cup, each child pours the plaster carefully onto the moistened sand, making certain that each scooped-out area is filled with the plaster. A toothpick or broomstraw is inserted and withdrawn at random in the plaster's surface to aid in the escape of any trapped air bubbles. The plaster is allowed to dry undisturbed for several hours, if not overnight. Then the finished piece of sand sculpture is lifted out of the carton and any excess sand is removed from it by lightly brushing the sculpture's surface with a dry paint brush.

Veneer prints. Materials needed include: airplane glue; sheets of plywood of various dimensions (8″ × 10″); different textures of paper, i.e. oatmeal, stencil, several grades of sandpaper; different textures of fabric, i.e. net, waffle-weave, embossed, Indianhead; yarn; string; toothpicks; masking and adhesive tapes; paper doilies and any textural materials that are flat and which the children find interesting. X-acto knives used under close teacher supervision and linoleum block cutting tools are also helpful. Several brayers (rubber rollers with handles), sheets of glass, linoleum block printing inks, turpentine and newsprint are needed for making the prints themselves.

A design is lightly drawn on the plywood with a pencil or is transferred to the plywood from a drawing. Flat textural materials such as paper or fabric are cut to fit the different areas of the design and are then glued firmly in place on the plywood. *All* edges of textural materials must adhere to the plywood. There should be some repetition of texture throughout the design. If the outline of any area is to be emphasized, glue yarn, toothpicks or string around the edge of that area. For negative lines and areas (which will appear white on final prints), an X-acto knife or similar tool can be used to cut away the surface of the plywood itself. Whenever possible the texture of the plywood should be utilized in the design, as a sky, a background for a landscape, still-life or abstract. The textural areas of the plywood can be emphasized by repeatedly dampening the grain of the wood with a moistened sponge prior to application of the ink.

When the glue is dry, ink is applied to the veneered surface in the same way that it is applied to a linoleum block: ink is squeezed onto the glass pane from which the brayer picks it up and transfers it to the plywood sheet's veneered surface. The completely inked surface is covered with a piece of newsprint which is then rubbed gently but firmly with the heel of the hand, the fingers, and the bowl of a spoon. The corner of one edge of the newsprint is grasped and pulled diagonally toward the opposite corner, thus lifting off a copy of the finished veneer print.

The use of more than one color of ink can be attempted once the student is satisfied with his trial print.

Ink is removed from the plywood's surface, as well as from brayers and glass panes, by the frugal application of turpentine with soft cloths.

● *Lincoln Delivered Gettysburg Address 1863*   [19]

You may obtain 25 copies of this famous speech, with portrait of Lincoln, for $1.00 from

>   The Barre Granite Assoc.
>   P. O. Box 481
>   Barre, VT 05641

● **Dog Week**   [Begins with the Sunday of the Last Full Week in September]

The American Humane Association offers a complete Humane Education classroom kit (HE-700) with posters, bookmarks and teaching suggestions for $1.50. They also have several brochures on dogs *(Care of Dogs* (G1-1004) 7 cents, *First Aid for Dogs and Cats* (GI-1002) 5 cents, *Care of the Outdoor Dog* (G1-10011) 7 cents, *Sit Heel Down Stay Come* (G1-1025) 5 cents, and dog books *(The Dog You Care For* (SP 1801) $1.25 and *The Dog for You* (SP 1803) $1.25. A Rental film list (HE-750) n/c and Selected Films on Animals (HE–751) $1.25 are also available from:

>   AHA
>   P. O. Box 1266
>   Denver, CO 80201

Please add 20% of net for shipping costs (25 cent minimum).

Bulletin Board

(Provide a map of the world near this information)

Here are some things you may not know about dogs. *How long have dogs been around?* The dog family has been on earth about 15 million years! *Why does a dog pant?* A dog pants to help him cool off when he's hot. He breathes hard with his tongue hanging out and this brings air into his body. This air cools his insides! *Why does a dog wag his tail?* Tail wagging is one way a dog "talks." His tail wags when he's glad to see you. Watch some dogs' tails. See if you can tell what their tail wagging means: "Wow, am I happy!" "Ok, who are you and what do you want around here?" "This is *my* part of town!" "Ok, you're a lot bigger than I am. This is *your* part of town. . . ." *Why does a dog turn around and around before he lies down?* Long ago all dogs were wild and slept outside in the tall grass. They turned around and around to flatten the grass and make soft beds. Today most dogs are tame, but they are born with the memory° of how to make beds in tall grass even though they don't need to anymore! *Can dogs see colors?* Your dog can smell things very far away. He can hear sounds you can't hear. But he can never tell red from green! Everything looks black, or white or gray to your dog! *Can all dogs bark?* Many wild dogs cannot bark. The wild dingos in Australia (os-trā-lee-uh) can't bark. Use this map and find where dingos live. The basenji (bu-sen-jee) of Africa can yodel when he's happy, but he can't bark. Use this map to find where basenjis first lived. The dogs that lived around the camps of early American Indians did not bark either. Only after the settlers came to America and dogs were tamed, did they begin to bark. (What do you think this means?) Find America on this map too.

°This memory is called instinct (in-steenkt). This is also the reason dogs gobble their food. They are born with the instinct to gobble food fast before some saber tooth tiger comes and takes it away from them!

Dog Riddles:

1. When is a yellow dog most often going to enter a brick house?
   (When the door's open)
2. What is taller sitting down than standing up? (A dog)
3. When is a dog's tail not a dog's tail? (When it's a-waggin' [a wagon])

● *American Indian Day*   [26]

The American Indians are not a single people with a single way of life. This basic fact makes it difficult to teach about Native Americans in generalized terms. Each American Indian group has its own singular way of life. The Bureau of Indian Affairs recognizes 266 Indian tribes, pueblos and groups (plus 216 Native Alaskan communities). About 250 Indian languages exist today. In 1974 there were 266 Indian reservations in the United States.

Help the children to see beyond the usual stereotype of the American Indian dressed in feathers, riding a pinto, hunting buffalo and living in a teepee. Start by exhibiting a U.S. map that shows the different Indian groups (one dollar from U.S. Govt. Printing Office, noted below) and supplement this with good slides, photographs, documented quotations and authentic recordings. Some good sources of these are:

1. The Museum of the American Indian (Heye Foundation Broadway at 155th St. NY, NY 10032) offers helpful monographs and slide kits for classroom use, postcard sets reproduced from tinted lantern slides and 1500 different books about Indians. Write to request their list of publications (25 cents), photography leaflet (15 cents) or book catalog ($1.00).

2. A good overview of American Indian information appears in the three-page *Information About Indians* produced by the Bureau of Indian Affairs. It answers such questions as, "How many Indians are there in the US?" (About 543,000 in 1973—U.S. census) and "May Indians vote?"(Yes, as of 1962 when New Mexico's disenfranchising interpretations of the State Constitution were found unconstitutional and Indians were permitted to vote as they had been in all other states since 1954.) Also available are an American Indian Calendar ($2.25) and descriptive bibliographies covering such subjects as Indian origins, food, wars, ceremonials and a Book List for Young Readers. The BIA does not handle sale of these publications—make checks payable to (and order from):

> Superintendent of Documents
> U.S. Government Printing Office
> Washington, D.C. 20402.

3. Long-playing records of authentic tribal music can be obtained from the Music Division, Library of Congress, Washington, D.C. 20540. Write and ask for their current price list.

4. The Rough Rock Demonstration School (Navajo Curriculum Center, Star Route One—Box 246, Rough Rock, AZ 86503) will send you a publications list which includes Kinship Packet ($2), Navajo Games and Culture Activities ($5) and Arts & Crafts ($1.50).

5. The Native American Materials Development Center (407 Rio Grande, NW, Albuquerque, NM 87104) offers some cross-cultural materials such as pottery and basketmaking posters, picture cards and a Clan filmstrip and tape. Write and ask for current price list.

Native American-Inspired Art Projects

Sand painting is an impressive ceremonial art. The designs made with colored powders are profoundly sacred and are a part of formal healing ceremonies which can be executed only by Navajo medicine men. There are a 1000 different sand painting designs and one medicine man may know several hundred sacred patterns. Each is directed towards the cure of a specific illness. Each detail of a painting must be executed perfectly and in a specific sequence, the slightest variation or deviation would be considered unseemly and could have serious negative consequences.

The ground or a large skin is smoothed and a neutral background color is sifted onto it. The medicine man holds each colored powder in his clenched fist and builds up designs by letting the trickles of sand escape down the second joint of his first finger. The thumb is used to stop the sand flow. The medicine man refers to no drawing but the one he carries in his mind.

When the design is finished, the patient sits on it in order to come into direct contact with the spirits. When the ritual is completed, the sand-painting is destroyed from the center out, following the order in which it was made. The powders, now contaminated by the illness they have absorbed, are carefully gathered up and removed to the north side of the medicine lodge.

[IMPORTANT: The students should understand that the sand-paintings made in the classroom are simply decorative variations of a *serious* ceremonial art.]

Young children can paint with slightly thickened poster paint directly onto squares of sandpaper or they can use crayons on sandpaper. These drawings can then be pressed on the reverse side with a warm iron in order to allow the colors to bleed onto one another.

Older children can dye fine builder's sand or sieved sand from a lake or river (Sand from a seashore must be washed several times in large amounts of water and then spread out on newspapers to dry). Mix the sand with the coloring agent in small baby-food jars.

A speedy way is to half-fill baby food jars with sand. Add a few drops of food coloring. Put on jar lid and shake jar. If color is too dark, add more sand. Lay down newspapers. Draw a simple design on smooth wood or tagboard. Place board on the newspapers. Start at top and apply thin coat of white glue in a small area. Cover with sand. Shake off excess and return to its jar at once. Use that color of sand everywhere else it is needed and then take a new color. Start at top of tagboard and repeat process until entire board is filled.

Indian Kickball*

The Hopi Indians of Arizona play kickball as a part of a spiritual ceremony. Each team represents a different Kiva (religious shrine) and prays for endurance before starting the mile-long race. The race course is over rough hilly ground along which the Hopis kick a *stone* ball!

---

*This kind of game as well as 82 others appear in *Games of the World: How to make them, How to plan them, How they came to be,* edited by Frederic V. Greenfeld, Ballantine Books, NY 1975.

Each team has 3-6 players and their own kickball painted with a bright stripe to distinguish it from the kickballs of other teams. Two or three teams can play at once, depending on the width of the race course used. The students should understand exactly where the race course lies, and the course itself should be rather long with interesting turns and twists. A three-inch rubber ball can be used by each team. Teams stand several yards apart at the starting line, with each team grouped around its kickball. At a given signal the race begins! One player hoists the ball with a lifting kick of his (right) foot and the team races after it with a different player kicking the ball the second time. No hands are used.

[IMPORTANT: This is a *cooperative* sport and all players help advance the ball—no one player may kick it twice in a row. The game ends as one team succeeds in getting its ball over the finish line.]

Native American Cooking

These two unusual Native American cookbooks can provide recipes for classroom cooking. Let your class change the ingredients to metric equivalents. Many students will enjoy preparing these foods and sampling unique unfamiliar flavors.

Indian Cooking ($1.50) by Frances Lambert Whisler (3405 Kelly's Ferry Road, Chattanooga, TN 37419) emphasizes Cherokee Indian foods using modern day ingredient equivalents.

Eskimo Cook Book (60 cents) was compiled by students of Shishmare Day School (Alaska Crippled Children and Adults, Inc., Box 2432, Anchorage, AK 99510).

SEPTEMBER ACTIVITIES

Language Arts:

I have observed that a Letter is never more acceptable than when received upon a rainy day.—*Charles Lamb, Sept. 9, 1826.*

Pen-Pal Projects

This is a good time to initiate pen pal projects. Bulletin board displays of pictures, coins and stamps (covered by sheets of clear acetate

plastic to discourage the disappearance of valuables) can stimulate student interest in (international) correspondence.
Sources include:

Dear Pen Pal
P. O. Box 4054
Dept. UF
Santa Barbara, CA 93103

No fee. Pen pals from U.S. and abroad
Ages 8-12
Send name, address, age & sex
Sponsored by *Big Blue Marble* TV Show

League of Friendship
P. O. Box 509
Mt. Vernon, OH 43050

50 cents each
Ages 12-25
Send 50 cents with stamped self-addressed envelope

International Pen Friends
P.O. Box 340
Dublin 12, Ireland

Provides special services for teachers, school classes and the blind. Ages 10-up

International Federation
   of Organizations for School
   Correspondence & Exchanges
(FIOCES)
29 Rue d'Ulm
Paris 5e, France

Will not send pen pal names,but will send the name of an organization that maintains pen pal addresses for the country in which child is interested

Reader Exchange
Learning
530 University Ave.
Palo Alto, CA 94301

Free. Send a description of student, class, and your name & address (60 words or less). Info should be valid for up to 6 months (printed at editor's discretion) and every respondent should get a reply.

A permanent classroom chart might be made to display these pen pal writing suggestions:

When writing letters abroad, *remember:*
***Answer promptly.* You'll be most enthusiastic about writing on the day you receive a letter from your pen pal.**

Write legibly. You have to keep in mind that your penmanship will be unfamiliar to your pen pal.

Tell all about yourself. Tell about your family, friends, school, home, hobbies, pets, favorite books, sports. Be careful not to sound as if you're boasting; be sincere about what you write; be polite.

Don't use slang. Foreign pupils will often not be familiar with slang (and as a rule children from other countries write in a more formal manner than we do).

Avoid controversial subjects. Don't talk about things that might make your pen pal uncomfortable, e.g. comparisons of religions, political views.

Suggest exchanges: Think about things you'd like to exchange— photos, coins, stamps, slides, drawings, shells, tape recordings.

Learn your pen pal's birthday: Be sure to send him/her a card or small gift.

The teacher can distribute a mimeographed sheet of leading questions to assist the writer in eliciting information from his/her pen pal.

Here's a method you can use for becoming pen pals with another class in a different (exotic) state. Go to your (state) library reference room where the U.S. phone books are kept. Choose a phone book from a state or states that will interest your students. Look in the Yellow Pages under *Schools—Elementary—Academic*, and then copy down the names and addresses of two or three (private) elementary schools. Next, write a brief letter addressed to the principal of the school,° stating how your class has written some stories and poems which you have photocopied and are enclosing in booklet form. Request that these be given to a similar grade-level class that might enjoy reading them and be interested in corresponding further with your students. Usually, that's all it takes, but don't mention anything to your class until you have a positive answer (occasionally a principal will not pass on your letter and in this case, simply write again to a second school). Once correspondence has begun (ask and answer lots of good questions), you can exchange drawings, photos, postcards, tapes, rocks, shells, pressed plants, coins, stamps, local folk stories, recipes and newspapers. Ask that the teachers also enclose printed notes telling what the children in each school are doing, saying, planning. If answers are quickly and faithfully prepared,

---

°or you may address the envelop to "A [fourth] grade class interested in being pen pals with a class in e.g. (*San Francisco, CA.*) (Substitute your own grade and city.)

this activity can lead to a level of enrichment and student-bonding seldom experienced in Social Studies classes.

September Math:

During the year, be sure that the students have a chance to see math in action by *using:* money, mileage indicators, thermometers, road signs, telephones, scoreboards, menus, street numbers, measuring cups and spoons, tape measures, rulers, counting games, register receipts, scales and road maps. Have them ask parents how *they* use numbers in their occupations or in their free time. Then take the class on a "field trip" around the block to see the variety of ways numbers are used in the neighborhood.

Older students can be shown how inflation works. Also, ask them to calculate: If you gave away a penny a minute, how much would you have spent in an hour? In a day? In a week? In a month? In a year? How long would it take for you to give away $100,000, 1/2 a million dollars? If there are 200 million people in America, and you wanted to divide a billion dollars among us equally, how much would each of us get?

September Puppet:

Puppet pattern and variations: You can give a cloth (felt) hand puppet form (8″ × 9″) to each child and let him/her glue on felt facial details, fur scraps, thick yarn hair, sequins, or tie on yarn hairbow or neckties.

Here are some variation possibilities and suggestions.

Provide the kids with lots of felt, cloth and fur scraps, buttons, metallic Christmas tree garland, sequins, feathers, lace, thin leather, yarn, scissors and Elmer's Glue. Encourage the kids to come up with their own very individual creations.

Helpful Hints to Teachers:

Fit one or two plastic containers for tableware into your top desk drawer. Use the little compartments for organization of—and easy access to—paper clips, pins, map tacks, tape, string, and so forth.

If your children ask "Why do we have to learn letters and writing?" help them see that decoding gives us power—that we decode every day to send and get other kinds of messages. We "read" traffic-lights, ambulance sirens, the "Golden Arches," and car taillights. Get them to see that they're already decoding lots of words such as *STOP, up, down, Men, Women* and *Free!* Build on any knowledge they already have. Ask the children to find examples in their neighborhoods of each letter you study.

Numbers can be handled in the same way. Use examples of football jerseys, house and car license numbers, baseball uniforms, telephone numbers and prices of their favorite foods. In this way, the students will begin to *understand* why they need to learn letters, numbers and writing.

Get weekly use of (or a subscription to) *T.V. Guide*. Study it each week and post an eye-catching "What's on T.V. This Week?" sign. Emphasize science, geography programs or cartoon specials (they're practicing listening skills, hopefully). Get the children to be aware of "good stuff on the tube!" Encourage them to contribute mini-posters advertising good programs that they are enthusiastic about.

Make a small sign for the inside top drawer of your desk. Tape it where your eyes will occasionally fall on it. The sign should read:

They can because they think they can.—Virgil (70-19 B.C.)

Set aside in a classroom cupboard the materials and equipment for one or two specific projects. On a day when you need a pick-me-up, one of these projects can be brought out, and the enthusiasm it evokes will be natural. An example of such a lesson might be the experiment below.

Volcano experiment. Purchase some crystals of ammonium dichromate at a chemical supply store. From 2 colors of modeling clay, make a realistic-looking crater on a large smooth rock. The crater should be about 6″ across at the base and 2-1/2″ across at the summit. Hollow out the crater so that it can easily hold 1-2 teaspoonfuls of the crystals. Following a discussion of volcanic action, during which such words as *lava, magma, pumice, igneous, vent, molten, dormant, extinct* are introduced, have a classroom display of volcanic power. Encourage the children to watch for different aspects of an eruption: What happens to the lava that is initially thrown upward? Where is lava most likely to flow? How is pumice formed? Strike a wooden match and insert it into the mouth of the crater, igniting the crystals. Viewers should stand clear of volcano until eruption has ceased.

Make a large bar graph on the chalkboard by listing each student's name. Give every child the same three addition problems and five minutes in which to work them. Allow the class to correct these problems, and then put the results on the graph. Repeat this procedure with subtraction, multiplication and division problems. This is an appropriate lesson to present when the children have become tired of the routine Math period.

Occasionally, prepare a mimeo of incorrect grammar, spelling, punctuation examples which you have taken from *their* written work. The fun of recognizing a sentence and identifying its author will help to enliven language review lessons for your class.

Younger children are delighted to receive a little special attention on their birthdays. Buy a box of trick birthday candles (the type that re-light whenever they are blown out) from a magic shop. Announce to the class that this is a special birthday candle that cannot be blown out. Let the birthday child make a wish and blow out the candle. Verbally encourage the candle to re-light (or profess a lack of confidence in its powers). Once it has re-lit, the candle may be "blown out" a second time or permanently put out by pinching its wick. Little children look forward to this "special attraction" each birthday.

Some teachers find that it's very helpful to reserve the last 20 minutes of each day for a "pow-wow" during which students talk over the day's successes and near-misses and take time to add a few lines to the individual journal each of them keeps.

Rosh Hashana, the Jewish New Year, often occurs in September. It is traditional to serve apple slices dipped in honey at this time in anticipation of sweetness for the year ahead.

October

Plaguey twelvepenny weather
—Jonathon Swift, Journal to Stella, Oct. 26, 1710

††   National Newspaper Week: first or second Sunday

1   James Earl Carter, Jr., 39th U.S. President, was born in Plains, Georgia in 1924.

Roger Maris hit his 61st home run of the season for the New York Yankees: a major league baseball record, 1961.

2   King Richard III was born at Fotheringhay, England, 1452.

First black U.S. Supreme Court Justice, Thurgood Marshall, was sworn in, 1967.

3   Child Health Day

First woman senator, Rebecca L. Felton of Georgia, was appointed to a brief term in the U.S. Senate on this day in 1922.

U. S. Navy Commander Walter Schirra, Jr., orbited the earth almost six full times in the Project Mercury Capsule, 1962.

4   Rutherford B. Hayes, 19th U.S. President, was born in Delaware, Ohio in 1822.

Frederick Remington, artist of life in the southwestern U.S., was born in Canton, New York, in 1861.

Dick Tracy comic strip was first published by *The New York Daily News*, 1931.

Space Age began as the USSR orbited the first artificial satellite, "Sputnik," 1957.

5   Chester A. Arthur, 21st U.S. President, was born in Fairfield, Vermont 1830.

First T.V. broadcast of a Presidential address was made from the White House by Harry S. Truman, 1947.

6   First public showing of his motion pictures by Thomas A. Edison in West Orange, New Jersey, 1889.

First talking feature film made its world premier in New York City: Al Jolson spoke in "The Jazz Singer," 1927.

George Westinghouse, manufacturer-inventor, was born in Central Bridge, New York, 1846.

Thor Heyerdahl, explorer, was born in Larvik, Norway, 1914.

7   First U.S. railroad, The Granite Railway (a horse-and-gravity powered operation), began service at Quincy, Mass., carrying granite to nearby Milton, 1826.

Denmark's King Christian X defied the Nazi occupiers of his country by attending a service in a synagogue in Copenhagen where he said, "If the Jews are to wear the Star of David, then we shall all wear it. You are all Danes. You are all my people."

†† Fire Prevention Week (National Fire Protection Association, 470 Atlantic Ave., Boston, MA 02210) is always held during the week of October 8th, anniversary of Great Chicago Fire, 1871.

8   First no-hitter baseball game was pitched by Don Larsen of the New York Yankees in 1956 in a game against the Brooklyn Dodgers (Final score: 2-0).

9   Leif Erickson Day commemorates landing of Viking explorer on North American mainland in about 1000 A.D.

10   William A. Anders, U.S. astronaut, was born in 1933 in Hong Kong.

Limited nuclear test ban treaty went into effect, 1963.

Spiro Agnew resigned as U.S. Vice President, pleading "no contest" to the charge of evading U.S. income taxes, 1973.

11   Pulaski Memorial Day, authorized by President Truman, 1946, to honor the Polish nobleman, Casimir Pulaski, who died on this day in 1779 while fighting for American independence during the Battle of Savannah in Georgia.

Eleanor Roosevelt, U.S. diplomat, humanitarian and first lady, was born in New York City in 1884.

12   First sighting of the New World (San Salvador, one of the eastern Bahama Islands) was made by Christopher Columbus on this day in 1492. Columbus Day is now observed on the second Monday of the month.

On this day in 1973, President Nixon nominated House minority leader Gerald Ford as Vice President.

Quotation of the Day: I'm a Ford not a Lincoln.
—Gerald Ford on his nomination to the vice presidency, 1973.

13   Molly Pitcher, heroine of the Revolutionary War, was born in Carlisle, Pennsylvania, 1754.

14   William the Conqueror, at the Battle of Hastings, conquered England for the Normans in 1066.

Dwight D. Eisenhower, 34th U.S. President, was born in Denison, Texas in 1890.

First live T.V. broadcast from a spaceship in orbit: U.S. "Apollo 7," 1968.

15   Poetry Day

16   Queen Marie Antoinette of France was guillotined, 1793.

Oscar Wilde, writer, was born in Dublin, Ireland, 1854.

On this day in 1859, Abolitionist John Brown raided Harper's Ferry, Va., and seized the hotel, arsenal, firehouse and thirty citizens. His objective was to free the nation's blacks and establish them in a black republic.

> *Quotation of the Day:* I pity the poor in bondage that have none to help them; that is why I am here, not to gratify any personal animosity, revenge or vindictive spirit.
> —*John Brown at Harper's Ferry, 1859.*

17 On this day in 1933, Albert Einstein came to America as a refugee from Nazi Germany.

18 Canaletto, artist, was born in Venice in 1697.

Alaska Day marks transfer of Alaskan Territory from Russia to the U.S., 1867.

U.S. Department of Health, Education and Welfare stopped all use of cyclamates in foods, 1969.

19 Yorktown Day marks the surrender of Lord Cornwallis at Yorktown, Va., which ended the Revolutionary War, 1781.

National Forest Products Week, by Presidential proclamation, beginning on the third Sunday of October.

20 PT Barnum opened his Hippodrome housing the "Greatest Show on Earth" in New York City, 1873.

Saturday Night Massacre: anniversary of that night which became the turning point in the Watergate Affair. On October 20, 1973 at 8:24 PM it was announced that President Nixon had discharged Watergate Prosecutor Archibald Cox and Deputy Attorney General William Rickelshouse. The Attorney General Elliot Richardson resigned and demands for the impeachment of President Nixon began. These demands were to continue until President Nixon's resignation on August 9, 1974.

21 Edison Lamp Day commemorates invention by Thomas A. Edison of the incandescent electric light, 1879.

> *Quotation of the Day:* The longer it burned, the more fascinated we were. . . . There was no sleep for any of us for 40 hours.
> —*Thomas A. Edison*

Dizzy Gillespie, musician, was born in Cheraw, South Carolina, in 1917.

American Education Week, beginning with the Sunday before Veterans Day (N.E.A., 1201-16th St., N.W., Wash., D.C. 20036).

††   Veterans Day, third Monday in October.

23   First woman to solo in a plane, Blanch Scott, reached a height of twelve feet, 1910.

24   United Nations Day commemorates the adoption of the United Nations Charter in 1945 (United Nations Association of U.S.A., 345 East 46th St., New York, NY 10017).

Anthony van Leeuwenhock, maker of microscopes, was born in Delft, the Netherlands, 1632.

††   National Cleaner Air Week, beginning with Sunday of last full week of October (Air Pollution Control Association, 18 East Fourth St., Cincinnati, OH 45202).

††   Standard Time begins at 2 AM on the last Sunday in October. "Spring: forward . . . Fall: back!" (Mnemonic device).

25   First coast-to-coast non-stop air service: TWA, 1930.

26   The Erie Canal between Hudson River and Lake Erie was opened in New York State, 1825.

28   On this day in 1260 AD, Chartres Cathedral was completed, Paris, France.

Captain James Cook, explorer, was born in Marton Village, England, 1728.

King James III was crowned King of England, 1760.

29   Sir Walter Raleigh, charged with participating in a plot to oust King James I, was executed in London, 1618.

30   John Adams, 2nd U.S. President, was born in Quincy (Braintree), Massachusetts, on this day in 1735.

31   Halloween.

National UNICEF Day observed on behalf of United Nations Childrens' Funds (U.S. Committee for UNICEF, 331 E–38th St., New York, NY 10016).

Nevada was admitted into the Union as the 36th State, 1864.

October

In the early Roman calendar, October was the eighth month:
octo=8 in Latin

OCTOBER QUOTATIONS

†† Newspapers are the world's mirrors.—*James Ellis*

I fear three newspapers more than a hundred thousand bayonets.—*Napoleon Bonaparte*

Congress shall make no law abridging the freedom of speech or of the press.—*The U.S. Constitution.*

Our liberty depends on freedom of the press, and that cannot be limited without being lost.—*Thomas Jefferson*

Eternal vigilance is the price of liberty.
—*Oliver Wendell Holmes*

We live in the midst of alarms; anxiety beclouds the future; we expect some new disaster with each newspaper we read.
—*Abraham Lincoln, c. 1863.*

3 With a good heredity nature deals you a fine hand at cards; and with a good environment, you can learn to play the hand well.
—*Walter C. Alvarez, M.D.*

Half the secret of resistance to disease is cleanliness, the other half is dirtiness.—*Anonymous*

> *Nature requires 5*
> *Custom allows 7*
> *Idleness takes 9*
> *and Wickedness, 11.*
> —*Hours in bed, Mother Goose*

4   Space travel is utter bilge.—*Sir Richard Vander Riet Wooley, 1956*

I knew there was something in the nature of homesickness called nostalgia, but I found that there is also a homesickness for the earth. I don't know what it should be called but it does exist. There is nothing more splendid . . . than Mother Earth on which one can stand, work and breathe the wind of the steppes.—*Major Gherman Titov, Soviet cosmonaut*

10 All wars are civil wars, because all men are brothers. . . . Each one owes infinitely more to the human race than to the particular country in which he was born.—*Francois Fenelon*

More and more, the choice for the world's people is between becoming world warriors or world citizens.—*Norman Cousins*

14 Neither London nor Abilene, sisters under the skin, will sell her birthright for physical safety, her liberty for mere existence.
                                           —*Dwight D. Eisenhower*
(Address at Guildhall when he received the Freedom of the City of London, July 12, 1945.)

15 Poetry comes with anger, hunger and dismay; it does not often visit groups of citizens sitting down to be literary together, and would apall them if it did.—*Christopher Morley*

Even when poetry has meaning, as it usually has, it may be unadvisable to draw it out. . . . Perfect understanding will sometimes almost extinguish pleasure.—*A. E. Housman*

Poetry is what Milton saw when he went blind.—*Don Marquis*

16 Experience is the name everyone gives to their mistakes.
                                                  —*Oscar Wilde*

17 One thing I have learned in a long life: that all our science, measured against reality, is primitive and childlike—and yet it is the most precious thing we have.

Nationalism is an infantile disease; it is the measles of mankind.

The World War after the next one will be fought with rocks.

I live in that solitude which is painful in youth, but delicious in the years of maturity.
                                               —*Albert Einstein*

Education Week—Happy is he who knows the reason for things.—*Virgil*

"Why," said the Dodo, "the best way to explain it is to do it."
     —*Lewis Carroll, Alice in Wonderland, Chapter 11*

The institution we call "school" is what it is because we made it
     that way. If it is irrelevant, as Marshall McLuhan says; if it
     shields children from reality, as Norbert Weiner says; if it
     educates for obsolescence, as John Gardner says; if it does not
     develop intelligence, as Jerome Bruner says; if it is based on
     fear, as John Holt says; if it avoids the promotion of significant
     learnings, as Carl Rogers says; if it induces alienations, as Paul
     Goodman says; if it punishes creativity and independence, as
     Edgar Friedenberg says, if in short, it is not doing what needs to
     be done, it can be changed; it *must* be changed.
     —*Neil Postman and Charles Weingartner*

24   We, the peoples of the United Nations, determined to save suc-
     ceeding generations from the scourge of war, which twice in our
     lifetime has brought untold sorrow to mankind, and to reaffirm
     faith in fundamental human rights, in the dignity and worth of
     the human person, in the equal parts of men and women and of
     nations large and small . . . and for these ends to practice
     tolerance and live together in peace with one another as good
     neighbors . . . have resolved to combine our efforts to ac-
     complish these aims.
     —*Preamble to the Charter of the United Nations.*

30   Yesterday, the greatest question was decided which ever was
     debated in America; and a greater perhaps never was, nor will
     be decided among men. A resolution was passed without one
     dissenting colony, that these United Colonies are, and of right
     ought to be, free and independent States.
     —*John Adams in a letter to Mrs. Adams; July 3, 1776.*

You are apprehensive of monarchy; I, of aristocracy. I would,
     therefore, have given more power to the President and less to
     the Senate.—*John Adams to Thomas Jefferson.*

OCTOBER EVENTS

● *National Newspaper Week*   [Begins 1st or 2nd Sun.]

When a student argued that he could "read well enough" because he could read the newspaper, here's how one teacher handled it:

"Further discussion led to an agreement that Mike would cut out front-page stories and write down the questions he thought anyone reading the stories should be able to answer. Mike also wrote out the answers. Our agreement was that he would do 7 questions and answers and have them "approved" by two people of his choice.

"This activity led to a NEWSPAPER SRA (Stupendous Reading Activity) KIT! The approvers became enthusiastic and wanted to participate in Mike's activity. Soon, all three were pasting up the articles and setting up separate cards for questions and answers. (You can use heavy card stock such as tagboard. My students cut up old file folders.)

"Before long, other students had joined in the activity, but each one tended to select an area of special interest. One girl chose to do Dear Abby columns. One boy did a whole series of political cartoons, while another preferred comic strips. A boy chose want ads such as the example below:

WANT ADS

Garden Tractor For Sale—Exl Cnd.
All Acc. Call p.m. only 383-1956

Questions:
1. What does Exl Cnd. mean?
2. What does All Acc. mean?
3. When would you call?
4. What area of the city is the
   383 telephone exchange?

"By the time nearly everyone had become involved, they began to see a real need for organization. A big, cardboard box was decorated with John Hancock-style signatures. With Magic Markers, the children color-coded each section.

"Upon completion, this was the best SRA kit I have ever seen *because virtually every student did every exercise* (either while the kit was being prepared or while they were approving each other's work).

"There were many arguments about the questions and answers, so we set up a procedure for correction, improvement and upgrading. When differences were not able to be resolved, two forms were used.

"The amount of learning resulting from this activity was astounding. Each day, 5-15 newspapers were brought in. By the time the students had divided the sections, selected the articles, written the questions and answers, done the cutting, pasting and gave and received approval, they had read much more than they would have from a prepared kit." *

[NOTE: Two activity sheets (with 21 activities) which use newspaper comics, cartoons, & visuals, are offered free from The Hartford Courant, 285 Broad St., Hartford, CT 06115.]

● *Child Health Day*   [3]

Bulletin Board or Learning Center

Post a sturdy full-view mirror and several smaller mirrors. Beside one, secure this sign:

Because we eat so many processed foods, tooth decay is a big problem today. We know we should go to the dentist and brush often, but just *how well* do YOU brush? Here's a system that will pay off in fewer or NO cavities! Get yourself a little egg timer; turn it over and brush 'til the sand runs out. That way you're sure to brush three minutes!
Try to brush after each meal.
When you've finished with your teeth, lightly brush the surface of your tongue! This helps clean off bacteria that could spread throughout your mouth.
Look at your teeth now. How clean are they? Can you see any bits of food down by the gums? If so, go home tonight and "brush up" on your dental health habits!

Beside the long mirror post a sign:

Use THIS mirror to see how you stand. Try to remember to stand tall. Your whole body feels better when you do.

---

*Reprinted from "SRA - Stupendous Reading Activity," pp. 4-5, *The Raspberry Report Card*, Vol. 1, No. 14, March 25, 1974, edited by Ann Severance P.O. Box 12212, Nashville, TN 37212.

The materials below can be incorporated into this center:
You can get a free copy of "Food of Our Fathers" (ages 8-up), "The Thing the Professor Forgot" (ages 4-11), "Bread Puzzle" (ages 5-7) by writing to:

ITT Continental Baking Co.
P.O. Box 731
Rye, NY 10580

A jazzy activity-coloring book called "Soozie says, Only Sick People Need Drugs" (Teacher's Guide) is offered by U.S. Dept. of Justice, Drug Enforcement Administration, Washington, D.C. 20537.

- *The Space Age Began with Orbiting of Sputnik, 1957*   [4]

If you would like to introduce model rocketry into your teaching, here's how:
Write, saying that you are a teacher, to: Estes Industries, Inc., Penrose, CO 81240, and they will send you a free Astron Alpha rocket which you or older students can build. (You will need a launching system. These are sold at hobby stores or can be ordered from Estes Industries for $15.) Included with the rocket are a brochure of teaching publications, a teacher's guide and a model rocketry catalog that lots of kids will love to read.
Making a space-age time line is one good way for students to acquaint themselves with the history of rocketry. The kids can use an encyclopedia (look under Space-craft, History), or if they want to make a U.S. space-age time line they can use pages 62 and 63 of *Apollo*, a free publication of NASA, Office of Public Affairs, Washington, D.C. 20546.
Many beautifully illustrated books are available from NASA (at no cost), as well as information about the NASA space science education project and free NASA films.

- *First Public Showing of Movies, 1889*   [6]

All kids love movies. Here are four sources for hundreds of *free* films.

U.S. Dept. of the Interior
Washington, D.C. 20240

Farm Film Foundation
Washington, D.C. 20005

U.S. Consumer Safety Commission
Washington, D.C. 20207

Association Films, Inc.
866 Third Avenue
New York, NY 10022

It is always best to preview a film before showing it to your class. This will ensure that the film is not just a vehicle to push a commercial product. To help you become aware of such plays, you may want to read "The Fortune 500 Goes to School: Corporation in the Classroom" by Scheila Harty, a Sierra Club reprint available from The Sierra Club, 530 Bush St., San Francisco, CA 94108.

If you have money with which to rent films, request the catalog from Films Incorporated, 733 Green Bay Rd., Wilmette, IL 60091. (Rentals average $20 a film and this company offers some beauties.)

● *Fire Prevention Week*   [Includes October 8]

The Great Chicago Fire began on October 8, 1871 when Mrs. O'Leary's cow allegedly kicked over a lantern in the barn at 137 DeKoven Street. The fire swept over 21,000 acres, burned 17,000 buildings, killed hundreds and left 98,000 people homeless.

"Up the Ladder" is a reading drill game for young children. It requires a simple paper ladder with nine rungs, each of which has a pocket in it, and packets of reading word cards (ten to a packet). Each card will be of a size to fit in the ladder rungs. The child takes a packet of words and tries to climb the ladder by reading a word and placing it in the first rung of the ladder. Child may only insert words read correctly. Should child miss one word he/she can try the next until he/she has attempted all the words in the packet. "How high up the ladder can *you* go? Who can climb back down?"

Get a copy of the Fire Safety brochure from the Dept. of Housing & Urban Development, Washington, D.C. 20410. It features 32 dangerous situations involving fire. Cut out each of the examples, put them in a plastic fireman's hat and let each student take one. Children then use these situations/precautions as the basis for writing creative stories. Encourage the students to use different approaches when writing these stories, such as an emergency ward entry, a hurried phone call report, an eyewitness trying to save someone, a fireman or ambulance driver's impression, and so on.

- *Columbus Day*   [12]

When Columbus set sail, he was not worried that his ships might fall off the edge of the world. He had read many times "Imago Mundi" which summarized the geographical knowledge of that time and which included many demonstrations that the earth was round. What Columbus did fear was "monsters of the deep" which could destroy his ships and eat his crew members. (He was also afraid that his men might run out of fresh water before he could reach the Canary Islands again.)

Have students make paintings and drawings that show how the earth, sky, sea, space might have looked if Columbus *had* sailed to the edge of the world. These drawings might also include sea dragons, monsters and fantastic marine life.

Dramatic play. This can be introduced at this time of year, using Columbus as the initial theme. Each month will afford opportunities for the use of this technique if you find it useful in working with your particular group.

". . .[D]ramatic play in the classroom is an educational technique under which the children explore an area of human experience (1) by reliving the activities and relationships involved in that experience in their own way, (2) by acquiring, under teacher guidance, needed information and skills and (3) by increasing the satisfactions inherent in play that is meaningful and extensive. Dramatic play encompasses the following procedures:

1. The introductory situation is an arranged environment planned by the teacher.

2. Children explore the arranged environment and are permitted to respond in their own way, to manipulate tools and materials and discuss them.

3. A story may be read by the teacher to further the interest of the children in the selected area and to provide initial data for use.

4. Children are invited to play out any part of the story or set their own situation.

5. First play is spontaneous and unguided, but is carefully observed by the teacher.

6. Play is followed by a sharing period in which satisfactions are expressed or dissatisfactions are clarified, under teacher guidance, into statements of questions and expressed needs.

7. Planning for meeting the expressed needs includes the processes of problem-solving, making of rules, assignment of work to be done. [Steps 8, 9 and 10 are particularly suitable to culmination of Social Studies units.]

8. A period of extension of experience through such activities as research, excursions, firsthand processes and utilization of multimedia ensues before, and beside, further play.

9. Play proceeds on higher levels (involving more accurate activities and more interrelationships and interpretations) as a result of enriched experience.

10. This is a continuous and expanding procedure, progressing on an ascending spiral that may, in the upper grades, eventuate, after weeks of growth, into a structured drama."*

Dramatic play may be facilitated by collecting, and then keeping in the classroom, a box of small simple props such as assorted hats, costume jewelry, eye glasses (or frames), shoe-boxes, a flashlight, wooden spoons, coffee cans, a baby blanket or a few pieces of fabric. The use of such devices as signs, drawings, guidelines, crepe paper (to indicate a stream or the sea), and notation of important facts and dates on the chalkboard can also enliven these sessions.

[IT'S A FACT: The rulers of Spain gave Columbus the money for his first voyage. It cost what today would be about $20,000. As a result of the discoveries made by Columbus, the Spanish treasury (in the form of gold and treasure) was amply repaid. For every dollar spent on Columbus' journey, ten thousand dollars was gained!]

- *Poetry Day*   [15]

> *No one spoke,*
> *The host, the guest*
> *The white chrysanthemums.*
>   —*Ryota (1718-1787)*

William Carlos Williams wrote poems that can be enjoyed, read and understood by all ages of children. Obtain copies of the following poems written by Williams, and share them with your class:

This is Just to Say
The Red Wheelbarrow
Between Walls
The Locust Tree in Flower

Other works of poetry which students might enjoy could include: *The Serpent,* by Theodore Roethke, *The White Horse,* by D. H. Lawrence, *The Velvet Shoes,* by Elinor Wylie.

> *If I keep a green bough in my heart*
> *The singing bird will find it*
>   —*Chinese*

- *Albert Einstein Arrived in America, 1933*   [17]

What scientist turned down the chance to be a president? Albert Einstein! Soon after Israel became an independent nation, its leaders sought out Einstein to be their head of state. He answered by saying that he did not feel qualified to meet demands of a position involving human relations. It would be better if he continued his study of the physical world, in which he described himself as "having a little comprehension."

- **Edison Lamp Day**   [21]

Thomas Edison did not actually invent the light bulb. He perfected one in 1879—fifty years after Humphrey Davey produced an arc light and years after Joseph Swan made a crude light bulb.

What Edison did was spend years in research and experimentation in order to greatly improve the light bulb by discovering a superior filament.

In science the credit goes to the (one) who convinces the world, not to the one to whom the idea first occurs.—*Sir William Osler, 1849-1919*

- **National Forest Products Week**   [Beginning with the Third Sunday in October]

Project Learning Tree:

The American Forest Institute and the Western Regional Environmental Education Council have collaborated to develop a project which elementary and secondary teachers could use in helping students understand their interdependence with the total forest community and develop the knowledge, skills and commitment all citizens need if society is to use resource lands wisely for the long-term benefit of all.

Based in Boulder, Colorado, this project is now available in 20 states (from Maine and Rhode Island, to Florida, New Mexico and California). Project Learning Tree has a helpful periodic publication, *The Branch*, and inservice workshops at which the *K-6 Supplementary Activity Guide*, an outstanding resource book, is provided at no cost to teachers. Write P.L.T. (and request sample pages from the guide) to get on their mailing list.

Project Learning Tree
Salina Star Rte.
Boulder, CO 80302

The Forest Service (U.S. Department of Agriculture, Washington, D.C. 20250) offers free materials to help you teach about Forest Conservation. Write, requesting their catalog (FS-28) and *Suggestions for Incorporating Forestry Into the School Curriculum* (FS-62). These materials are more staid in tone than those offered by P.L.T., but order them and use the most lively of the ideas suggested.

(The following information is written at fourth-grade level and can be duplicated for use with middle-grade students.)

Until 200 years ago, paper was made from rags. After a while, it got hard to find good rags. And paper made from dirty old rags was not very good to write on. (It was a *bad* time to try to make books!)

Then, one spring day in 1719, a French man named Reumur (Rō-moor) took a walk in the woods. He went by an empty wasp's nest. He stopped and looked at it. Reumur saw that the nest was made of PAPER! How had a wasp made paper? There were no rags in the WOODS!

So Reaumur began to watch the wasps. He saw them rip off little bits of wood. They seemed to eat the wood. The wasps flew back to where the nest was being made. There they would each spit out a little sheet of paper onto the nest. The bits of wood had been made into paper while they were inside the wasps!

Reumur saw that *we* could make paper from wood. We would just (1) Chop up trees into little bits (2) Wet these little bits with water (3) Chop them up again (4) Add glue (5) Roll the material out flat (6) Let it dry.

Without paper we could not have

All buildings are first planned on paper. It takes one ton of paper to plan a tall building! That walk in the woods 200 years ago made this a new life for all of us!

Paper Making in the Classroom

You will need fine meshed wire screen, a large flat aluminum frozen-food pan, a second aluminum pan that can fit inside the first, a dishpan that will hold 10 quarts of water, 30 sheets of inexpensive facial tissue (not wet strength), 2 sheets of blotting paper the size of the first pan, liquid starch, measuring spoon, a blender or eggbeater, a sharp knife or tin snips, a rolling pin and an electric iron.

Trim the screen to fit inside the first pan. Cut most of the bottom out of the first pan, leaving only a 1/2" ledge that will support the screen. Cut out the entire bottom of the second pan, leaving only the sides. This is the mold for the paper.

Rip up the tissues and put them in the dishpan. Add 1 tablespoon instant starch mixed with 10 quarts of water. Use the blender or beater to beat until thoroughly mixed into pulp.

Put the screen in the bottom of the first pan. Set second pan on top of it. Hold the mold firmly on the screen. Dip pans and screen sideways into the pulp mixture. Clean off extra pulp around the edges of the mold. Disassemble pans and lift out the screen. Put the wet screen between the pieces of blotting paper. The paper will stick to the blotter. Remove the screen. Replace the blotter atop the paper. Use the rolling pin to press out extra water.

Finally, use a warm iron to press the paper which is still between the two pieces of blotting paper. Trim the edges of the sheet if you like, and —voilá! Handmade paper!

Repeat process. (Try using colored facial tissues to get pastel-tinted paper.)

• *Halloween* [31]

Halloween is an ancient celebration, a combination of a Druid autumnal festival and Christian feast day, and dates from the 7th century.

Etymology

In medieval England spiderwebs abounded in castles, huts and along forest paths. It was a common experience in those days to accidentally walk into a spiderweb and have it catch on your face and hair. People of that time joined "coppe" (head) and "web" (net) as a name for the spider's mesh trap. Over the years the name "coppe web" has gradually become simplified to cobweb.

There was a great deal of violence in 14th century England. Charles II organized civic watches to help protect the citizens. Each of these officers carried a lantern at night and soon jokes were being made about "Jack of the Lantern." Eventually, a shortened form of the expression became popular and then began to be used to describe a child's lantern made of a hollowed-out turnip or gourd. Now linked with Halloween, this imaginary watchman has become a holiday institution.

In the last years of the 15th century, Price Ulad of Wallachia went mad and executed 23,000 Turkish prisoners whose heads were then posted around his castle. Ulad's father's name was Dracul, meaning "The Devil" and Ulad's name became Dracula, "Son of the Devil!"

During medieval times "Soulers" roamed the streets of England, praying, singing hymns and asking for alms. In return for the money, the Soulers were to pray for the donor's relatives who might be in Purgatory. "Trick-or-treating" is an outgrowth of these Soulers' parades.

Bulletin Board Suggestions

For attention-getting titles, burn the edges of letters you have cut from construction paper or burn the sides of a sheet of paper on which lettering appears.

A display for older students is shown here. Appropriate vocabulary enrichment words are printed on the ghost shape. On the second day of this display, definitions are made to float at the side of the ghost. By this time the class should be familiar with the words and ready to match them with correct definitions.

Halloween Language Arts:

Try telling chain stories with younger children. Give a signal (ring a little bell) to remind a child if he/she fails to follow a logical sequence

If your students are familiar with Alfred Hitchcock films, discuss the technique Hitchcock often uses of leaving the plot unresolved. Why is this technique effective?

The following lists can be used in different ways. They can be duplicated and cut crosswise into 30 strips. These are put into a large sack and drawn out by the students, who then use each slip as the basis for a creative writing assignment. Or, you might supply three sacks, one for People, one for Places and one for Things. The lists are copied and cut apart into thirty slips for each category. The children draw one of these slips from each sack and write a story around the three slips drawn. Or, you can suggest that they trade some of their slips with friends to secure a story outline that especially interests them.

People	Places	Things
Witchdoctor	Darkest Africa	Voodoo charm
Dracula	Castle in Transylvania	Hovering bats
Ghost	Haunted house	Rattling chains
Vampire	Gothic castle ruins	Mists from the swamps
Werewolf	Graveyard	A smell of blood
Mummy	The tombs in Egypt	A smell of mold
Zombies	The cellar	Vulture bodyguard
Hunchback	A belfry	Deformed features
Frankenstein	A mad scientist's laboratory	Struck by lightning
Abominable Snowman	The Himalayas	Fur covered body
Dr. Jekyl & Mr. Hyde	English doctor's office	A cup of strange green liquid
Sorcerer	Castle dungeon	Crystal ball
Warlock	An altar with a fire burning on it	A cup of blood
Witch	A dark, windy hillside	A savage black cat
Ghoul	A crypt	Moldy coffin
Ogre	A damp stinking moat	Green scaley arms
Minotaur	A desert island	A labyrinth
Banshee	The windy plains	A scream that curdles your blood

People	Places	Things
Dragon	A medieval kingdom	A black knight on horseback
Giant	A far-off land not found on maps	A cage that you are locked in
Cyclops	Your bedroom at midnight	A rattling window
Loch Ness Monster	A Scottish mist-covered lake	A sea monster's cold breath
Big Foot	The thick woods	A cave on the far side
Man from another planet	The desert in New Mexico	A U.F.O.
King Kong	The Empire State Building	A thunderstorm
Headless Horseman	Pitch dark road	A racing black stallion
Medusa	A cliffside cave with statues of humans	13 green vipers
Spider Woman	An attic covered in huge spider webs	7 pet black widow spiders
Prehistoric Monster	Steaming jungle	A bog of quicksand
Roc	A cliff over the sea	Flames

Here are some Creative Writing self-starters:

1. Conduct an interview with a witch (or any other supernatural creature).
2. The night I was locked in the Wax Museum.
3. How ESP saved my life.
4. I Married a ——————.

5. My Own Private Ghost
6. The Mummy's Revenge
7. The Walking Dead
8. Letters from Outerspace
9. House of the Snake People

[IT'S A FACT: Bats are the only mammals that have the ability to actually fly.]

Halloween Riddles:

1. Where does Wolfman keep his car? (In the barking lot)
2. If you worked in a mortuary, what would you call your free time? (Coffin breaks)
3. What kind of people go to Heaven? (Dead people)
4. What holiday do vampires celebrate to show their gratitude for all the good food they've had this year? (Fangsgiving)
5. What is a vampire's favorite fruit? (Neck-tarines)
6. What does Frankenstein do on Mother's Day? (He sends a dozen roses to the Electric Company)
7. What kind of boats do vampires like best? (Blood vessels)
8. What would you have if you crossed a Frankenstein with a Werewolf? (An electric fur coat or a pinball machine that bites!)
9. Was Frankenstein upset when his neck bolts came loose? (You better believe it. He was so mad that he lost his head.)
10. What's the name of the famous Halloween building in New York City? (The Vampire State Building)
11. Why is a turkey like a ghost? (Cause he's always a-gobblin!)

12. What kind of beans do werewolves like? (Human beans!)

13. If you asked a mummy for change for a quarter and he only gave you 2 dimes back, what happened? ('Egypt' you.)

14. What would you get if you crossed a mummy with a vampire? (Either a flying Band Aid or a gift-wrapped bat)

15. Why is the letter E like death? (Because it's always at the end of life. . . .)

16. If Frankenstein were a gardener, what flowers would he grow? (Mourning gories, merry ghouls, sin flowers & shriek peas)

17. What happened to all the flowers Frankenstein planted? (They grue-some)

18. What would Dracula hate to have for breakfast? (He hates stakes at sunrise. They're sure to give him heartburn.)

19. Why does Frankenstein love good riddles? (Because they keep him in stitches!)

Halloween Reading:

Kids love to read about scary things. Here is some spooky but informative material you may want to use with your class. It is written on a fourth-grade level and can be read aloud to younger students, used as a listening activity.

The Loch Ness Monster

Loch° Ness is in Scotland. It is the biggest lake in Great Britain. It's about 24 miles long, a mile wide and 975 feet at its deepest. The walls of

---

°Loch means "lake" in Scottish.

Loch Ness are rippled, so there are lots of good places for a sea monster to hide! The water is not clear. It is full of silt, tiny bits of mud and plants.

In 1933, a highway was built along Loch Ness. Since then, hundreds of people, and many scientists, say they have seen the Loch Ness monster. Their reports are very much alike: The monster is about 20 feet long with 1 or 2 humps, a long thin neck and a tiny head. He's dark brown or greyish-black, and he swims real fast!

Everything known about the monster was fed into a computer. The computer said that the best time to see the monster would be June, July or August when the water in the Loch is its clearest. The best place to see him would be at the mouth of a river or in a quiet bay because this is where there would be the most fish for him to feed on. (He must eat fish, we know, because there aren't enough plants in Loch Ness to feed him.)

Cameras were set up at river mouths and in quiet bays. Sonar was used to report whenever anything big was coming near. Sonar sends out a string of beeping sounds. When these sounds hit something they bounce back. This is an echo. If you can tell the time between a sound leaving and a sound returning as an echo, you can measure how far off a moving thing is.

Five times the sonar has reported a large thing coming near and the cameras have started turning. But, so far, the scientists have only gotten very unclear photos—and no real answers to the mystery of the Loch Ness monster.

Discuss this information with the class. What ideas do they have about monsters, both real and imagined? What is the latest info on Nessie?

Halloween Math:

The Gypsy's Crystal Ball.

If you work this puzzle correctly, it will spell out your fortune!

Count the letters in your first name. If the number of letters is 6 or more, subtract 4. If the number is less than 6, add 3. The result is your key number. Start at the upper lefthand corner of the rectangle and check every one of your key numbers, left to right. Then read the messages the letters under the checked figures give you.

Now try making up a crystal ball of your own . . . this can be a real challenge!

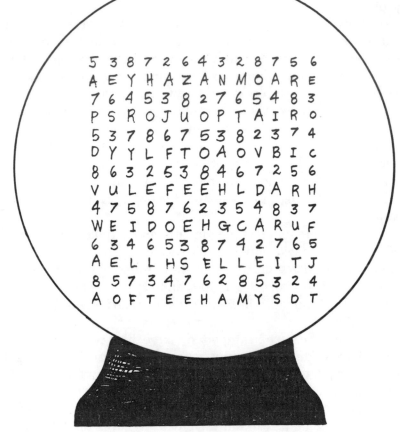

Halloween Pretzels

Etymology

Pretzels were first made by a European monk who gave them to children as a reward for having learned their prayers well. "Pretzel" comes from the Latin "pretiola": little reward. The shape actually refers to the crossed arms of children who are praying. Pretzels came to America on the Mayflower and they were used by colonists for trade with the American Indians. They were also used in games. Two Pilgrim children would hook fingers through the pretzel, make a wish, and pull! The child with the larger piece would supposedly get his/her wish.

Give each child a copy of this recipe with the blanks. Have them change the measurements to metric and be sure they have metric measuring cups and spoons to use while preparing the pretzels. Check the metric conversion table on page 24.

Wierd Creature Pretzels
Makes 2-25 critters

Pretzels are good for you. They are rich in proteins and minerals.

1 cup (_____) warm water (scant cup if honey is used)

2 pkg dry yeast

2 T (_____) raw sugar (or 2 T (_____) honey and a pinch of soda)

3 cups (_____) unbleached flour

2 tsp. (_____) baking soda

1 egg

3 T (_____) poppy seeds

butter, coarse (sea) salt, almond slices, sunflower seeds, Cheerios, cocktail toothpicks

Put the water in a bowl. Add the yeast. Stir until it's dissolved. Add raw sugar. Stir. Add flour slowly. Stir until dough is stiff. Knead dough 5 minutes. Make dough into a ball and put it in an oiled bowl. Cover with a piece of wax paper and a towel and put in a warm dark place for 30-35 minutes, until it's double in size.

While the dough rises, heat oven to 400°F (_____). Fill a big pot with water and the baking soda. Butter cookie sheets. Put the dough onto a floured table top and use a rolling pin to roll dough into a square 1/4"-1/2" (_____) thick. Use a dull knife to cut dough into pieces. Take a piece of dough and form it into a wierd monster shape. Don't try to make any details on it yet, just get a good body shape.

Use a slotted spoon to lower the critter into the boiling water. Let it stay 5-10 seconds. Then take it out and put it on the cooky sheet. Now you can use the Cheerios and nuts to make its eyes, teeth or fangs. The toothpicks can make other details—hair, spines, whatever you want.

Put a small name tag just under your creature so you will know which is yours. Brush the top of your critter with beaten egg and sprinkle salt on his back!

Bake 12-15 minutes until golden brown.

Answers for Metric Equivalents:

> 1 cup = .24 liters (1.)
> 2 T = 30 milliters (ml.)
> 3 cups = .72 l.
> 2 tsp. = 10 ml.
> 3 T = 45 ml.
> 1/4″–1/2″ = 6-10 millimeters (mm.)
> 400°F = 204° Celsius (°C)

Halloween Science:

Do You Know Your Bones?

Provide the display or learning center with: a large jointed cardboard Halloween skeleton, a "Visible Woman" and/or "Visible Man," *The Bone Picture Book* (Elementary Science Study, McGraw-Hill Book Co., Webster Division, 1221 Avenue of the Americas, NY, NY 10020) or any picture books that show detailed photos or drawings of skeletons, discarded X-rays (skull pictures) from a local hospital, paper, pencils, brads, scissors, tagboard, Elmer's Glue and *lots* of bones. You and the students can collect these bones from a butcher or you can ask the high school biology department to loan you some bones. A stewed chicken, if not boiled overlong, will provide numerous small strong bones for the students to use.

Post a sign that reads:

> **Why is it impossible to say how many bones there are in a human body? For one thing, babies have more bones than adults. Grown-ups usually have 206 bones while babies have up to 300! Lift this skull to learn why.**

The answer under the skull reads as follows:

> **Children have 5 vertebrae at the base of the spine that become one bone (the sacrum) in adults. The skull of a baby is divided by six gaps or**

"soft spots." In about two years the skull bones grow to fill in these gaps, reducing the number of parts of the skull.

Other reasons are that some of us have four tiny vertebrae in our "tail bone" at the end of our spine, while some of us have five.

Some people are born with an extra rib—this usually happens to boys (3 times as many males as females have extra ribs), so some adults have 207 bones in their bodies!

Another sign reads:

Did you know that some of your bones are not in your skeleton? How's that possible? Lift this legbone (the *radial*) to see how:

The answer under the leg bone reads:

The hyoid bone near your voice box is not connected to any other bones and the six ossicles in your inner ears are also not connected to the rest of your skeleton!

Other signs and answers read:

What is bone made of? (A bone is made of calcium. It is really a kind of very hard tissue.)

Why do we need bones? (Bones hold the body up and allow it to move. A bone is a kind of food supply system, too.)

Then have the students use the bones accumulated and do the following exercises:

1. Look at these bones. Can you find the shoulder blade, a breast bone, a rib? Look at the Visible Human (or a diagram) to tell you how each of these bones look.

2. Can you guess why the rib cage has to stick out so far? Find two different pelvises. Can you imagine what kind of animals each came from? Note how the jaw on the head works and then look to see how your forearm can turn over completely while your upper arm stays still.

3. Use the tagboard and brads to make your own moveable skelton. It can be a human one or a dinosaur or a fish or an animal you make up. (Just be sure the bones would work in the body.)

4. Make some drawings of bones or of skeletons or take some of these little bones from this box and build a bone sculpture. Turn it around and around to see that it looks good from every angle.

Herp-Osteo Specimens offers a large variety of articulated skulls and skeletons to museums and schools. Of specific interest: snake sheds and eye-covers, rattlesnake skulls, small collections of bones for children to examine or assemble themselves. Write, requesting a price list and indicating your specific interests, to:

Herp-Osteo Specimens
3919A West Magnolia Blvd.
Burbank, CA 91505

Halloween Art:

Mask Making

A mask with a chin: Divide a 12″ × 13″ piece of butcher paper or oaktag into half and into quarters. In the bottom quarter fold in both bottom corners to meet at the center of the line. Then fold up the bottom point so that it, too, meets at the center. Staple folds in place. Then cut out a semi-circle at the center. Open out this bottom part and it becomes the chin.

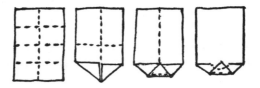

Each child then puts on a mask and marks where the eyes, nose and mouth are located.

A chart of basic outlines for features can be displayed. Let the students come up with as many outline suggestions as possible before posting the chart.

> Eyes ○ ◑ ◖ ◖ ◗ ◗
>
> Noses V ⊎ ◡ ⊎
>
> Ears ⌒ ⌒ ⌒ ⟨
>
> Mouths ⊤⊤ ◢ ◡ ∿

Once a child has decided on the basic forms, he/she cuts around nose outline and lifts up flap, cuts out mouth and eye shapes. Curled paper eyebrows or lashes may be added. Masks can be colored with felt tip pens or poster paint. Raffia or crepe paper hair or beards can be attached around sides of the mask. Using this technique, each child should have a unique mask.

Tissue-paper decorated masks: Tissue-paper overlays can be very effective in decorating a mask. Students draw a face shape and hat on tagboard and cut it out. Eyes are cut out about 2-1/2" apart. Use rubber cement to adhere several loosely overlapped layers of different colored tissues around the eyes, to define nose, cheeks or lips or to serve as eyebrows. This technique can be used to add color to *partial face mask.*

Patterns can be worked out on newsprint and then transferred to tagboard. Noses flap over and are lightly curled to stay down in place. Birds, cats, Martians and devils can be adapted to this basic design. Once mask has been cut from tagboard and decorated, child pastes hole reinforcers over two side holes and ties an elastic band to holes to hold mask onto head.

Dover Press offers two fine books of Halloween masks: "Cut and Color Paper Masks" by Michael Grater (23171-2) for $1.50 and

"Cut and Make Monster Masks in Full Color" also written by Grater (23576-9) priced at $2.00.

Funny Ol' Owls° can be made by young children—again, with a lot of variety possible in the finished pieces. Let the children look at lots of owl pictures in encyclopedias and bird books. Discuss how the wings grow out of the shoulders, where the tail attaches, how the eyes and beak are situated on the head. Then let the children pick two 6″ × 9″ pieces of construction paper offered in a range of colors. Children fold each paper in half lengthwise and draw a body shape to fill half of one sheet. Refold paper and cut out. Then draw wings to fill half of the second sheet of paper.

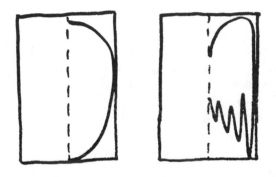

Let the children themselves come up with the wingshapes. They may want to refer back to pictures in books if they can't "remember how a wing goes." Refold paper and cut out wings. Let the kids experiment until they each find the way their wings look best on their owls' paper bodies. Glue down wings. Head and tail are cut from scraps. Each should be cut from a paper folded in half in order to assure symmetry. Glue these in place. In order to avoid stereotyping owl features, children can again refer to books when they're cutting out beaks and feet. White, gold and black paper should be provided for the children when they cut out the owls' eyes. If you have a source of tiny fluffy feathers (an old feather pillow?), these can be added to the funny ol' owls with many comic results.

[IT'S A FACT: The owl cannot move its eyes! In order to look to the side, the owl must turn his head. This head-turning sometimes makes the owl look as if his head is almost twisting off.]

°From the book, PORTFOLIO OF LOW EXPENSE ART LESSONS by Anne Martin. © 1977 by Parker Publishing Company, Inc. Published by Parker Publishing Company, Inc. West Nyack, New York 10994.

Halloween Make-Up

A safe and variable Halloween mask is one made of make-up. Stage make-up can be purchased at a costume store, or you can make your own with kitchen supplies. You will need:

2 t. white shortening   glycerin

5 t. cornstarch   food color

1 t. white flour   cocoa

For the basic white mixture, cream together the first three ingredients. Add a few drops of glycerine to make it creamy, and then add food coloring as desired. For a brown mixture, blend together 1 t. white shortening and 2-1/2 t. unsugared cocoa.

A thin line of red lipstick right below the eyes makes your eye look bloodshot and scary.

After the Halloween festivities, remove the make-up with cold cream or baby oil.

Halloween Games:

The Witch and the Warlock. One child is the witch and one is the warlock. The rest of the kids are divided equally among "the cats" and "the bats."

They go to opposite sides of the play area. When the witch and warlock call out "Bats" all the bats fly to the opposite side of the area and the witch and her partner catch as many as they can. Those caught join the Witches' Covey. Now the action is repeated with the covey calling out "Cats" and all the cats fleeing to the opposite side. Play continues for 10 minutes or until everyone is a witch—whichever.

Poison ball pass. This is a good lead-up activity for teaching kickball or basketball skills. The children make a circle and number off by twos, forming two teams in this way. Give the ball to one child. At the sound of a whistle, the ball is passed rapidly around the circle from player to player.

When the whistle blows, the ball stops. The team of the player who last held the ball gets a point *against* it. At the sound of the whistle, play resumes. At game's end, the team with the lower score wins.

[**VARIATIONS: As children's skills improve, put two balls in play across the circle from each other and/or lengthen the distance between players.**]

Halloween Party:

Children, in committees, are encouraged to do the majority of the planning. A time schedule is set up as a guide for these committees, e.g.: 2:15, recess: children may be dressing in their costumes in the restroom or cloakroom. Supervision may be needed. 2:30, everyone is in his seat. 2:35, short games, a story. 2:55, on the dot— refreshments (soft "spooky" music may be played as a calming device). 3:10, napkins discarded, everyone seated. 3:15, dismissal; clean-up committee remains in classroom (to wash paint off windows).

Decorations. The classroom windows have been painted with Halloween motifs, (a combination of kitchen cleanser mixed with poster paint). The cleanser facilitates window-washing on Friday afternoon. Torn tissue paper ghosts may have been lightly glued atop these paintings. Small scraggly tree branches have been suspended from light fixtures; brightly colored shapes (bats, owls, witches, moon) twirl on threads tied to these branches. The children can draw a large graveyard scene on the chalkboard, using only yellow and white chalks. This drawing might be done during free time on the day of the party.

Entertainment. Games should be kept fast-paced, quickly rewarding and controlled. This helps prevent younger children from becoming overly excited.

During the recess prior to the party you will hide peanuts in the shells all around the room. A few of the peanuts are tied with orange and black ribbons. When the children come back into the room they each get a plastic or wax paper sandwich bag and are told to look for the nuts around the room and to go and collect them. Mention that the orange and black ones are special. These are rewarded with *Casper the Ghost* comic books (or *Spiderman* or *Sesame Street* or *Dark Shadows*).

For the next game each child takes a strip of paper and designs a witch's nose. They color these and print their name at the top of each. Then they play "Pin the Nose on the Witch" with the understanding that this game is just for laughs and that everyone will get a prize (homemade fruit leather: pg. 350).

Refreshments. Children can vote on the choice of food prior to their party. It need not be elaborate, because an abundance of sweets will probably be consumed that evening. Treat suggestions include: hot or cold apple juice (see October Recipes at back of book); cupcakes in which foil-wrapped fortunes and tiny prizes have been baked; caramel apples; doughnuts with icing faces.

Two notes to the teacher. (1) Try to keep the day of the party as calming in mood, and as organized in method, as you can. (2) Bring an extra mask or two (or a sheet) for "that one child who couldn't have a costume this year."

● *Nevada Admitted to the Union, 1864*   [31]

Etymology

Nevada gets its name from a Spanish word which means "snow covered." The Spanish conquistadores first called the mountain range bordering this state The Sierra Nevada ("snow-clad mountains"). Nevada was named after these mountains.

OCTOBER ACTIVITIES

Class Pumpkins

If you are able to contact a farm-produce market, you can often purchase, or even order in advance, a tiny pumpkin for each child in your class. Then, armed with a spoon, each child can carve out his own jack-o'-lantern. You can walk around the room and slice off the tops of pumpkins with a knife, but usually the handle of the spoon can be used by the child himself to open the top. Newspapers are spread on each desk so that the seeds can be saved (recipe follows) and as an aid to clean-up.

As the pumpkins are scooped out, discuss the layers of the shell, the way in which the pumpkin grew from a blossom and the importance of water to the growth of the pumpkin.

The basic geometric shapes can be listed on the front board so that the children can use them as a guide to cutting features in their pumpkin. Also, remind the children to bore a small hole with a pencil in the lid of the jack-o'-lantern in order to allow the candle's smoke to escape.

Toasted Pumpkin Seeds

Thoroughly wash and clean the seeds. Drain them well on paper toweling. Sprinkle the bottom of a cookie sheet with a solid layer of salt. Arrange the seeds in a single layer on the salt. Place the cookie sheet in a moderately low oven (300°) for 40-45 minutes or until the seeds are lightly browned. Allow to cool in the pan.

Flower Bulbs

Now is the time to plant bulbs indoors. Hyacinths should bloom by Christmas; daffodils, tulips and mauve crocus are also usually successful. (Yellow crocus will not bloom indoors.) Plant bulbs in special fiber purchased at a nursery, or in a bulb jar (which need not be set in a dark place until roots appear and so allows class to watch growth).

Vegetable Faces

Maybe you'd like to try a variation on pumpkin jack o' lanterns. Young children can have lots of fun carving funny faces on turnips, potatoes, acorn or butter squash or even large apples! (Later, a vegetable soup can be made with these Halloween vegetables.)

Look Ahead Chart

Looking ahead to other Holidays: You may find it useful to discuss the form below with other teachers. Compare their ideas with your own. This can help you clarify your sense of the Holidays and how you can most effectively integrate Holiday themes into classroom learning situations.

HOLIDAY	MEANING OF HOLIDAY	HOW CHILDREN SEE IT	HOW SENSITIVE, CONCERNED TEACHERS MAY BEST PROVIDE MEANINGFUL HOLIDAY EXPERIENCE	
			In the Classroom	Suggestions to the Parents
HALLOWEEN				
THANKSGIVING				
HANNUKAH				
CHRISTMAS				

Your students can give their parents a Holiday gift that will become a family keepsake, but they will have to begin these now. Order a Small Fry Original (Tile or) Plate Kit ($3.95 each). Have each child use the special paper and markers provided to create a personal design for a gift plate or tile. Return the papers to Small Fry Originals with 5 dollars for 21-30 drawings and in up to 4 weeks your class will receive beautiful bright reproductions of their drawings laminated to white Melmac type plastic dishes or tiles. (9 dollars for 30 Holiday gifts!)

Small Fry Originals
Plastics Manufacturing Co.
2700 South Westmoreland
Dallas, TX 75224

A Puppet Theatre in the Round

This is a fine classroom addition and you can use it year after year. Choose a sturdy card table. Measure it and fit it with a sewn box made of felt. The box has no bottom. The front and back panels have 2 layers of felt in contrasting colors. One will become the flaps and the one beneath becomes the stage.

Felt is not inexpensive. You may consider using another heavy-weight cloth in place of felt.

Slit the front and back and tack flaps back as shown.

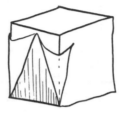

This will afford two big stages, one front and one back and the small holes on the sides can be mini-stages.

Use Elmer's Glue to carefully adhere bright colored felt details and trim to the felt box. The children can design and execute decoration of the theatre. A felt-covered cardboard marquee or front piece can be added or four towers or a series of flagstaffs or signs.

The children can sit all around this theatre. The puppets just pop out on all sides. The small holes on the sides can become peep shows during intermissions: an underwater show (goldfish in a bowl), a wild animal with a sign: DANGER This one bites! (a mirror placed flush against inside of opening). The kids can come up with their own variations!

November

†† National Children's Book Week, dates vary (Children's Book Council, 175 Fifth Avenue, New York, NY 10010)

†† Cat Week, first Sunday of November (American Feline Society, 41 Union Square, New York, NY 10003)

1 First weather observations made by U.S. Weather Bureau, 1870.

Authors Day originated by Nellie McPherson in 1928.

First test explosion of H-Bomb was held at Eniwetok, Marshall Islands, 1952.

†† Election Day is the first Tuesday after the first Monday in November.

2 James Polk, 11th U.S. President, was born in Mary County, Tennessee, 1795.

Warren G. Harding, 29th U.S. President, was born in Corsica, Ohio, 1865.

North and South Dakota were admitted to the Union as 39th and 40th states, 1889.

3   Vilhjalmur Stefansson, explorer, was born in Arnes, Canada, 1879

First Presidential election in which citizens of the District of Columbia were allowed to vote, 1964.

4   Will Rogers Day marks the birth of this cowboy humorist, in Oolagah, Oklahoma, 1879.

On this day in 1971, four men completed a raft ride across the Pacific Ocean from Ecuador to Australia.

5   Eugene V. Debs, Socialist leader, was born in Terre Haute, Indiana, 1855.

Ida Tarbell, investigative journalist, was born in Erie County, Pennsylvania in 1857.

First U.S. patent for an automobile was issued to George B. Seldon of Rochester, New York, 1895.

6   On this day in 1860, Abraham Lincoln was elected President of the USA.

James Naismith, inventor of basketball, was born in Ontario, Canada, 1861.

On this day in 1928, Herbert Hoover became the 30th president of the United States (Hoover Presidential Library Association, Inc., P.O. Box 359, West Branch, IA, 52358).

7   Marie Curie, scientist and winner of two Nobel Prizes, was born in Warsaw, Poland, 1867.

First woman elected to the U.S. House of Representatives: Jeannette Rankin of Montana, 1916.

The Russian Revolution, led by Nikolai Lenin, overthrew the Czarist government, 1917.

Quotation of the Day: "Comrades, the workers' and peasants' revolution . . . has taken place. . . . From now on, a new phase in the history of Russia begins."—*Nikolai Lenin*

Museum of Modern Art opened in New York City, 1929.

President Franklin D. Roosevelt was elected to a fourth term of office, 1944.

8   The Louvre, great Paris museum, whose construction was begun in 1204, was opened, 1793.

Montana was admitted to the Union as the 41st state, 1889.

9   First instance of a U.S. president leaving the United States while in office: President Theodore Roosevelt sailed on a U.S. battleship for the Panama Canal Zone, 1906.

11   Washington was admitted to the U.S. as the 42nd state, 1889.

Armistice Day commemorates the signing of the armistice between Allied and Central Powers at 5 A.M. on this day in 1918 in Marshal Foch's railway compartment in the Compiene Forest, France.

Quotation of the Day: "The Armistice was signed this morning. Everything for which America fought has been accomplished. It will now be our fortunate duty to assist by example, by sober, friendly counsel, and by material aid, in the establishment of just democracy throughout the world."

—President Woodrow Wilson,
in a letter to the United States.

12   Elizabeth Cady Stanton Day marks the birth of this feminist in Johnstown, New York, 1815.

14   Favorite Author's Day

On this day in 1889, Nellie Bly (Elizabeth Cochrane), reporter for the *New York World,* set off to outdo Jules Verne's hero in *Around the World in Eighty Days.* She did it in 72!

15   Georgia O'Keeffe, artist, was born in Sun Prairie, Wisconsin, 1887.

Marianne Moore, poet, was born in Kirkwood, Missouri, 1887.

16   Paul Hindemith, composer, was born in Hanau, Germany, 1895.

Oklahoma Statehood Day commemorates Oklahoma's admission to the Union as the 46th state, 1907.

17   Queen Elizabeth I succeeded to the throne of England, 1558.

Suez Canal opened, 1869.

Quotation of the Day: "In all my years of public life I have never obstructed justice . . . Your President is no crook!"—*President Richard Nixon, 1973.* (Less than a year later, on August 9, 1974, President Nixon, threatened with impeachment, resigned his Presidency.)

18   Antarctica discovered by U.S. Navy Captain Nathaniel Palmer, 1820.

19   On this day in 1620, the Mayflower arrived off Cape Cod, Massachusetts.

James A. Garfield, 20th U.S. President, was born in Orange, Ohio, 1831.

††   National Stamp Collecting Week, third Monday (American Stamp Dealer's Association, 147 West 42nd Street, New York, NY 10036)

20   First child, Peregrine White, a girl, was born to the Pilgrims in the New World, aboard the Mayflower off Cape Cod, 1620.

Senator Robert F. Kennedy was born on this day in Brookline, Massachusetts, 1925.

On this day in 1967, the population of the United States reached 200 million.

21   On this day in 1864, President Lincoln sent a letter of condolence to Mrs. Bixby, whose five sons were killed in the Civil War: "I pray that our Heavenly Father may assuage the anguish of your bereavement and leave you only the cherished memory of the loved and lost, and the solemn pride that must be yours to have laid so costly a sacrifice upon the altar of freedom."

22   The nation's gallant young leader, John Fitzgerald Kennedy, was assassinated as he rode in a motorcade through the streets of Dallas, Texas, 1963.

On this day in 1971 Elgin Long became the first person to have flown over both the North and South Poles.

23   Abigail Adams, wife and mother of U.S. Presidents, was born in Weymouth, Massachusetts in 1744.

Franklin Pierce, 14th U.S. President, was born in Hillsboro, New Hampshire in 1804.

First fossil bones were discovered in the Antarctic, 1969.

†† Thanksgiving is the fourth Thursday of November.

24 Father Junipero Serra, missionary-explorer, was born in Majorca, Spain in 1713.

Zachary Taylor, 12th U.S. President, was born in Orange County, Virginia in 1784.

Women from 21 states of the Union convened in Cleveland in 1869 to organize the American Woman Suffrage Association. The chairperson was vigorous women's rights leader, Lucy Stone; the main speaker was Julia Ward Howe.

25 Indian Heritage Day

26 First lion to be seen in America was exhibited in Boston, 1716.

On this day in 1864, Charles Dodgson sent an early Christmas gift to 12-year-old Alice Liddell. It was a handwritten story he had created for Alice, called *Alice's Adventures Underground.* (Today we know the story as *The Adventures of Alice in Wonderland* and Dodgson by his pen name, Lewis Carroll.)

Eugene Ionesco, playwright, was born in Slatany, Rumania, 1912.

28 On this day in 1520, Ferdinand Magellan entered the Pacific Ocean on his way around the world, the first European to sail the Pacific from the east.

29 On this day in 1922, Lord Carnarvon of England and his American assistant, Howard Carter, discovered the tomb of King Tutankhamen in Egypt.

First flight over the South Pole was accomplished by Richard E. Byrd and crew in his tri-motored Fokker plane, 1929.

30 Winston Churchill, former Prime Minister of Great Britain, was born on this day in Oxfordshire, England, 1874.

Quotation of the Day: I have never accepted what many people have kindly said, namely that I inspired the nation. It was the nation and the race that had the lion's heart. I had the luck to be called upon to give the roar.—

—*Sir Winston Churchill on his 80th birthday.*

Shirley Chisholm, U.S. Congresswoman, was born in New York
City in 1924.

November

For the Romans, November was the 9th month: *novem* = 9 in
latin. ("November; n. The eleventh twelfth of a weariness":
Ambrose Bierce, *Devil's Dictionary*).

NOVEMBER QUOTATIONS

---

††   The two most engaging powers of an author are to make new
things familiar, familiar things new.—*Thackeray*

Another damned thick, square book. Always scribble, scribble,
scribble, Eh, Mr. Gibbon?
—*William Henry, Duke of Gloucester, to Henry Gibbon*

Oh . . . my desire is . . . that mine adversary had written a book.
—*Job 31:35*

1   What the scientists have in their briefcases is terrifying.
—*Nikita Krushchev on the first A-Bomb test*

I'd be astounded if this planet is still going by 50 years from now. I
don't think we'll reach 2000. It would be miraculous.
—*Alistair Cook*

We are going to have to find ways of organizing ourselves
cooperatively, sanely, scientifically, harmonically and in
regenerative spontaneity with the rest of humanity around
earth. . . . We are not going to be able to operate our spaceship
earth successfully nor for much longer unless we see it as a
whole spaceship and our fate as common. It has to be everybody
or nobody.—*Buckminster Fuller*

Man has lost the capacity to foresee and forestall. He will end by
destroying the earth.—*Albert Schweitzer*

When I was a boy I was told that anybody could become President; I'm beginning to believe it!—*Clarence Darrow*

2   I am a man of limited talents from a small town. I don't seem to grasp that I am President.—*Warren G. Harding*

4   My folks didn't come over on the Mayflower, but they were there to meet the boat.—*Will Rogers*

5   While there is a lower class I am in it; while there is a criminal element, I am of it; while there is a soul in prison, I am not free.
        —*Eugene V. Debs, September 14, 1918.*

7   The workers have nothing to lose in this revolution but their chains. They have a world to gain. Workers of the world, unite!—*The Communist Manifesto 1848, last words.*

     From each according to his abilities, to each according to his needs.—*Karl Marx, 1875*

††   Thanksgiving. In regard to the moral character generally of our ancestors, the settlers of New England, my opinion is that they possessed all the Christian virtues but charity; and they seem never to have doubted that they possessed that also.
        —*Daniel Webster, October 14, 1826*

29   At first I could see nothing, the hot air escaping from the chamber causing the candle flame to flicker, but presently, as my eyes grew accustomed to the light, details of the room within emerged slowly from the mist, strange animals, statues, and gold—everywhere the glint of gold. For the moment—an eternity it must have seemed to the others standing by—I was struck dumb with amazement, and when Lord Carnarvon, unable to stand the suspense any longer, inquired anxiously, "Can you see anything?" it was all I could do to get out the words, "Yes, wonderful things."—*Howard Carter*

NOVEMBER EVENTS

- *National Children's Book Week*   [Dates Vary]

Bulletin Board Suggestions

Are You Ready for a Good Laugh? Illustrate the board with lots of photos of children's paintings, drawings of people laughing. Ask students to write short descriptions of funny book characters, amusing story situations, or their favorite humorous books.

Perhaps you'd like to give the class some suggestions for unusual ways in which to share their latest reading experiences. Here are a few:

1. Give a flannel-board talk. Cover a big piece of cardboard with (padded) flannel. Cut out characters and objects in the story from felt, or paper. In the latter case, lightly glue another felt piece to the back of each cut-out. Move characters, objects on flannel board as you tell the story.

2. Prepare a monologue from the story. This will help you see what it's like to put yourself in another person's place.

3. Make a comic book out of the story you read. Put it somewhere in your room where others will read it.

4. Make a painting or cut and paste pictures to illustrate: the best part of the story, the way it ended, a real sad part, the funniest part of the story or the sequence of what happened in the book.

5. Older students might be given the job of casting Hollywood or TV actors and actresses as characters in the book. Each role should be described in terms of physical characteristics, mannerisms and emotional and intellectual descriptions. Each casting decision should be justified by referring to an actor's previous experience or specific abilities that would make him especially suitable for the part.

6. Two or three students work together to make a slide projector and hand-made slides to use in illustrating their book reports (see page 104).

7. Older students could be asked to give their (written) responses to these suggestions:

- Locate passages that reveal the author's point of view.

• See if you can find the sentence or paragraph that best summarizes the whole story. What is the *theme* of your story?

• Find two to four sentences that tell the most important things that happened in the story. In what part of the story did you locate these sentences? How did they help in building the plot?

8. Ask older students to explain what makes a literary classic. (It holds your interest, it is well-written, warmly human, and has a very basic appeal to readers.)

• *Cat Week*   [Beginning with First Sunday in November]

Bulletin board suggestion: Use the Halloween mask idea (page 68) to quickly construct six or seven different sizes and colors of (striped, spotted) cats. Have students help make these.

The cats will be used on a bulletin board entitled: **This is Cat Week. I Bet You Didn't Know These Things About Us!**

Use the cats to point up the written areas of display. Answers are discovered by lifting up balloons which are stapled or glued to background paper on which answers are written.

Make certain students can reach the balloons.

How long have cats been around? Fossils of cats have been found which are 2 million years old!

Who had the first pet cats? About 5,000 years ago wildcats were first tamed. The Egyptians had pet cats 4,000 years ago. But probably there were no pet cats in Europe until after 1000 A.D.

How can cats see in the dark? In the dark the pupils in my eyes open very wide. This lets in lots of light so I'm able to see more at night than *you* can.

Why does a mother cat hide her babies? Newborn kittens are helpless. Their eyes are not strong. We hide our kittens to keep them safe and to keep bright light from hurting their eyes.

City life is hard on a cat. How is it making the cat family change? City cats are growing darker in color than cats that live outside cities! Scientists say this change is genetic°—it's evolution°° at work! Cats show changes faster than people do because there about 15 generations of cats during one human generation. Scientists think that city cats are getting darker because a city cat needs to keep away from many enemies (dogs, other cats, people) and darker fur helps him keep out of sight more easily.

When did cats win a war? (Ha! I bet I got you on *this* one!) In 600 B.C. the Persians were trying to take the Egyptian city of Memphis. But the city walls were too thick and high and the Persians couldn't get in. In those days the Egyptians felt that cats were like gods. The Persians didn't believe this at all. So the Persians rounded up a lot of cats and began throwing them over the walls of Memphis. The Egyptians were in a panic! They couldn't stand to see their gods hurt and although they

°(je-ne-tik) of the beginning of something.
°°(ev-ō-lū-shun) the development of an animal from its first stage of life on this planet to its present or final stage.

were stronger than the Persians, the Egyptians gave up their city in order to save the cats!

Cat Riddles:

> **What small chest is full of mouse bones?**
> (A cat's: This is a 19th century riddle.)
> **What does a cat become after it is six months old?**
> (seven months old)

- *First Weather Observation Made by U.S. Weather Bureau, 1870* [1]

Just as there is folk art and folk medicine, so there are folk methods for predicting the weather:

- When skunk cabbage grows tall (6-7 feet high) it means a severe winter is ahead.
- When deer and elk come down from the high country and blackbirds and hummingbirds head south before the cold, it means there will be deep snows.
- Common daisies and white water lilies close their petals as rain approaches.
- If the dandelion opens later than 7 A.M. or closes earlier than 7 P.M., watch for rain.
- Thin, delicate onion skins mean a mild winter.
- An abundance of wild berries, or acorns, means there will be heavy snowfalls.

What folk weather signs can your class add to this list?

Science Experiments

Cloud-making: You will need a milk bottle or a clear glass gallon jug, matches and a candle.

Explain the three main classifications of clouds:

Stratus: 1. means "layer"

             2. these clouds look like an even layer of gray or white paint over the whole sky.

             3. these are usually low clouds.

Cumulus: 1. means "pile"

             2. these clouds look like piles of fluffy cotton.

             3. they are called fair weather clouds.

Cirrus: 1. means "curl"

             2. these clouds look like curls of smoke.

             3. they are always high above the ground, usually 8-10 miles high.

             4. often they are running before a storm.

             5. they are always made of bits of ice.

Let the students come to the chalkboard and draw illustrations to go with each description of clouds.

This demonstration is hard to see if you are not right next to the person who is making the cloud. If it is possible, have the students pair off in the classroom and have each two make a cloud in their own milk bottles or jugs. This way it is easier for them to see what is explained below.

How to Make a Cloud in a Bottle

1. **Use hot water to wet the inside of a clean (milk) bottle.**

2. **Drop a lighted match into the bottle: it goes right out and leaves a trail of smoke. This smoke is made of many tiny specks. The moisture can condense around these specks. (Stand with your back to the light in order to see what happens.)**

3. **Then suck air out of the bottle. A 'cloud' forms inside! The bottle clouds up. But once air gets inside the bottle again, the cloud will disappear.**

4. What made the cloud appear in the bottle? When you sucked air from the bottle, the remaining air expanded to fill up the space and it became a little cooler. This made the water vapor condense, forming a cloud of little drops. When warm air gets into the bottle, the cloud is warm and the drops of water evaporate.

Conclusion: Clouds form when the air cools and some of their moisture condenses. When the cloud meets warmer air, the moisture in the cloud evaporates.

• *Ida Tarbell, the Original "Muckraker," Born 1857* [5]

In a revealing series of articles written in 1902, Ida Tarbell, a newspaper reporter, took on John D. Rockefeller and his Standard Trust monopoly. Her articles were very popular with the public and eventually led to the break-up of the Rockefeller oil monopoly. Enraged oil profiteers called her "Miss Tarbarrel" and made up a brand new English word to describe her: they called her a muckraker (muck is dirt, filth, wet fertilizer)! We now use the word muckraker to describe anyone who searches for and charges or exposes corruption by people in public positions.

• *Montana Was Admitted to the Union, 1889* [8]

Etymology: the word "montana" is a Latin noun meaning "a mountainous area."

• *Elizabeth Cady Stanton Day* [8]

Born on this day in 1815, Elizabeth Cady grew up to be an intelligent young woman, but in those days college degrees were not given to women. So she studied law with her father, who was a judge. But because she was a woman, she could not get a license to practice law.

While in her father's office, she learned of the many laws and discriminations there were against women. In 1848 with her friend Lucretia Mott, she held a women's rights convention in Seneca Falls, New York. This was the beginning of our modern women's rights movement.

Elizabeth Cady Stanton had great charm, intelligence, humor and courage. She was the mother of seven children and she successfully ran a large, loving household. All her life she worked for the emancipation of women. Today we honor her nearly 200 years after her birth.

Some definitions and their distinctions:

- *Suffrage:* the right to vote.
- *Suffragette:* a woman who militantly supported women's right to vote.
- *Feminism:* the theory that women should have political, economic and social rights equal to those of men.
- *Feminist:* a supporter of feminism.
- *Women's Liberation:* the movement dedicated to the realization of feminism.
- *Women's Rights:* the rights claimed by, and for, women: those of equal privileges and opportunities with men.

• *Favorite Author's Day* [14]

Take the class to the library and let them look through the books until each has found a favorite (contemporary) author. Make a list of these. Have them each compose a letter to their favorite author, making sure to use correct letter form. Interesting comments about the author's work, questions, a drawing, or a photo could be included.

You can secure the addresses of authors by finding the author in Current Biography (addresses follow each article) or by locating the publisher of the author's work and addressing the letter to the author in care of the publishing firm.

• *National Stamp Collecting Week* [The Second Week in November]

Year after year, the U.S. Postal Service gets thousands of letters filled with advice about who to put on U.S. commemorative stamps. Some of the most unusual have included:

- A salute to Whooda Tom, the world's greatest hog caller.
- A tribute to "Acrefoot" Johnson, a legendary barefoot Florida mailman.
- A stamp honoring the devil and other forces of evil. To be issued in Hell, Michigan.

If any of your students would like to design a stamp, here are three rules to remember.

1. Except for a President, a person must have been dead 10 years before he or she can be honored on a stamp.

2. No anniversaries of colleges, towns or cities can be used as they are just too numerous.

3. Don't write your Congressman for help. Send your suggestions to:

> The Citizens' Stamp Advisory Committee
> Stamp Development Branch
> U.S. Postal Service
> Washington, D.C.

Students interested in stamp collecting may write for a free Stamp Selection Booklet. Write to:

> U.S. Stamp Information Service
> P.O. Box 23501
> L'Enfant Plaza Station
> Washington, D.C. 20024

A stock list of stamp issues and a booklet describing U.S. postage stamps and postal stationery is available by writing:

> Philatelic Sales Division
> U.S. Postal Service
> Washington, D.C. 20265

Please include a self-addressed stamped envelope 3-3/4 × 8-3/4.

- *Oklahoma*   [16]

Etymology

The name Oklahoma is derived from the Choctaw Indian words "okla" meaning "people" and "humma" or "homma" meaning "red." So Oklahoma means the red people, the Native Americans.

- *First Fossil Bones Discovered in the Antarctic, 1969*   [23]

Archaeologists digging near the South Pole found fossils of Lystrosaurus, a four-foot reptile that lived 200 million years ago in parts of South Africa and Southern Asia. Finding the fossils supported the theory that Antarctica was once part of a land mass that included what is now South America and Australia.

Etymology

The Greek word "arktos" meant "bear" and "arkitkos" refers to the constellation of the Great Bear which revolves around the northern part of the earth. In these words is found the ancestor of "arctic."

Materials for building walls and fences were scarce in Medieval Europe and so, often, farmers made use of ditches, moats and trenches for draining their lands and penning their animals. In Latin, these dug-out areas were called "fosses." Often, as he was tilling the soil, a farmer would find a bone or tooth in a shovelful of earth. These bones and teeth were called "fossils" because they were objects found in fosses. It took a long time, but eventually scientists were able to prove that fossils were actually remains of plants and animals that had lived in prehistoric times.

Student-made fossils. (If possible, have actual fossils on display.) Make up a batch of Sand Clay. Wrap it in plastic wrap and then in foil to keep it moist. Have each child collect small objects to use in their fossil-making: small shells, feathers, leaves and bones work very well. A student may work to construct a small prehistoric animal by gluing tiny bones, feathers, toothpicks or balsa wood strips together. Each child gets a lump of sand clay. Let the children experiment while making impressions in the clay. Some children may want to build small prehistoric creatures *from* the clay. Let the clay dry well before moving the student-made fossils.

Sand Clay

2 cups sifted sand   Cook over medium heat, stirring
1 cup cornstarch   constantly for 5-10 minutes: until
1-1/2 cups cold water   mixture is very thick.
                            Turn onto a plate and cover with a
                            wet cloth. Cool.

• *Thanksgiving* [Fourth Thursday of the Month]

Etymology

Widespread travel was restricted until the days of the Roman Empire. Then it became quite common in large cities to see a sailor or merchant wearing odd clothes and speaking a curious strain of Latin. Such a foreigner was called a peregrinus (stranger). This word entered the English language as pilgrim.

William Bradford, first governor of the Plymouth colony, searched for a title for his group. It was made up of radicals who had left church and state to make their homes in the New World. Bradford happened upon the reference to pilgrims in the Bible: Hebrews 11:13, and he used this word to describe his small band of strangers who, for conscience's sake, had come here as Pilgrims in 1621.

The Spanish explorers discovered many new plants and animals here in the New World. Among these was a big bird domesticated and raised by the Pueblo Indians of the Southwest. When this bird was brought to Europe in about 1519, it created a sensation. Nothing like it had ever been seen there before, and many people thought it so curious that they felt it must have come from Turkey—a land of mystery to Europeans at that time. So the bird became known as a "turkey" from its supposed land of origin.

Early settlers in America found the forests thick with turkeys which weighed 50 or 60 pounds apiece. They soon learned that the male birds chattered loudly and continuously while searching for mates. Hunters learned to imitate these cries and would lure the big birds within shooting distance. It became a joke on the frontier that turkeys were completely immodest, filling the air with sounds of their lovemaking and so any person who spoke bluntly and openly was said to be 'talking turkey.'

Many of our impressions about the Pilgrims are stereotyped and even incorrect. See how many misconceptions these facts will dispel:

1. Plymouth Colony existed for just 72 years, from 1620 to 1692, when it merged with the Massachusetts Bay Colony.

2. Half of the original 100 Mayflower passengers died the first winter they were here.

3. The Pilgrims were able to establish a colony here in the New World after all other groups failed largely because of a lucky accident. After the Pilgrims landed, they sent out a scouting party which discovered a 10-bushel store of seed corn that had been hidden by the Indians for use in spring planting. The corn was buried under sand in a place that is today called Corn Hill. This corn° eventually saved the colony from starvation during the long New England winter.

4. For the first ten years, the Pilgrims did NOT have spinning wheels, candle-dipping, horn books or diamond-paned windows.

5. Bright colors, not somber greys, were typical of Pilgrim clothing. Household inventories and Plymouth Colony court records list bright colored clothing more often than that of black or grey.

6. The average household consisted of 9 to 10 people. The main room of a cabin was crowded and untidy, as it was filled with tools, drying plants and stacks of hides. Little real furniture was available.

Thanksgiving Language Arts:

Give each young child a long thin lined sheet of paper. Ask the kids to write their names at the top of these papers and follow with: I am thankful in 198__ for: Then they complete this sentence on each line with the name of something for which they feel grateful, such as "We can afford to buy our groceries," "Grandma and Grandpa write me letters," "We don't have much homework tonight."

These lists will give insights into your students' thoughts and feelings and may also indicate personal spelling words they need to practice.

°(Today maize, or 'Indian' corn, provides more people with more calories than any other plant.)

Discuss the names of the different parts of a turkey and ask the students to copy this list below or hand out sheets on which it is written.

Turkey Quiz

What part of a turkey:

1. is another way to spell "a short story"?   T __ __ __
2. is another way to spell a part of a sentence?   C __ __ __ __
3. does a farmer tend most carefully?   C __ __ __
4. do you often use in the A.M.?   C __ __ __
5. comes in the mail at the end of the month?   B __ __ __
6. is used in a band?   D __ __ __ __ __ __ __ __

(Answers: Tail, Claws, Crop, Comb, Bill, Drumstick)

Thanksgiving Reading:

This is a Tewa Prayer for well-being. The Skyloom refers to small desert rains that resemble a loom hung from the sky:

> *Oh our Mother the Earth, Oh our Father the Sky,*
> *Your children are we, and with tired backs*
> *We bring you the gifts that you love.*
> *Then weave for us a garment of brightness;*
>
> *May the warp be the white light of morning,*
> *May the weft be the red light of evening,*
> *May the fringes be the falling rain,*
> *May the border be the standing rainbow.*
>
> *Thus weave for us a garment of brightness*
> *That we may walk fittingly where the birds sing,*
> *That we may walk fittingly were the grass is green,*
> *Oh our Mother the Earth, Oh our Father the sky*
> —*Tewa*

This translation is from *Songs of the Tewa* by Herbert J. Spinden and is used with permission of the Palace of the Governors Print Shop, a working exhibit of frontier presses. The Print Shop offers *Skyloom* and other Native American poems on beautiful broadsheets, four to a package for $2. Also offered are reproductions of old newspaper pages,

"WANTED" posters, and 19th century handbills (from 25¢ to $1.25). For information write:

> The Print Shop
> Palace of the Governors
> Museum of New Mexico
> Santa Fe, NM 87501

The Winter Count. A calendar-like device used by the Sioux Indians. It measured time by winters rather than by European years and is the most extensive North American historical record known.

Painted on the tanned side of a buffalo hide, each year of the Winter Count was represented by one pictograph or glyph. Each glyph is a primitive representation of a person, place, or event of that year.

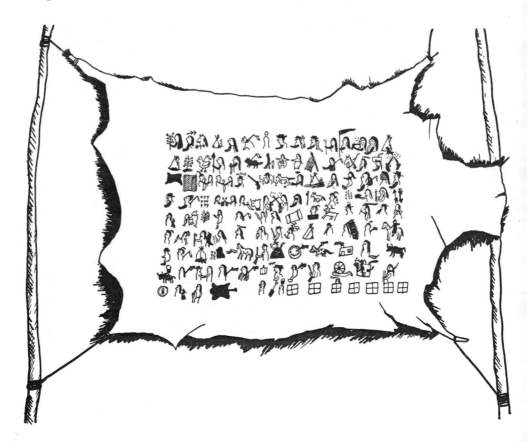

Talk with the students about glyphs and codes and about the different ways of keeping track of one's life.

Thanksgiving Math:

Enrichment. Here are two recipes for classroom cooking experiences. Very young children will enjoy communal preparation of their own cranberry sauce.

Cranberry Sauce

2 pkg cranberries (8 cups)

4 oranges

2 cups sugar (or honey)

Chop the cranberries into fine pieces, peel and chop the oranges; put the sauce into small sterilized jars. This sauce makes nice little gifts to say "thank you" to the office secretary, school custodian, or parents.

Thanksgiving Soup

a whole chicken

water

winter vegetables

salt

herbs (thyme, oregano,
    parsley, bay leaf)

Look at the chicken and talk about it: see how the joints work, notice the parallels between birds' bodies and our own. Then put the chicken into a big pot with water to cover. Simmer. Strain out all bones when meat begins to fall off.

Scrub and cut up vegetables. Peel only the ones that must be peeled. Use carrots, potatoes, onions, turnips, celery, and possibly mushrooms.

Add herbs. Talk about how the leaves of each plant taste, and differ in appearance.

Add sea salt: a pinch or so.

Continue simmering soup for two or three hours. Cool. Serve the Thanksgiving Soup in sturdy (non-waxed) paper cups at the end of a dark day.

Thanksgiving Art:

Cake frosting paint. Made by mixing 1 cup powdered tempera with 2 tablespoons wallpaper paste. Then add 1/4 to 1/2 cup liquid laundry starch to improve the consistency.

Children use tongue depressors or popsicle sticks or plastic knives to spread the paint onto a piece of white or colored cardboard. Then they model their cake frosting paint into three-dimensional designs or paintings, such as Thanksgiving landscapes.

Thanksgiving Culmination:

The Faribault State Hospital in Faribault, Minnesota (55021) is a facility for developmentally disabled children and adults, specifically those who are mentally retarded. The Director of Community Services, Mr. R. Douglas Olson, says:

> I'm sure you realize that the needs in hospitals such as ours are endless, and volunteer assistance is always needed. Letters, cards and small gifts are some of the best remembrances our people can enjoy, as long as they are regular. Let me propose a project for your (fourth) graders:
>
> Perhaps they would like to "Adopt A Building." This would mean that we would give each of your students a first name of a resident, age, birthdate and a short statement of what they like. Your students would then remember them with small gifts on special occasions as well as cards once a month through the school year. We'd attempt to provide you with names on a one-to-one basis.
>
> Our residents are all older in years than your (fourth) graders, but most enjoy pre-school to grade school activities because of their mental inabilities. Adopting a Building is a good way of getting children to recognize a need to be their brother's keeper.

Contact Mr. R. Douglas Olson if your class is interested in participating in such a project.

If your class would like to share with homeless children, write to your State Department of Social Services (located in your state capital) for the address of foster care institutions in your state.

● *Indian Heritage Day* [25]

Etymology

Heritage means the culture and tradition handed down to us by our ancestors. Heritage comes from the Latin word "hereditas" which also gives us the word "heredity", the passing on from parent to child of certain resemblances or characteristics.

Native American Poetry

Here are two poems by Indian students at Crown Point Public School in New Mexico:

The Squaw Dance

What a big fire!
Long logs, short logs,
They have chopped down
For the squaw dance.

People are sitting on the logs.
Some are drinking coffee.
People are getting ready to dance.
Some are watching.
　　　　　　　　—Gary Martinez

The Little Hogan

The little hogan on the mesa,
All alone standing against the wind.
The little fire burning in the hogan,
Sheep outside quietly lay asleep in the cold.
The winds blow the trees making sad sounds.
　　　　　　　　—Eugene Perry

If you enjoy writing, occasionally contribute your own poems for the class bulletin board, not for comparative purposes but to show the children that you, too, enjoy writing poetry and sharing your work with others.

Cinquain

Classroom
Dark eyes and hair
Murmur of native tongue
Lessons in white man's speech and thought
Two worlds
            —Anna Lee Dowdle
            5th grade teacher
            Crown Point Public School, N.M.

Art Ideas:

Painting with yucca* brushes. One stalk of yucca will yield 2–3 brushes. Split each stalk into 2–3 long pieces. Cut stalks in half if they are very long. Use a knife to slit and separate the end pieces: fibers will be used as brush "bristles." Chew the end fibers to soften and loosen them, or roll a round rock over them, using a kneading motion. Continue to chew or roll the end fibers until they bend easily and are brush-like.

Break hard clay into a fine powder. Put this into a paper cup and cover it with water and soak it for awhile. Stir until the mixture is paste-like. Add water gradually until clay-paint has the consistency of butter-milk. Add 1 teaspoon Elmer's Glue to a half-filled small paper cup of the mixture and stir. One little paper cup can provide sufficient paint for 3-4 students. The children trade colors back and forth until each has use of several colors. Clay paints must be stirred *often.*

Painting with Clay Colors. Do some research, looking at pictures of pictographs, pottery designs, Winter Counts and symbols used on baskets, silver jewelry and in beadwork. Paintings should be as authentic in design as possible. Use only natural brushes and natural paints. *No* pencils, please!

Students can choose to make one of the following:

- **A mural using pictographs (historic or original)**
- **Round medicine shields of cardboard**
- **Hide paintings on crumpled brown paper (from large grocery sacks)**

---

*Other natural materials should be experimented with until a natural brush from your area is achieved. Of course, regular classroom paint brushes may be used.

- A personal life history Winter Count of his/her own life
- Illustrations for American Indian tales or myths

Quiet corner tepee. The following suggestion for a quiet corner for young students is not intended to replicate an actual Indian tepee, and children should not think that it does. But it is quick to construct and it's a dandy change for the children, providing a quiet place to read or write a poem or just get off on their own for a bit.

You'll need two six-foot 2 × 2's (for the door frame), two discarded sheets, a heavy duty stapler and felt-tip pens. Lean the 2 × 2's in an inverted V-shape against a corner in the room.

If the children are young, have them decorate the sheets, giving them felt tip pens and reference books with pictures of early American Indian teepees. Let them use Indian symbols on the sheets or make up glyphs. The sheets can be dyed tan rather than being decorated, if you prefer.

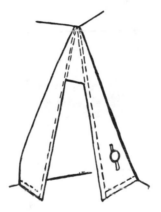

Next, staple the cloth taut between the 2 × 2's and the walls. The teepee can be folded against a wall when it is not being used. (See October, American Indian Day for other suggestions.)

- *Lewis Carroll sent Alice in Wonderland to Alice, 1846*   [26]

Lewis Carroll created an intricate and unique underground world for the setting of his book. Have the children each design a strange eccentric land in picture-form, and from these drawings, let them build a tale that takes place in their unusual countries.

NOVEMBER ACTIVITIES

Reporting on Student Work

In an examination, those who do not wish to know ask questions of those who cannot tell.—*Sir Walter Alexander Raleigh, 1861–1922*

Give one of these to each of your students prior to the end of the first report period:

1. What *do* you like about (subject).
2. How do you think (subject) could be improved?
3. What do you think was most helpful?

       reading about it?   field trips?

       seeing films about it?   film strips?

talking it over?   Uni-paks?

homework lessons?   learning centers?

special projects?

Number these in the order that you think they were most helpful.

4. **Write anything you may have to say about (subject).**

Read the answers carefully. Speak privately with any students whose answers warrant a consultation.

November Reading:

Blends

In teaching the sounds of the blends (sh, ch, th, wh), you can duplicate the following drawing to help a child remember that *sh* says "sh-h-h-h!"

Blend card games. Once the sound of *sh* has been learned, the student goes through magazines and cuts out pictures that illustrate this blend (*shoe, shirt, shoulder, shore, shiney, shampoo, shorts, shack, ship, short, shouting, etc.*). Each of these pictures is then glued to a file card. (The letters *sh* are printed in big letters on an equal number of file cards.)

This procedure is repeated with each of the blends (ch, th, wh).* When 30 or more cards have been completed, they are all put together and shuffled.

Individual children can then practice their recognition of the blends by grouping the cards into their four separate piles. Another child, or you, can check these blend piles to see that they have been correctly made.

Four or five children can play card games using these blend cards and following the rules of "Go Fish" or "Animal Rummy."

---

*You may choose to introduce this game using only two blends on the cards, adding the other two blends as the students gain confidence with the first two.

Try to jot down some of each young child's conversation (never anything embarrassing, of course). Transfer these to strips of paper and post them around the room.

The class will be surprised, and feel flattered, to see their words recorded, and appearing on public display.

Some children may want to tackle independent reading projects. Ask them to devise a "grant form" which one must fill out in order to obtain an independent reading "fellowship." This form would ask the area of interest, reason for this interest, what the applicant wants to learn and some questions he/she hopes to answer, who may be of help, how the acquired knowledge can be used, what the grant will hopefully lead to and approximately how long will be needed to complete the project.

November Science:

Slide Projector

You will need: a camera lens, a shoebox and lid, a flashlight with a good strong beam, 3 strips of 1-1/2' × 4" corrugated cardboard, a mat knife and scissors.

First, cut a hole in the middle of both ends of the shoebox: do this by drawing a line connecting opposite corners of one end of the box and where these lines cross, draw a circle, just big enough to hold the camera lens. In the other end of the box, again draw lines connecting opposite corners and make a round cut-out just big enough to hold the handle of your flashlight.

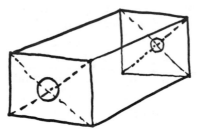

You may need to make a cardboard support.

Place the box (with inserted lens and flashlight) so that it is facing a wall five feet away. Put the lid on the box. Turn out the lights and switch on the flashlight. Adjust the position of the box by moving it back and forth until the image on the wall is in focus.

Hold a slide inside the box and move it around until its image on the wall is in focus. Draw a line on the bottom of the box to show the position of the slide at this point. This line marks the place you will put the slide cartridge.

To make the cartridge, cut holes in the 3 strips of corrugated cardboard. Now glue the strips together. Your slides should fit right into these pockets.

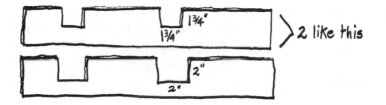

You need to be able to slide the cartridge back and forth in the projector so cut slots on both sides of the box (and lid, too, if necessary) right along the line you drew on the bottom of the box.

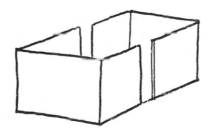

Put the lid on the box. Put a slide in the cartridge, slide it into place and project the slide! (You may have to cut off a bit from the bottom edge of the cartridge if the slide is being shown too high.)

Fun with a Magnet

A little lesson in magnetism (display with a big magnet and a jar on big and little paper clips).

Use this magnet to see how many paper clips it can make come to it.

How many little paper clips can you pick up at once? Now how many big paper clips can you pick up? What is the most paper clips that you can pick up at once? How many clips does that leave in the jar?

Make a graph on the graph paper to show each of the things italicized above.

> We know that the magnet loves the lodestone, but we do not know whether the lodstone loves the magnet or is attracted to it against its will.—*Arab physicist of the 12th century*

A Winter Flower Garden

You will need a clay pot with good drainage, potting soil, bulbs,° patience. Add soil to pot until the bulbs (pointed ends up) rest on it with their tops one inch below pot rim. Add more potting soil to cover. Water thoroughly. Store in cool (NOT freezing) place for 12 weeks. Keep soil moist, but not wet. Bring out into the warmth and light and watch your winter garden bloom and grow!

November Math:

Practice counting by twos, threes, fives, or tens (a self-teaching, self-correcting device!) Use long strips of tag board, 1″ × 15″. Make these into number lines. Then, take a paper punch and punch out all the numbers in a series, such as 2-4-6-8-10-12-14 and so on.

Let's Count by 2s!   1 O 3 O 5 O 7 O 9 O 11 O 13 O 15

The student then puts her/his paper under the number line and writes in the missing numbers. Then the number line is removed and the student looks at the paper. The student should see that he/she has just been counting by twos! The work can be checked by turning over the number line and noting the missing numbers which are written beside the holes.

°Many bulbs are *poisonous* so, of course, children should not try to 'taste' them!

December

†† Hanukkah (moveable Jewish Festival of Lights, November or December)

1 First gas station opened: Pittsburgh, Pennsylvania, 1913. On their first day of business they sold 30 gallons. Before this, gasoline was purchased in stables and garages.

On this day in 1955, Mrs. Rosa Parks, a black seamstress of Montgomery, Alabama, was arrested because she refused to give up her front section bus seat to a white man.

2 On this day in 1804, at the Cathedral of Notre Dame, Napoleon Bonaparte crowned himself Emperor of France. Just as Pope Pius VII raised the jeweled crown to place it on Napoleon's head, Bonaparte snatched the crown from him and placed it on his own head!

On this day in 1823, President James Monroe presented *The Monroe Doctrine* to the world.

Quotation of the Day: We should consider any attempt on their (the European powers) part to extend their system (of government) to any portion of this hemisphere, as dangerous to our peace and safety. *—President James Monroe.*

On this day in 1859, John Brown was hanged in the public square at Charleston, Virginia for his raid on Harper's Ferry in October. The old man was very calm before and during his ordeal and, while being driven to the gallows, he looked at the passing view and said "This *is* a beautiful country."

First self-sustaining nuclear reaction was achieved at the University of Chicago, 1942.

On this day in 1954, the U.S. Senate voted to censure Senator Joseph McCarthy (R., Wisconsin) for his conduct.

3   Illinois was admitted to the Union as our 21st state, 1818.

First human heart transplant was performed in Capetown, South Africa, by Dr. Christian Barnard on Louis Washkansky, who lived for 18 days following the operation, 1967.

4   First "Thanksgiving Day" in America, Berkeley Plantation, Virginia, 1619.

5   Martin Van Buren, 8th U.S. President, born 1782. (He was the first native born U.S. President.)

Christina Rossetti, poet, was born on this day in London, 1830.

Quotation of the Day: I love best to have each thing in its season only and enjoy doing without it at all other times. It is the greatest of all advantages to enjoy no advantages at all.
                                        —*Henry D. Thoreau, Dec. 5, 1856.*

6   On this day in 1889, people throughout the South were saddened by the news of the death of Jefferson Davis, in New Orleans.

7   Giovanni Bernini, architect, was born on this day in Naples, Italy, 1598.

Willa Cather, writer, was born on this day in Winchester, Virginia, 1873.

9   John Milton, poet, was born in London, 1608.

On this day in 1917, Jerusalem, after centuries of Moslem rule, was surrendered by Turkish troops to the British during World War I.

10 United Nations Human Rights Day marks the adoption of the U.N. Declaration of Human Rights, 1948.

Quotation of the Day: All human beings are born free and equal in dignity and rights. . . . Everyone has the right to freedom of thought. . . . Everyone has the right to freedom of opinion and expression.—*United Nations Declaration of Human Rights, 1948.*

Mississippi was admitted as the 20th U.S. state, 1817.

First distribution of Nobel Prizes, 1901, on the anniversary of the death of Alfred Nobel (1896). The peace prize is awarded in Oslo and the other Nobel Prizes are awarded in Stockholm. (On this day in 1964, the Reverend Martin Luther King, Jr., non-violent leader in the fight for civil rights in America, was awarded the Nobel Peace Prize; he became the 12th American and the third black to win this peace award.)

Quotation of the Day: I accept this award today with an abiding faith in America and an audacious faith in the future of mankind.—*Martin Luther King, Jr., 1964.*

11 Indiana was admitted to the Union as our 19th state, 1816.

On this day in 1946, UNICEF (United Nations International Children's Emergency Fund) was established.

12 On this day in 1792, Beethoven paid 19 cents for his first music lesson from Franz Joseph Haydn in Vienna.

Marconi sent first radio signal across the Atlantic, 1901.

13 On this day in 1642, New Zealand was discovered and named by Abel Tasman of the Netherlands.

14 On this day in 1799, George Washington died at Mt. Vernon, Virginia.

Quotation of the Day: To the memory of the man, first in war, first in peace and first in the hearts of his countrymen.
—*Eulogy to Washington by Col. Henry Lee.*

Alabama became the 22nd state to join the Union, 1819.

Shirley Jackson, American writer, was born in 1919.

15   Nero, Roman emperor, was born on this day in Antium, the
          Roman Empire, 37 A.D.

          Bill of Rights Day marks ratification of first 10 amendments to the
          U.S. Constitution, 1791.

          Quotation of the Day: Congress shall make no law respecting an
          establishment of religion, or prohibiting the free exercise
          thereof; or abridging the freedom of speech, or of the press; or
          the right of the people peaceably to assemble, and to petition
          the Government for a redress of grievances.
                                                        —*First Amendment.*

          On this day in 1890, Sitting Bull, Chief of the Sioux Indians, was
          shot and killed in South Dakota following a dispute with the
          federal troops.

16   Jane Austin, writer, was born on this day in Steventon, England,
          1775.

          Margaret Mead, anthropologist, was born on this day in
          Philadelphia, Pennsylvania, 1901.

          On this day in 1916, Gregory Rasputin, "The Mad Monk," who
          maintained a great influence over the Czar and Czarina of Rus-
          sia, was lured to the palace of a Petrograd noble where he was
          murdered by poison and his body was sunk beneath the ice of a
          nearby canal.

          Arthur C. Clarke, science fiction writer, was born on this day in
          Somerset, England, 1917.

17   Wright Brothers Day marks the first successful airplane flights in
          history when Orville and Wilbur Wright soared over the sand
          dunes near Kitty Hawk, North Carolina for twelve and fifty-
          nine seconds, respectively.

          Quotation of the Day: The first flights with the power machine
          were made on December 17, 1903. Only five persons besides
          ourselves were present. . . . Although a general invitation had
          been extended to the people living within five or six miles, not
          many were willing to face the rigors of a cold December wind in
          order to see, as they no doubt thought, another flying machine,
          not fly.—*The Wright Brothers.*

18   First commercial nuclear power plant in U.S. began supplying electricity to Shippingport, Pennsylvania, 1957.

19   First issue of Benjamin Franklin's *Poor Richard's Almanack* was published, 1732.

On this day in 1963, the U.S. launched the 19th Explorer Satellite.

20   First state to secede from the Union, South Carolina, voted unanimously to do so at a special convention in Charleston, 1860.

The Union of Soviet Socialist Republics was formed by fourteen Communist states, in Moscow, 1922.

21   First time that the Pilgrims set foot on American soil, Plymouth, Massachusetts, 1620.

Benjamin Disraeli, writer and Prime Minister of Great Britain, was born on this day in 1804.

Winter solstice.

22   International Arbor Day (International Arbor Day Committee, 931 East Jefferson St., Tallahassee, FL 32301).

On this day in 1938, a Coelacath, a fish thought extinct for 65,000,000 years, was caught off the coast of South Africa.

Quotation of the Day: We buried Abraham Lincoln and John Kennedy, but we did not bury their dreams or their visions.
 —President Lyndon B. Johnson, ending the nation's month of official mourning, 1963.

23   First transistor is invented by John Bardeen, Walter Brattain and William Shockley, 1947.

24   The Ku Klux Klan, a secret fraternal society, is founded on this day in 1865, in Pulaski, Tennessee.

Quotation of the Day: Twas the night before Christmas and all through the house, not a creature was stirring—not even a mouse.*—Clement C. Moore, Dec. 24, 1822.*

25   Christmas Day.

First monarch of Great Britain to be crowned in Westminister Abbey, William the Conqueror took his throne this day in 1066.

On this day in 1776, George Washington led his troops across the Delaware River to Trenton, New Jersey, for his surprise attack on the Hessians camped there.

First performance of "Silent Night" (which had been written the night before by the village schoolteacher, Franz Gruber) is heard in the village church in Oberndorf, Austria, 1818.

President Johnson's Christmas gift to the South in 1868: "An unconditional pardon and amnesty to all who directly or indirectly participated in the late rebellion."

First appearance of the character Sherlock Holmes in *Beeton's Christmas Journal*, 1887.

26   General George Washington's troops defeated the Hessians at the Battle of Trenton, in the American Revolutionary War, 1776.

28   Iowa was admitted to the Union as the 29th state, 1846.

Woodrow Wilson, 28th U.S. President, was born on this day in Staunton, Virginia in 1856.

29   Andrew Jackson, 17th U.S. President, was born on this day in Raleigh, North Carolina in 1808.

Texas was admitted to the Union as the 28th state, 1845.

30   On this day in 1853, U.S. negotiator James Gadsden signed an agreement with Mexico for the U.S. to purchase 45,000 square miles of land south of the Gila River (the southern portion of Arizona and New Mexico) for $10,000,000. This was called the Gadsden Purchase.

31   Ellis Island, in New York harbor, became the receiving station of all immigrants entering the U.S. on the Atlantic Coast. (From 1892 through 1954, 16,000,000 immigrants entered the U.S. there.)

The end of World War II was officially announced by President Harry S. Truman, 1946.

December

This is the tenth month in the calendar of ancient Rome; in Latin 'decem' is ten.

DECEMBER QUOTATIONS

2 History

. . . is a set of lies agreed upon.—*Napoleon Bonaparte*

. . . is mostly guessing; the rest is prejudice.
—*Will and Ariel Durant*

. . . is indeed little more than the register of the crimes, follies, and misfortunes of mankind.—*Edward Gibbon*

. . . is bunk!—*Henry Ford*

. . . is a bucket of ashes.—*Carl Sandburg*

. . . is a cyclic poem written by Time upon the memories of men.
—*Percy Shelley*

The monuments of the nations are all protests against nothingness after death; so are statues and inscriptions; so is history.
—*Gen. Lew Wallace*

Who would be cleared by their (un-American) Committees? Not Washington, who was a rebel. Not Jefferson, who wrote that all men are created equal and whose motto was rebellion to tyrants is obedience to God. . . . Not Lincoln, who admonished us to have malice toward none, charity for all; or Wilson, who warned that our flag was a flag of liberty of opinion as well as of political liberty or Justice Holmes, who said that our Constitution is an experiment (and) that we should be eternally vigilant against attempts to check the expression of opinions that we loathe and believe to be fraught with death.—*Henry Steele Commanger.*

Patriotism. Do not . . . regard the critics as questionable patriots. What were Washington and Jefferson and Adams but profound critics of the colonial status quo?—*Adlai Stevenson.*

5
> *Who has seen the wind?*
> *Neither you nor I:*
> *But when the trees bow their heads*
> *The wind is passing by.*
> *—"Sing Song"*

Better by far you should forget and smile
Than that you should remember and be sad.
—"Remember", Christina Rossetti

14   I thank you for your attention. You had better not take any more trouble about me but let me go off quietly.
—Last words of George Washington (to his doctors)
Dec. 14, 1799

15   True, there is government harassment, but there still is that relative freedom to fight. I can attack my government, try to organize, to change it. That's more than I can do in Moscow, Peking, or Havana.—*Saul Alinsky*

The death of a democracy is not likely to be an assassination by ambush. It will be a slow extinction from apathy, indifference and undernourishment.—*Robert Hutchins*

Freedom is not enough.—*Lyndon Johnson*

16   Hope is a good breakfast, but it is a bad supper
The remedy is worse than the disease.

They are all discoverers that think there is no land,
  when they can see nothing but sea.

Some books are to be tasted, others to be swallowed, and
  some few to be chewed and digested.

—*"Of Studies," Jane Austin*

20   Sincere diplomacy is no more possible than dry water or wooden
     iron.—*Joseph Stalin*

31   *Ships that pass in the night*
     And speak to each other in passing;
     Only a signal shown and a distant voice in the darkness;
     So on the ocean of life we pass and speak one to another.
     Only a look and a voice,
     Then darkness again and a silence.

—*Longfellow*

A General Word about December Events

Think through your ideas in response to the following questions:

- Can you state concisely what Christmas means to you? What does it mean in our culture today?

- What aspects of Christmas can be meaningful to your students who are non-Christians?

- How much of this can be part of your December teaching plans? During this season outside activities accelerate and multiply. How can you use the activities presented here to lessen or to channel pre-Christmas excitement in young children? And which might be used to prevent older students from wasting December in a mounting spiral of over-activity?

DECEMBER EVENTS

Here are a few suggestions for helping you to "keep the peace" during this exciting pre-holiday time:

1. Provide very young students with an opportunity for experimenting with water and/or sand. Few activities are as calming as sand table or water play. These can soothe over-excited children while they are experimenting with liquid measurement, action-reaction, water surface tension and liquid volume.

2. Read stories by candle light (or a luminaria*) in a darkened room.

3. Allow ample time for everything, from hanging up coats to eating lunch and painting. There is often just too much hurry during the Holidays.

4. Let young children paint at easels. Keep these set up and supplied with paint and paper all the time.

5. Plan to spend as much time as possible with each child individually.

6. You might consider putting off the decoration of your classroom until a few days before vacation to avoid over-stimulation. Let the children do the decorating *themselves.*

7. Presents and parties and Santa Claus should not be held over the heads of the children. They are given presents because they are loved . . . not because they have behaved in ways pleasing to adults.

● *First Self-sustaining Nuclear Reaction, 1942*   [2]

Older students may write for "*A Layman's Brief Guide to Nuclear Power*" and "*Radiation and Man*" which is in a comic-book format and is free from:

> Canadian Nuclear Association
> 65 Queen St. W Suite 1120
> Toronto, Ontario M5H-2 M5 Canada

---

*Page 139 explains how to make a luminaria.

An Action-Reaction Demonstration.°

You will need: a cardboard tube such as a stiff mailing tube or an empty paper towel core, about 30 cm long; a bolt or weighted dowel rod, 0.61 cm in diameter, 15 cm long with a notch in one end; several 0.61 cm dowel rods, 10 cm long; a strong rubber band with a relaxed length one-fourth that of the tube; a heavy thread or string about twice the length of the tube.

Procedure: Notch both ends of the mailing tube. Tie the string through the tube (weight it with an alligator clip but remove after threading the rubber band through the tube). Wrap a portion of the rubber band around tube end and have the remainder on the inside of the tube. (See Figure 1) Pull the string until the rubber band is stretched to about 2.5 cm from the other end. Secure the string by passing it through a notch and wrapping it around the end of the tube several times, finally applying a half-hitch or two. Load tube with notched dowel rod, and place the loaded tube on the dowel rods when all is ready.

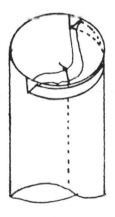

Figure 1

Demonstration: Ask for predictions as to what will happen when the string is burned (Figure 2). What quantitative results can be procured with this device? Can students improvise refinements to increase accuracy of demonstration? What would happen if this were done on the corner of a table so that all parts end up on the floor? Instead of the dowel rods, **(don't substitute glass rod or tubing)** substitute a

°As it appeared in Science Bulletin by Bev Graham, Science Specialist, N.M. State Dept. of Educ., contributed by Mr. George McBane of Dexter, New Mexico.

roller skate, or suspend the tube as a ballistics pendulum. Could a Polaroid camera help in getting quantitative results? What happens if a piece of conduit is used? A piece of pipe?

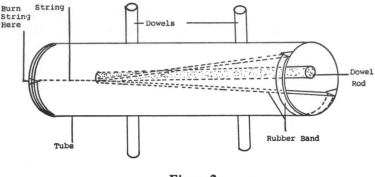

Figure 2

- ***Illinois Admitted to the Union, 1818*** **[3]**

Etymology:

    The name "Illinois" is the French form of Iliniwen, meaning "men," the name of a tribe of Algonquian Indians who lived in this region when the first Europeans arrived.

- ***Mississippi Admitted to the Union, 1817*** **[10]**

Etymology

    The name, taken from the river which forms the boundary of this state, may be Choctaw meaning "beyond age" or Illinoian, meaning "great water" or "father of all waters."

- ***First Distribution of Nobel Prizes, 1901*** **[10]**

    The money for the Nobel Peace Prize comes from a bequest of $9,200,000 left by Alfred Nobel at his death in 1896. The inventor-philanthropist got the start of his huge fortune from the sale of dynamite and other explosives. He accidentally discovered how to make dynamite by mixing nitroglycerine with inert substances. By the end of the 19th century every major nation was buying the death-dealing smokeless powder produced in Nobel's factories.

Nobel prizes are awarded for outstanding work done in the fields of physical science, chemistry, literature and in medical science or physiology.

Acceptance of his responsibility in magnifying the capacity of people to kill one another is said to have been the main force behind Nobel's establishment of the Peace Prize.

- *Indiana was Admitted to the Union, 1816*   [11]

Etymology

The word Indiana means "land of the Indians."

- *First Radio Signal Sent Across the Atlantic, 1901*   [12]

Italian inventor Guglielmo Marconi set up wireless telegraphy experiments on top of Signal Hill in Newfoundland. He succeeded in receiving and clearly understanding signals from Poldhu Station, England, on this day in 1901.

The Marconi system of telegraphy was used extensively during the First World War. During the last years of his life Marconi experimented with microwaves which he believed held the secret of television. Guglielmo Marconi died in 1937 at the age of 63.

OSCAR is an acronym for Orbiting Satellite Carrying Amateur Radio. OSCAR is an active communications satellite that can bring the space age into your classroom. It makes communication possible with cities and continents up to 5,000 miles apart. To learn more about OSCAR and how you can utilize this program in your classroom, write for free materials to:

> The American Radio Relay League, Inc.
> 225 Main St.
> Newington, CT 06111

- *Alabama Admitted to the Union, 1819*   [14]

Etymology

The word Alabama comes from the Choctaw Indian language and means, roughly, "the thicket clearers."

● *Bill of Rights Day*   [15]

An exact full size facsimile (31″ × 33″) of the original parchment document can be obtained for 70 cents° (no stamps) from:

> General Services Administration
> (NAPC)
> Washington, D.C. 20408

● *Wright Brothers' Day*   [17]

"The chilly December day two shivering bicycle mechanics from Dayton, Ohio, first felt their homemade contraption whittled out of hickory sticks, gummed together with Arnstein's Bicycle Cement stretched with muslin they'd sewn on their sister's sewing machine in their own backyard in Hawthorn Street in Dayton, Ohio, soar into the air above the dunes and the wide beach at Kitty Hawk."°°

The Academy of Model Aeronautics offers a teacher's guide to teaching about the Delta Dart. Upper grade teachers may find it helpful. Ask for a free copy from:

> Academy of Model Aeronautics
> 815 Fifteenth St., NW
> Washington, DC 20005

"Planes from Past to Present" is a free set of eight black and white (7″ × 11″) stills of commercial planes made from 1926 to 1971. The accompanying book *Inside United Airlines* would be of interest to students who plan a possible career with a commercial airline. Write for these materials to:

> United Airlines
> P. O. Box 66100
> Chicago, IL 60666

● *First Issue of Poor Richard's Almanack, 1732*   [19]

Etymology

Our word "almanac" comes from Arabic (al = the + manakh = weather). Early almanacs emphasized astronomical data, weather

---

°price subject to change without notice.
°°From John Dos Passos, *The Big Money*. Used by permission of Elizabeth H. Dos Passos.

forecasts and useful information pertaining to farming, housekeeping, and moral enlightenment.

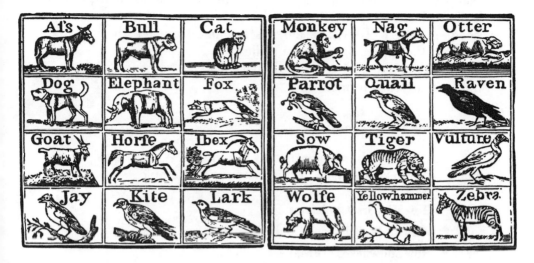

Ask the children to discuss the meaning of each of the following proverbs:

- Look before you leap.
- A penny saved is a penny earned.
- A bird in hand is worth two in the bush.
- He who hesitates is lost.
- Penny-wise and pound-foolish.

- *Winter Solstice* [21]

This is the day of winter solstice when the sun is farthest from the equator and its apparent northward motion along the horizon ends. In Latin *sol*=sun and *sisto*=to stand still.

Discuss non-deciduous trees and make a collection of cone and needle samples. From these, the children can learn to identify the 7 most common genera (Arborvitae, Pine, Yew, Hemlock, Fir, Spruce, Juniper). Emphasize the difference between the shapes of the trees. Use pictures from a seed or nursery catalog to illustrate a mix-match quiz or a bulletin board display. Remind the children that the shape of the needles begins with the same letter as the name of the tree: the fir has flat needles; the spruce has square needles.

Talk about "cold" and its relativity. Discuss how snow, sleet, hail and rain are each formed.

December Language Arts:

Have the children honor this day by writing "Winter Tales" to "explain" certain phenomena of this season. For example:

- How We First Got Icicles
- Why the World Grows Cold in Winter
- How Snowflakes Are Made
- Why Winter Nights Are Long

The children might write a winter story with a friend, each contributing ideas to the tale as it progresses.

[IT'S A FACT: When Wilson Bentley photographed more than 5,000 snowflakes, he discovered that (1) each presents a beautiful hexagonal pattern, and (2) no two are alike.]

Physical Education Suggestion:

This is a good time of year to add a Fitness Corner to your room. Post a list of suggested ways for students to use this corner so they can work off extra energy and tension. Include a few safety precautions.

1. Run in place 32 times.
2. Broad jump and measure how far you traveled.
3. Jump rope 28 times.
4. Now do "hot peppers" as long as you're able.

Hopping, throwing, striking, high-jumping, catching and use of balance beams can also be included. It's probably best to suggest just three activities at first, gradually adding to the list with time.

December Science:

Students can write to the address below for outstanding educational materials concerning wool. Eight actual samples of this fiber (from raw wool and a test tube of lanolin to the finished fabric) and an informative booklet will be sent to you free by:

Pendleton Woolen Mills
P.O. Box 1691
218 S. W. Jefferson
Portland, Oregon 97201

● *Hanukkah* [A Moveable Holiday in November or December]

"Hanukkah" means dedication and is the Jewish Festival of Lights or of Dedication. It was begun two thousand years ago in 165 B.C. by Judas Maccabeus to honor the rededication of the Temple in Jerusalem which three years earlier had been desecrated by a Syrian conqueror.

Hanukkah lasts eight days, and at sundown of each day candles are lighted—one on the first day, two on the second, and so on until the eighth evening. It is a happy holiday, and special songs are sung each evening.

The problem of Christmas-Hanukkah in the public schools. How subtle and complicated a problem it is! ... [Without the usual Christmas curriculum] what do you do with the children from Thanksgiving until Christmas? How do you decorate the classrooms and hallways? It is not a question of "equal time, equal space" for Hanukkah ... School is not the place for religious observance.

Since winter is a time for holidays in all religions, the school time could well be spent in studying comparative religion on various levels. There is a big difference between learning about a religion and being compelled to celebrate its festivals. (Tableaux, replicas, displays, prints could be researched and executed.)

The only caution that must be made is that the exhibit should be prevented from deteriorating into "Christmas Around the World," thereby portraying Hanukkah and all midwinter festivals of other religious groups as though they were mere variations on the Nativity story.*

Of course, the way you choose to treat Hanukkah and all holidays special to specific groups, depends upon the ethnic and religious makeup of your class and your community.

A Hanukkah dreidel is a toy top with four sides. Each side has a Hebrew letter which are the first letters of the words "A great miracle happened there": "nes gadol (godol) haya (ha-ya) sham (shawm)."

One way to play with the dreidel is to put out some peanuts (in the shell) as the "pot." If the letter "nun" (noon) appears, you get nothing; if "gimmel" appears, you take all; if "hay" appears you get half the pot; and if "shin" turns up you must put one peanut back into the pot.

Your students may enjoy preparing a small Hanukkah repast. It would be fun to invite your Room Mother or the principal to come to help you enjoy the festivities. The candies can be made well in advance. The cake(s) can be baked that morning, or even the day before, and a batch of the potato latkes, fried in an electric skillet, can be kept warm in paper towels, while additional latkes can be fried up on the spot, as there is a demand. Plastic forks and paper plates and napkins will also be needed.

Katowes Cake

Katowes is an old riddle-puzzle game that must be answered in numbers totaling 44. The measures for ingredients in this cake total 44—the number of candles lighted during Hanukkah.

16 tablespoons (1 cup) flour

1 teaspoon baking powder

1 teaspoon grated orange peel

3 eggs

16 tablespoons orange juice

7 teaspoons confectioners' sugar (optional)

Stir flour, baking powder and orange peel until well mixed; set aside. In the large bowl of a mixer beat eggs 10 minutes or until very thick and lemon-colored. Gradually beat in sugar until very

---

*Reprinted by permission of Schocken Books Inc. from THE HANUKKAH BOOK by Mae Shafter Rockland. Copyright © 1975 by Shocken Books Inc.

thick and light. Fold in flour mixture about a third at a time. Gently fold in orange juice. Turn into very well greased 9-inch fluted tube pan. Bake in preheated 325° oven 50 minutes or until toothpick inserted halfway between edge of pan and tube comes out clean. Cool in pan. Invert on rack. Remove pan. Sprinkle with sifted confectioners' sugar. serves 12.

NOTE: Cake shrinks in cooling.

Sesame-Seed Candies
(See appendix for metric equivalents)

1 cup sugar

1/3 cup honey

1/2 teaspoon ginger (2 tsp. fresh grated. Don't include any big fibers)

Dash of salt

3/4 cup sesame seeds

1/2 cup finely chopped nuts

In large saucepan mix sugar, honey, ginger and salt. Stir over low heat until sugar dissolves. Bring syrup to boil (wash down any sugar from sides of pan with pastry brush dipped in water). Cook over medium heat *without stirring* until mixture reaches soft-crack stage (270° on candy thermometer); remove from heat. Stir in seeds and nuts. Pour into greased 15×10×1-inch jelly-roll pan. Spread thin with wet knife. While still warm cut in diamond-shaped pieces. Cool completely. Separate candies and place on waxed paper. Cover loosely with another sheet of paper. *Let dry overnight.* Makes about 36.

Potato Latkes (Pancakes)

10 eggs	1-1/4 teaspoon pepper
15 tablespoons flour	Oil
7-1/2 teaspoons salt	Parsley sprigs

30 medium potatoes, peeled and shredded*

5 medium sized onions, shredded coarse

(Accompaniments: applesauce, sour cream)

In a large bowl mix potatoes, onion, eggs, flour, salt and pepper. In large electric skillet heat enough oil to coat bottom of pan. Drop batter by 1/4 cupfuls into oil. With back of spoon spread evenly to 3-inch pancakes. Cook over medium-high heat until golden brown

---

*Keep covered with water to prevent discoloration.

and crisp, turning once. Drain on paper towels. Place on warm platter, garnish with parsley. Serve at once with desired accompaniments. Makes 28-30 latkes.

Nursing Home Visit

You might consider taking your class to visit a nursing home during this Holiday Season. If you do, here are a few suggestions:

1. First *you* go and check out the facility. Is it really an appropriate place for a class visit? Ask the administrators what small gifts or food your class might bring. Discuss their singing carols or giving a puppet show or a short play. If your class does visit, ask if you might meet the patients in the reception room.

2. Check with your principal and get his/her okay.

3. *Then* present the idea to the class and get their thoughts.

4. Notify the parents via a mimeo and get their okay. Children should understand in advance the kinds of elderly people they'll be meeting (e.g., bedridden, blind, deaf, in wheel chairs, sedated).

5. Help the kids write a follow-up letter to the nursing home patients and staff.

● *Christmas*   [25]

Germany is generally credited as being the country of the Christmas tree's origin. Some feel St. Winifred created the first tree; others say Martin Luther, one Christmas Eve, envisioned a candle-lit tree as he gazed at the starry heavens. The first authenticated mention of decorated trees occurs in an Alsatian manuscript (1604). It is also recorded that the German soldiers in the British army decorated evergreens to celebrate Christmas in 1776 at Trenton, New Jersey. But it wasn't until 1841 that decorated trees became popular here and abroad. In that year, Queen Victoria had a tree decorated for her children at Windsor Castle, at the suggestion of Albert, her German Prince Consort.

In pagan times, bonfires were built to keep the waning sun alive during winter solstice. Christmas tree lights, fires and candles may be descendants of those primitive blazes.

In the 12th century, St. Francis of Assisi, Italy, wanted to make the Christmas story come alive for the people of his church. So he constructed the first crèche scene. It was a doll in a simple manger set upon the grass near the church; live farm animals grazed by it. St. Francis also popularized carol-singing as he relied on the use of carols in the services held around the crèche.

The word "holly" comes not from "holy," but from "holm oak," the leaves of which holly resembles. The Christmas wreath commemorates Christ's crown of thorns. Pre-Christian legends held that witches despised holly and that they would stay away from any house where it was hung (as a wreath on the door).

A pre-Christian custom dictated that Roman enemies were to reconcile with one another if ever they met under mistletoe!

Why do we have turkey at this time of year? Because James I hated boar's head. His taste for turkey at Yuletide became popularized when, in 1603, he became the King of England.

Legend says that one Christmas another English king found himself snowbound. His cook had no idea what to prepare for a holiday meal. Then he had an inspiration; he collected all the supplies in the camp: stag meat and dried apples and plums. He threw in some flour, eggs and sugar and salt and wet these down with brandy and ale. Finally he took the resulting lump of dough, tied it in a cloth and boiled it. The outcome? The very first Christmas Plum Pudding!

Over 5,000 years ago, Mexican Indians made strings of popcorn for religious ceremonies. Even today you may see strings of popcorn decorating statues in remote villages in Mexico. The Native American Indians taught the Pilgrims how to plant and cook corn. Ever since the 17th century, popcorn has been a part of our Christmas celebrations.

Etymology

The "nog" in eggnog is short for "nogging," a small mug carved from a cylinder of birch. Old English taverns used to serve drinks at the table in noggins. Nog was also the name of a strong ale. The first eggnogs were made of milk curdled in ale or dry sack (the English name for Spanish dry sherry wine) and flavored with spices.

Christmas Bulletin Boards

Lettering suggestions:

1. Soak heavy yarn in starch and form letters (on wax paper or plastic wrap) while yarn is wet. Once dry and set up, lettering is posted on bulletin board.

2. Cut out felt letters and back each one with plastic foam from a meat tray so that letters will stand out in relief from the bulletin board once they are pinned in place.

3. Use strings of popcorn wound around straight pin outlines of words.

Theme Ideas:

The Heavenly Orchestra. Each child is asked to pick a different instrument of the orchestra (or hand out slips on which names of different instruments are written).

Strings						
Strings	1.	Violin	Woodwinds	7.	Clarinet
	2.	Viola		8.	Oboe
	3.	Cello		9.	Bassoon
	4.	Double Bass	Brasses	10.	English Horn
				11.	Trumpet
	5.	Piccolo		12.	French Horn
	6.	Flute		13.	Trombone
				14.	Tuba

Percussion (not all of these are used during every per-formance)	15.	Timpani°	22.	Bells
	16.	Bass Drum	23.	Celesta
	17.	Snare Drum	24.	Triangle
	18.	Tamborine	25.	Chimes
	19.	Castinets	26.	Tom-Toms
	20.	Cymbals	27.	Xylophone
	21.	Gongs		

Have photos and actual instruments on display. Let the children familiarize themselves with each instrument and how it is held when it is being played. A visit to the high school instrumental music department might be the easiest way to accomplish this. (Have class bring sketchbooks.)

Give each student a piece of 5″ × 7″ white butcher paper, scissors, glue, a blue crayon or felt tip pen, white and silver paper doilies, down (from a feather pillow), silver tinsel garland, white yarn, and silver stars. Ask each child to design a very special angel, playing the instrument assigned to him/her. Encourage variety in the creation of these angels.

Once angels and instruments are cut out and the glue is dry, ask the students to help you group the instruments into their four families: strings, woodwinds, brass and percussion. Name a few players who *have* to stand while playing their instruments. Why do the double basses stand at the back of the orchestra instead of with the other strings? Group the Heavenly Orchestra (in their correct positions) on the bulletin board. Later, you may also want to post some of this additional information on the bulletin board (see February Music, page 223).

°Kettle drums.

Here's an easy and attractive Holiday bulletin board display that will preserve classmade ornaments until they are to be taken home as special gifts (to the kids' families). Green felt strips are carefully stapled or adhered to the board with double-sided tape. Ornaments are pinned beneath the "branches."

Our holiday greetings to you! Several young students make a *large* painting of their school on butcher paper. All the windows and doors should be included. Pin this to a bulletin board.

Next, each child makes a small self-portrait of himself/herself, which will fit into a window or doorway of the school in the painting. Some of these self-portraits can also appear in the school yard or in front of the building if drawn at full-length.

Then, each student designs a small balloon (to appear above the head of the figure) in which his/her personal Holiday greeting will appear (Rejoice, Joy, Cheers, Glad Tidings, Peace, Cheerio, Happy Holidays, Season's Cheer and Pax are some possibilities).

Finally, each child finds a place on the bulletin board to pin his/her portrait and greeting to all classroom visitors!

How did we get these holiday traditions? Older students can research and illustrate a bulletin board that answers this question. Origins of the Christmas Tree, candles, lights, holly, mistletoe, fires, crèche scene, Santa Claus, presents, reindeer, sleigh, stockings hung by the fireplace, poinsettia, plum pudding, popcorn, eggnog, Yule log, bells and Christmas cards can all be researched°, and simplified drawings can

---

°The origins of many of these traditions are mentioned in this chapter.

be made to illustrate each tradition. Illustrations and written information should be kept quite large in scale to facilitate viewing. Students should experiment with placement of information until they are satisfied with the overall composition of the display. Give them assistance if it is needed.

Room Environment—Wall Decorators

A continuous narrative mural can be used as a runner above the blackboard: *Winter Celebrations from 3000 B.C. to the Present* and could include Egyptians decorating their homes with palm branches, symbols of life triumphing over death, Romans hanging little Bacchus figures on pine trees during a Saturnalian revel, Scandinavian myth of a service tree springing from blood-soaked earth where two lovers were violently murdered, the Druids worshipping oak trees and evergreens, the French knight who found a huge tree covered with burning candles and topped by the Christ Child, and so on.

Christmas customs around the world. Probably not all of these countries could be included on one mural. Perhaps you would use traditions from countries that represent the ethnic backgrounds of your students.

Belgium:	**Children leave carrot-filled (wooden) shoes out on St. Nicholas' Eve. The carrots are for the saint's white horse.**
China:	**Christmas Trees were called the Trees of Life and in some sections of this vast country "Old Christmas Father" brought gifts.**
Czechoslovakia:	**St. Mikulas comes down from Heaven on a golden rope and wanders the earth looking for good children. An angel in robes follows him and so does his servant Peter, who has become, through time, a red-tongued devil. On Christmas Eve the family sits around the tree and fortunes are told.**
Denmark:	**Julenisse, a Yule gnome, lives in the attic all year long (with a cat). He is tiny, jolly, white-bearded and well-loved. Rice pudding is left out for him on Christmas Eve. At 12 o'clock he comes down from the attic, bringing gifts. Evergreens decorate the house, windows, and rye and wheat decorate the barn and gates.**

England:	They have Christmas trees, caroling, mistletoe, holly and a big Christmas dinner. Gifts are found by the fireplace. Old English customs go back more than a thousand years, e.g., mummers dress in strange clothes and act out old stories and legends.
France:	The family goes to church on Christmas Eve and then has a big dinner before going to bed. Pere Noel brings children gifts on Christmas Eve. He is white-bearded, and wears white robes, carries a gold staff and comes down the chimney.
Germany:	Christmas Fairs have been held "by the well in the market place" ever since the days of the Crusades. Christmas trees are known to have been used in Strasbourg, Alsace in 1605 and lighted ones were used by 1740. On Christmas Eve, gifts are exchanged. Back in 1603, people costumed as angels and devils came and asked children if they'd been good. While the children knelt in prayer, the parents put gifts on the table behind them and these gifts were said to have come from Heaven.
Greece:	St. Basil brings gifts to the children of Greece and he is said to arrive in a ship.
Holland:	St. Nicholas and his servant Peter bring gifts to the children. St. Nicholas rides a horse and wears a red bishop's robes and a long white beard. Peter carries switches and toys and gifts. Children leave carrot-filled (wooden) shoes out on St. Nicholas Eve. The carrots are for the saint's white horse.
Italy:	The crèche scene, il presepio, is the center of the celebration. Christmas Eve is spent at church and Christmas Day there is a big dinner. Gifts are delivered on January 6 by a kindly old witch, La Befana, and lumps of coal are left for bad children. Kids have hung up their socks the night before.
Mexico:	From December 6 to Christmas Eve, "las posadas" are enacted. These show the quest of

Mary and Joseph looking for a place to rest, and friends gather each night in the patio of a different home to sing "las posadas," asking for admittance. Children carry the crèche scene. Later, children are blindfolded and they try to break a hanging gift-filled piñata. On January 6, the Day of the 3 Kings, the children put their shoes on the balconies or window sills to be filled by the Kings. Later that day there is another party, piñata, and play, and at night there is a cake made in the shape of a crown. Baked inside is a little doll of Baby Jesus, and it means good luck for the child who gets it in his piece of cake.

Norway: The animals are given special treats and people say: "Here's something to let you know that Yuletide is here my friend!" Wheat sheaves for the birds are tied to posts and houses for the birds. The Journey of the Queen of Lights is acted out from house to house. Star Boys go with her, bringing light to dark Norway.

Old Russia: Gifts were brought by Grandfather Frost (Dedush Ka Moroz). They were placed under a tree decorated with gilded walnuts and gay ornaments made by the family. The Christmas Eve feast began when the first star appeared.

Panama: Children write letters to Baby Jesus c/o Saint Peter (El Niño Jesus c/o San Pedro) promising good behavior and closing with love and kisses to Mary and Joseph.

Poland: When the first star appears, the gift-giving and feasting begins on Christmas Eve. Straw is put under the table cloth to remind the family that Christ was born in a manger. Villagers dress up as animals and go caroling; they receive food and drink in return.

Puerto Rico: Children leave a gift for the Wisemen's camels on January 6 (often this gift is a basket of flowers). They find their presents the next morning.

Spain: As the first star on Christmas Eve appears, lamps are lit in the windows. After breakfast the next morning, the family dances around the "nacimiento" (manger scene), singing carols. Every year, the Magi pass through Spain on their way to Bethlehem, and they leave gifts for good children who have put their shoes out on the window sills on the night of January 5.

Sweden: Little straw goats were the earliest Christmas gifts to Swedish children, and these are still important decorations today.

On December 13, a pretty young girl in a white gown, wearing a crown of candles, brings the family coffee and cakes. She is St. Lucia, Queen of Light. On Christmas Eve, an old bearded gnome, Jultomte, gives the children gifts wrapped in many layers of tissue paper and held together with sealing wax.

Syria: On January 6, the camel brings gifts to the children who have put out bowls of food and water for him. An old legend says that the camel was the youngest of the animals ridden by the Magi and finally he fell to the ground from weariness. The Christ Child later blessed him for his great efforts. In Syria each year, candles burn to guide the Child home from over the Judean hills.

Yugoslavia: (This country is made up of 6 republics and so customs differ within it): Children write letters to Jesus and the angels who bring them gifts on Christmas morning. Most of Yugoslavia burns a

Christmas log, which must be a young oak that falls to earth just as the sun rises on Christmas morning. It is ceremoniously carried home and placed in the fire next to the crèche scene. Corn and wine are sprinkled on the log and everyone wishes for a good harvest. A young man strikes the log with an iron rod until the sparks of good fortune fly upward.

Room Environment—Windows

Stained glass window. Have children paint window with a mixture of equal parts of Bon Ami,® Alabastine® (whiting) and dry tempera paint. Pour in enough water to make a creamy paste. Apply to window with small brushes, clean cloths or little pieces of sponge. Remove paint with a damp cloth.

Stained glass stars. You will need colored tissue paper (light green, aqua, pink, yellow), black construction paper, scissors, ruler, pencil, rubber cement, Elmer's Glue® and wax paper (or a plastic drop cloth).

Children fold and cut out simple star shapes from butcher paper (brown paper bags). These shapes are then traced (with ruler) onto black construction paper. Children cut out two shapes from the black paper for each ornament. Then they cut strips of different colors of tissue paper. These strips may be about 2" × 8" in length.

The work area is covered with wax paper or a sheet of plastic and the children lightly put glue on black cutouts and lay colored tissues flat across each cutout, overlapping different colors in a random, irregular way. The matching black cutout is dabbed with glue and placed on top of tissues, exactly covering the black cutout on the bottom. Weights (big books) are placed on top of the finished star. Later these are removed and any excess tissue around the edge of the star is trimmed away. Use rubber cement to attach stars to window: apply a coat of rubber cement to back of star shape; let dry. Apply rubber cement to window pane where star will be. Let dry. Press star onto window pane.

Buy some clear plastic storm window covering; it is sold in 36" and 42" widths and easily cut with scissors. Felt-point pens work beautifully on it. (Vivid hues are obtained by squirting ink from felt-point refill-can directly onto plastic.) Crayons give a rough texture; water colors mixed with gelatin give tints, pastels. To remove ink from an area, dip a cotton swab in shellac thinner and gently rub plastic. Finished compositions are adhered to classroom windows with double stick cellophane tape.

Room Environment—Door

Large bread Santas spell out WELCOME! Paint baked Santas with poster paint (or acrylics) and spray with clear plastic. Use heavy clear plastic thread (fishing-line) to sew letters to a large piece of illustration board and then staple or tack board to classroom door. (See page 345 for bread dough recipe.)

A beautiful pine cone wreath. You'll need a circular wire base (sold at many flower shops), dark brown acoustical tile cement (sold at hardware stores), lots of pine cones, dried pods, small branches of dried berries and Baby's Breath.

Children push the cones and pods tightly into the spaces between the outer and middle wire circles and then push cones into the spaces between the inner and middle wire circles. Tile cement is generously applied to middle area and cones and pods are pressed into cement to fill *all* spaces. Let cement dry for 24 hours. Accent some parts of wreath by inserting sprigs of berries or Baby's Breath. Add a cheery big bow to complete your classroom wreath.

Language Arts:

Have the children write paragraphs based on the following:

"All the things that Christmas means to me," or "This day means different things to each of us." A lovely blank verse poem or bulletin board could result from a compilation of parts of the paragraphs.

Mail-order gift catalogs can be collected, and young children can use them to cut out their favorite pictures, pasting them onto a sheet of paper. Underneath this they write or dictate to you a few sentences about these gift selections.

This is a season for sharing and giving. Discuss how you plan to give the gift of yourself and your feelings to family and friends. What presents could you make or recycle, instead of buying?

"The Year I Couldn't Find (or lost) the Christmas Spirit (and what happened then). . . .:" a story starter.

Little Christmas Tales for the [Second] Grade: These could be executed in tiny book format using the Dolch 220 Basic Word List and then be given to the lower graders as special Holiday Gifts from your class to theirs!

Crossword Puzzles

Have students create puzzles utilizing the most frequently misspelled holiday words: wreath, sleigh, icicles, poinsettia, reindeer, mistletoe, Bethlehem, creche, nativity, myrrh, frankincense, Jerusalem.

These puzzles can read horizontally or both up and down. The most successful puzzles can be duplicated and students can work on them during free time. You could furnish the students with (partially filled in) puzzle formats such as these:

Etymology

In 1535, Henry VIII was furious when the Catholic Church refused to give him a divorce from his first wife, Catherine of Aragon. He made plans to institute a Church of England and he set about plundering the rich monasteries in order to finance his plans.

The abbot of one of these Glastonbury monasteries, hoping to protect his possessions, decided to make a good-will gesture to the King. He sent his chief steward, John Horner, with a Christmas gift to King Henry VIII: deeds to 12 estates that belonged to the monastery.

When Horner returned, he reported how pleased the King had been with the gift. But the chief steward did *not* mention how he had kept the most valuable deed for himself—property worth 100,000 pounds! Horner was never officially punished for the theft, but England learned of his exploit and someone made up a rhyme to ridicule him: Little Jack Horner . . . stuck his thumb into "a Christmas pie" and pulled out a juicy "plum" for himself! Today "a plum" describes any highly desirable prize.

Christmas Poetry:

Check with your principal before using these poems as they might be considered, by some standards, too religious for use in a classroom setting:

The Friendly Beasts

Jesus our brother, Kind and good
Was humbly born in a stable rude;
The friendly beasts around Him stood,
Jesus our brother, Kind and good.

"I," said the donkey, shaggy and brown,
"I carried His Mother up hill and down;
I carried her safely to Bethlehem town,
  I," said the donkey, shaggy and brown.

"I," said the cow, all white and red,
"I gave Him my manger for His bed,
I gave Him my hay to pillow His head.
I," said the cow, all white and red.

"I," said the sheep with the curly horn,
"I gave Him wool for a blanket warm.
He wore my coat on Christmas morn.
I,"said the sheep with the curly horn.

"I," said the dove from the rafters high,
"I cooed Him to sleep so He would not cry,

I cooed Him to sleep, my mate and I.
I," said the dove from the rafters high.

And every beast, by some good spell,
In the stable dark was glad to tell,
Of the gift He gave Immanuel.
The gift He gave Immanuel.

*   —Unknown*

"Words from an Old Spanish Carol," by Ruth Sawyer (*The Long Christmas*, Viking Press, Inc., 1941) could also be read, as it is a natural companion-piece to "The Friendly Beast," including:

". . . . *One small fish from the river, with scales*
of red, red gold,
One wild bee from the heather,
One grey lamb from the fold,
One ox from the high pasture,
One black bull from the herd,
One goatling from the far hills,
One white, white bird.
And many children, God, owe them
grace, bringing tall candles to
light Mary's face. . ."°

Young students could make wonderful drawings and paintings in illustration of these poems.

Christmas Reading:

Try reading "The Christmas Mouse" (E. Wenning, Holt Publishing Co., 1959, $3.50) aloud to your middle-graders. It's entertaining and also explains the history of the carol "Silent Night." Older students may enjoy "A Child's Christmas in Wales," (as read) by Dylan Thomas. Some background and vocabulary build-up (i.e., jelly babies, etc.) will be most helpful.

Also, check "Journey of the Magi," by T. S. Eliot; "Star of the Nativity," by Boris Pasternak; "Carol for the Children," by Ogden Nash, and "Christmas in Cornwall," by Rosalind Wade, to see if they are appropriate for use with your class this year.

Younger children may enjoy making some Mexican Christmas luminarias: Put three inches of sand in the bottom of a (waxed) brown paper bag. Position a votive candle in the middle of the sand. The top of the bag can be rolled down to give the luminaria more stability. These look especially pretty at night in the snow. Residents of a nursing home would appreciate these gifts that they might enjoy from their windows.

Christmas records, such as the Charles Laughton narration of *Mr. Pickwick's Christmas* and *A Christmas Carol* can be taped and students can use these (with headphones) during free time, for quiet Holiday listening.

Christmas Social Studies Topic Suggestions:

The manufacture of candles, the difference between mass-produced and individually created products, the production of stained-glass windows, Church Arts, a study of toys (their history and present-day counterparts; children each design a toy, e.g., jack-in-the-box), Christmas Tree Farms.

Christmas Math:

This format can be used with young children as a felt-board play, on a chart, or as duplicated sheets, to help them review basic math skills. The directions would be altered to suit the math process involved, e.g., make each of these equations equal 12.

Listening Activity That Deals with Geometric Shapes

You may or may not choose to tell your students that the result of this listening activity should be a picture of Rudolph. You can say that "we're going to review the geometric shapes."

Give each child glue, scissors, a sheet of tan or brown or grey paper and small pieces of white, black or blue, and red or pink paper. Vary colors among children. Now explain that there is *no single correct way* for these (Rudolphs) to look. Just as in nature, these (deer) should all be a little different from one another. Add that they can decide whether to cut out big shapes or tiny ones, and thick or thin pieces, as long as the pieces themselves are of the right geometric shapes.

Cut a *big* tan or grey triangle. Cut 2 medium-sized semi-circles of the same color paper. Glue one medium-sized semi-circle to one of the corners of your triangle. Glue the other medium-sized semi-circle to the closest corner to the first circle of the triangle. Now cut out two small white circles. Cut out two smaller circles from the black or brown or blue paper. Glue one small colored circle inside each white circle. Now glue these inside the triangle between the corners with the semi-circles attached to them. Cut out a pink or red circle and glue it to the empty corner of your triangle. Cut out two long thin rectangles from the brown or black and glue them vertically above the two white circles. Now cut out 9 short rectangles, again from the same color (brown or black). Glue these at random, jutting out from the two vertical rectangles. What have we made? Can you tell? Hold up your Rudolph! How terrific that each one is different from everyone else's!

Students can create Christmas math problems involving different kinds of computation. These problems should be made as funny and outlandish as possible and T.V. personalities, fellow students, and people from school can be used as characters in the story problems.

Situations might involve the purchase of Christmas decorations, gifts, telegrams, long-distance phone calls, upkeep of unusual gifts, weight gained or lost as a consequence of Holiday eating, new clothes needed for a trip or a party, the cold weather, relative temperatures involved, graphs used to show snowfall at the North Pole, and so on.

Older students can have fun making classroom decorations based on equilateral triangles and pentagons. You will need drinking straws (i.e. Craftstraws packed 2000, 17″ length paper straws in a carton and distributed by CM Arts & Crafts, Inc., 9520 Baltimore Ave., College Park, MD 20740), long thin needles, scissors, and nylon thread.

To make these decorations:

1. Thread together five equal lengths of CRAFTSTRAWS and tie the two ends to form a pentagon, with corners A, B, C, D, E.

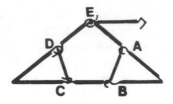

2. Thread two more lengths of CRAFTSTRAWS together and tie to the corners of A and B to form a triangle on side A B of the pentagon. Repeat on side C D and add a single length to corner E.

3. Draw together the tops of the two triangles and the single straw to form a cone.

4. Repeat as above to form a second cone, and add five more triangles to the sides of one of the cones. Bring together the above structure and the second cone by tying the apex of each triangle to the corners of the other pentagon.

An excellent instruction manual of many straw projects, "*Off We Go With Craftstraws*" is available from:

Sweetheart Cup/Straw Division
Owing Mills
Maryland 21117

Making Gingerbread People

Each child writes his name on a slip of paper and then receives a piece of wax paper for his desk top and a bit of flour. Using a large knife, cut dough into appropriate number of pieces. Once his hands are washed and his sleeves pushed up, each child gets a lump of chilled dough.

Gingerbread Dough
(for 30-45 cookies)

1/3 cup soft margarine

1 cup brown sugar   **Mix thoroughly**

1-1/2 cups dark molasses

1/2 cup cold water—Stir in

7 cups sifted flour

1/2 teaspoon EACH: salt

                     cloves

                     cinnamon   **Sift together**

                     allspice

                     ginger (fresh grated)

2 teaspoons soda are stirred into 1 T. cold water.

Chill dough. Roll out 1/3 inch thick and form into cookies. Decorate. Place on lightly oiled baking sheets. Bake at 350° for 15-18 minutes (longer baking will make brittle cookies).

Christmas Science:

Christmas Botany

American holly. This grows naturally from Massachusetts to Florida. In some places it reaches a height of 50'. At nurseries holly berries are sown and covered with mulch, and in the spring of the second year the seeds germinate. Holly is evergreen, shedding its leaves every third year.

Mistletoe. This is a parasitic air-plant growing on a host tree and manufacturing its own food. The roots of an air plant anchor it to the host tree; specialized rootlets of mistletoe delve into tissues of the host, drawing a water (and mineral) supply from it.

Christmas trees. Rather than buying a cut tree for the classroom, consider purchasing a living tree, such as a *Norfolk pine* which can then be enjoyed year round. (Lightweight ornaments should be used on a Norfolk Pine to avoid weighting down and damaging its branches.) *Balsam fir* has a symmetrical shape and its needles remain green even when dry. Its needles stay firmly attached, as they are arranged spirally on twigs and have no joints or brackets at their bases. Its cones stand erect on the boughs, giving a candle-like effect. *White spruce,* while liv-

ing, retains its bluish-green needles for 7 to 10 years! Once cut, it begins
to shed. *Cedar* has short, scale-like needles. Long-needled pines are
sometimes also used at Christmas.

Helping Birds

This is a fine time for the children to work together on a class project
such as "a gift for the birds." Such a lesson can induce quiet, thoughtful
working conditions that may initiate meaningful ecological discussions.

Here's a recipe suggested by the Audubon Society: mix equal parts
of melted beef suet and sugar syrup (3 parts water and 1 part sugar,
boiled together). Let the mixture cool to a soft, but manageable,
consistency and form into balls (about 3" in diameter). Roll the balls in
seeds, nuts, birdseed, bread crumbs, or any combination of the above.
Chill the balls in waxed paper until they are hard. Tie up the balls with
bright string for hanging on a tree, bush, outside a window, or on the fire
escape.

Comets and Meteorites

Some historians have suggested that the star of Bethlehem was, indeed, a comet. Send to these two addresses for free information
concerning comets and meteorites:

> Smithsonian Institute
> Astrophysical Observatory
> 60 Garden St.
> Cambridge, MA 02138
>
> The Manitoba Museum
>   of Man & Nature
> 190 Rupert Ave.
> Winnipeg, Manitoba R3B-ON2

(Request Astronomical sheet #5 and their list of available educational
materials.)

A Few Thoughts on Christmas Art

Year after year in their school experience, children have a
Christmas Art curriculum; try to develop plans that will alleviate boring
repetitions. What symbolic material comes with Christmas? Choose a
symbol and explore its meanings and possibilities for use in the
curriculum. What visual elements are especially a part of Christmas?
How can these be used in developing sensitivity?

When choosing gift or decoration projects for your class, be critical of the possibilities afforded for individuality of expression. Ask yourself if the project will give deeper meaning or understanding of old symbols—or is it more likely to perpetuate the cliche? Finally, what is the value of a "clever" idea when it is the teacher who initiated it?

Christmas Tree Ornaments

These ornaments may also be hung from light fixtures or along window casing or used to form a bulletin board display. Of course, in all cases, they should not be distracting to your class.

Easy star. Accordion fold a 10″ strip of paper (or a paper soda straw) into 9 equal folds. Glue ends together, forming star. Insert thread through a small hole in topmost point of star.

Five-pointed star.

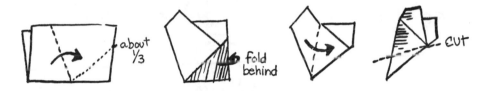

Six-pointed star. Fold a circle in half, fold this in half again. Fold this quarter of a circle into thirds. Cut on a slant as shown.

Any star at this point may have tiny holes and lacy edges cut, in order to make snowflakes instead of stars.

Paper snowmen. Let little children cut out these shapes either free-hand or by following a pattern.

Slits are made by teacher using a mat knife. Children add color, and details, and assemble.

Metallic paper strings of stars, hearts, circles. Identical pairs of stars, hearts and circles are cut out and pasted together with a thread or string in between. Silver or gold circles can be interspersed among the other shapes.

Finished strings are used like garlands on the tree or above windows.

Metallic balls. Children cut out 10 small circles of the same size (or they use legal seals available at stationer's). Each circle is folded in half and glued, one to another to form or the sections may be held together with glue to make

Use a needle to run a thread up through the middle of the ball for hanging.

Styrofoam meat tray ornaments. Wash and dry trays thoroughly. Perfect a shape (4- or 5-pointed star, a dove, an angel) on construction paper. Cut it out and lightly trace ornament onto meat tray.

Overlap two stars for a 3-D effect:

Use white glue to cement shapes together. Punch a tiny hole at point of star or other shape (near top of ornament) and thread nylon thread through hole. A light coating of glitter can be added to ornament (around edges) by applying a thin coat of glue and then sprinkling glitter onto the glue.

Satintone bell, balls, and chain. The entire class can work on this chain together. Use 1-1/4" Satintone Ribbon (which sticks to itself when moistened) and cut semi-circles 2-1/4" long from it. Moisten edges of semi-circles and press together to form a tiny bell shape. Strip off long lengths of ribbon 1/8" wide and string bells closely together. Use chain as garland on the tree.

The balls are made by first constructing 18 tiny bells as described above. Then moisten 3 of these and press them together to form a circle. Insert a ribbon loop, between the bells, for hanging. Add remaining bells, one at a time, around the original 3 until a ball is formed. Moisten each bell as you build the ball.

Pasta snowflakes and stars. Supply kids with a variety of macaroni shapes and white glue. Let them experiment with macaroni, each creating his/her own design of snowflake or star. Completed shapes are glued together and allowed to dry thoroughly before they are threaded with green or red yarn or ribbon loops for hanging.

Tiny braided Christmas wreath. Braid heavy green yarn and then glue it onto a small cardboard ring. Glue on silver shot candies. Adhere little red bow and hang by a silver cord.

Cornstarch hearts and flowers. Combine 3 cups cornstarch and 6 cups baking soda in a large pan. Stir in 3-3/4 cups water. Place over low heat and stir until mixture is the consistency of mashed potatoes. Remove from heat and cover with wet dish cloth. Allow pan to cool enough to touch.

Remove mixture from pan and knead until smooth and doughlike. On surface covered with waxed paper, roll out dough to 1/4″ thickness. Cut out shapes with cookie cutters. Also, using a sharp knife, cut out a centered 1-1/8″ to 1-1/4″ diameter hole in each shape. Pull away excess dough, knead into ball and use to roll out again. Make a centered hole through the top of each ornament using a large hairpin or an ice pick. Set ornaments on rack to dry overnight. Thin out some acrylic paint with water, use to paint ornaments and let dry. Add the date of the year in a bright color and let dry again. Brush on a final coat of polyurethane. Let dry completely and glue child's picture to back of ornament as shown.

Thread short length of ribbon or silver/gold cord through top hole. Knot ends to form a loop.

Gifts

Teacher's gift to class. Take your class caroling one evening (visit a local nursing home), and wind up at your house for hot chocolate and doughnuts.

Give the children a handmade piñata (as described in Christmas party suggestions later in this chapter).

Present your class with a set of holiday puzzles to be used during free time. Rubber cement a Christmas picture to tagboard. Press beneath books until dry. Paint the back of each puzzle with a different primary color to facilitate identification of pieces. Cut tagboard into pieces; each puzzle is kept in a hosiery box with a lid painted to match identifying color of puzzle it holds.

Advent calendar. Present your class with an Advent Calendar that begins with the first day of December and culminates on the last day of school prior to Christmas vacation. (Actual Advent Calendars, important in Europe and Scandanavia, mark the time from Advent Sunday until Christmas Day.)

A felt Advent calendar for young children. Each school day is marked by a child unpinning little plastic ornament (or wrapped box, star, or candy cane) and pinning it to the felt tree.

Large Advent calendar. Place flush against a window. It's made with a tagboard front and a tracing paper back. Each school day has a little window which gets opened out so that the light shines through. This calendar is usually teacher-made, although there may be a creative student(s) who would enjoy the challenge of designing and completing such a calendar for his/her classroom.

Magic shrinking keychain charm. Supply each child with a three-by-four inch piece of frosted acetate (available at hobby or art supply stores) and colored pencils, or a flat white styrofoam meat tray and waterproof felt tip pens. Students draw a (cartoon) figure, name, or design on the frosted side of the acetate piece or meat tray. This is then cut out with scissors. Use a paper punch to make a large hole near top of acetate or styrofoam piece.

Cover cookie sheets with aluminum foil and place pieces, colored sides up, on the foil. Preheat oven to 325° F (150° C) or toaster oven to 300° F. Bake for four minutes (one to three minutes in toaster oven). Plastic may wrinkle, curl, and then lay out flat in shrunken form. If piece sticks to itself, pull it apart, turn it over and reheat until it is flat. Remove cookie sheets with a hot pad and then quickly flatten edges of pieces using a metal spatula. Hold each piece flat until it is cool. A key chain or large jump ring is then threaded through the hole in each charm.

This gift key chain might be wrapped as a "julklap" (eliminating the dough step). A julklap is achieved by a Swedish and Danish method of wrapping small Christmas gifts: the key chain would be wrapped in fringed colored tissue paper, which is put in a little box that is tied up in bright paper and ribbon and this is wrapped in a long strip of colored cotton cloth to form a ball. Then a thin layer of dough is wrapped around it, completely covering the gift within. Dough is lightly browned in oven. This baked ball is pinned in a square of cloth and wrapped in white paper and tied with string. And there it is: a julklap!

Herbed vinegar. Buy white vinegar in gallon lots to save money. Each student has an attractive pint bottle that has been sterilized. To each pint of vinegar, student adds a sprig of fresh herbs: oregano, dill, rosemary or thyme. A clove of garlic is dropped into each bottle. A twisted peeling from a lemon, 6 whole cloves and 6 raisins are also dropped into bottle. Each bottle is then tightly corked and allowed to mellow for three to four weeks before using. Students may also design individual vinegar bottle labels, using 3″ × 4″ self-adhesive labels, which can be found at stationery stores.

Refrigerator magnets. To hold notes or pictures to any metal surface, young children design butterfly shapes, which are cut (with pinking shears) from 2 colors of felt, one shape smaller than the other.

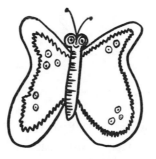

These are glued together securely. Two (thick) pipe cleaners are securely glued to felt, and a third (body) piece is cut from a dark color of felt. It is glued in place. Eyes and a smile may be added now. Tiny sequins or squares of glitter are glued onto the wings as decoration. Each completed butterfly is pressed under heavy books overnight. Four small magnets (1/3″ x 1/3″) (Pritt® Glue Magnets by Henkel Corporation, at 42 tabs for under a dollar in specialty and hardware stores) are glued to the top and bottom of the back of the butterfly. Students can make two or three butterflies as a gift to take home at Christmas.

Quick candles. Young children can make these Extra E-Z Christmas Candles; you'll need: 3 one-pound coffee cans, 1 five-pound coffee can, paraffin, old crayons, a knife, a hot-plate, water, hot pad and plumber's candles 1-3 per child.

> [NOTE: You should pour paraffin as it is very easy for children to get burned if they are not careful.]

Each one pound can is filled one-third full of melted paraffin. Crayon shavings are added to each can until paraffin is strongly colored: one can red, one blue, one green. Fill big can with water. Cans are brought to a table where each child holds a candle by its wick and dips it partway into the hot colored wax. Then candle is dipped in water to cool it. This process is repeated with different colors of wax. Each dip should submerge candle to a slightly different level so that a striped variegated candle will be the result.

A second method involves using any glass containers (jars or glasses), low-melting-point wax, metal core wicks and metal wick tabs, a candy thermometer, a double boiler, and an ice pick.

Cut the wire wick to the length you want and thread it through the button opening of the metal tab.

With a pair of pliers, press the prongs of the tab against the wick to hold it securely.

Heat the wax over water to 180° to 190° F. A candy thermometer will tell you this. Pour the wax, holding the wick above the center of the poured wax and letting it drop slowly to the bottom of your glass container. Use an ice pick to make sure the tab remains flat against the bottom.

Two Quick n' Easy Gifts

A babysitter information pad. Duplicate 20 sheets per student. Then kids punch 2 holes in the top of each sheet and make a colorful cover

Here's a pad for you to use when you go out at night. Have fun! Love, Ginny

BABY SITTERS INFO

You can reach me at......
We should be back by.....
If you have a problem call
.... at ....
Our nearest neighbor is
.... at........

Favorite stories:
Favorite toys:
TV Rules:
Food:
Bedtime:
(Allergies)

EMERGENCY #s
Our doctor:
Ambulance: ..
Fire....
Police...

and thread a piece of yarn through sheets and cover and tie a bow.

A shopper's helper. Duplicate 30 (4″ × 6″) sheets for each child.° (Adjust list to fit tastes of your students' families.) Leave extra space on sheets for shopper to use.

°Divide a ditto master sheet into thirds. Repeat list 3 times on master sheet so that you get 3 copies with each run.

Apples	Flour	Oranges
Bacon	Ice Cream	Onions
Bread	Lemons	Potatoes
Butter	Lettuce	Potato Chips
Cereal	Macaroni	Soft drinks
Coffee	Meat	Sugar
Eggs	Milk	Tea

Students punch holes and make covers and thread yarn through sheets and cover, tying yarn at the back of the folder. Each student writes a personal message on the cover, such as:

> **Here's a pad for you to use when you're going to shop for groceries. Hope it helps!**
>
> **Love,**
> **John**

Gift Wrapping Ideas

Collaged boxes. Have the children collect flat undecorated boxes; ask a department store to save some for you. Children use wide brushes to paint diluted Elmer's Glue on the box lid. Then they use their fingers to smooth on cut or torn colored tissue paper pieces. These pieces are overlapped to obtain shading and a feeling of depth. Next, a concrete design is introduced, such as a Christmas wreath, bells, holly sprigs or candles. The entire lid is given a new coat of glue and additional tissue pieces are placed on lid. Glitter may be lightly sprinkled on to paper to highlight certain areas. When the design is completed, using 3 or 4 colors of tissue, the edges of the box are trimmed of any overlapping tissue pieces.

Japanese-like dyed paper. * You will need: rice paper or any tough absorbent paper (even sturdy paper towels can be used), tube paints or food coloring, muffin tins, water, paper towels, pencils, rulers, scissors.

Children can fold the paper in nearly any direction—crosswise, diagonally or lengthwise—using an accordion-pleat technique. A folded packet is achieved. This cannot be too thick for dyes to penetrate, however.

---

*Carole M. McCarty, Seattle, and Kay L. Nation, Tokyo, originated the technique.

Put generous amounts of color in the water in each of the muffin tin areas. Children dip the corner or end of their paper into a dye bath. Paper is removed and excess color is pressed out between sheets of paper toweling. Experiment with length of time paper is in dye bath.

Dyed paper is unfolded carefully and laid to dry on paper towels. It can then be refolded and redipped to obtain unusual effects. Once dry, this paper is ready to use.

Batik paper. Each student will need two sheets of wrapping paper, old crayons, a dull knife, a bath towel, newspaper, and an iron. Spread out towel, and lay newspaper on top. Lay one sheet of paper on top of the newspaper; shave off many colors of crayons onto the paper. Make a lot of shavings and mix them up (sprinkle lightly with glitter). Place second sheet of paper on top of shavings. Quickly run a warm iron back and forth across top sheet of paper until shavings are melted. Open out two sheets of "batiked wrapping paper."

Santa sack. Each child will paint the front surface of a new flat. brown paper sack with red poster paint. Then, each student takes a piece of white railroad board and designs a face which is glued to the bag. Finally, the gift is put inside the sack and the top is tied with heavy green yarn.

Cards

A handmade card is a thoughtful gesture to extend to your Room Mother and any other persons whom the children wish to remember at this time.

Standard greetings. Joy; Peace; Noel; Rejoice; Season's Cheer; Happy Holiday; Glad Tidings; Yuletide Greetings. Children can be counted on to come up with personalized expressions of good cheer.

Card shape variations.

Icy blue Christmas cards. A crayon design message is applied heavily to a slick surfaced paper (fingerpaint paper, glazed shelf-liner paper or freezer paper)°. Then, a wash of icy blue ink is spread across the card's face to create a dramatic greeting card.

Soda straw accents. These can be achieved on a card by cutting short bits of colored plastic straws and gluing them onto a cut paper design to become the branches of a Christmas tree, the outline of a star, candles, the letters in NOEL, and so on.

°Sometimes a butcher will donate enough paper for the class to use.

Block-printing with adhesive-backed tape. Have each child create a simple design for a card (a bold outline of an angel, snowflake, holiday tiding, reindeer, holly leaf). Supply students with a roll of plastic foam or rubber weatherstripping tape (1/4 to 3/4 inch width) sold at building supply or hardware stores. Children use scissors to cut tape in different shapes.

[NOTE: Encourage experimentation, since mistakes can just be (carefully) peeled off!]

Tape is pressed onto a wooden block to form a design. Water soluble paint is then spread out on foil.

First, the student makes a test print. If no adjustments in design or lettering are necessary, then he/she tries printing on colorful construction or metallic paper. Repeat designs or multi-color patterns can be very effective on wrapping paper, too.

Santa with the moving arms. Each child constructs an armless Santa of cut and pasted paper, and glues it to the front of a (green or white) folded card. Each child gets six small paper clips and attaches them together, three at a time. One string of clips is tucked beneath each side of Santa's shoulders and taped in place. Then, glue is applied lightly to the underside of first two clips in each arm, and these are glued to the card, leaving Santa's forearms free-swinging. Paper cuffs and mittens are glued to each arm to complete these Santa cards.

Stamped holiday cards. Children use rubber stamp letters, halved fruit (apple, pear, cabbage heart) and carved spool ends to achieve a very personal greeting card. (Thank you, Susan M.)

Ask students to please remember to collect all their greeting cards after the Holidays. Once these have been brought to class they can be used in several ways:

1. Use them next year to create easy ornaments or gifs by cutting out pictures and backing with construction paper, punching a hole in them and adding a loop of colored string. Add glitter, metallic paper cut-out, paper doilies to personalize these. Small pictures may be cut out backed with construction paper squares to become Holiday tags for next year's gifts.

2. Young children can use the pictures from cards to practice sorting and alphabetizing. The greeting inside the card can be cut up into letters and words for young children to use to compose secret messages and tiny story books.

3. Donate holiday cards to a day care center, the children's ward or physical therapy department of your local hospital, or to the Red Cross—any of which can use such cards in their craft programs or work with young children.

December Physical Education

Santa's pack. This exercise also emphasizes listening skills. Each child is given a slip with a word on it that describes an article that would be in Santa's pack. Children are seated in a circle with no extra chairs. Standing child with master list of toy names begins telling a Christmas story (while walking around the circle). "Santa is filling his sack before starting on his journey. "He puts in a doll, a game, a teddy, a ball. . . ." As each child is named, he gets up and places his hands on the shoulders of the child immediately preceding him. Standing child continues walking around circle. When story teller mentions "reindeer" each child, including the story teller, tries to get a chair. The child left without a chair starts a *new* story and the game continues.

Candy cane relay race. Each team is given a red and white striped paper towel tube and a pencil. At a signal the first child in each team uses the pencil (no hands, please) to roll the candy cane down the floor to the opposite end of the play area. Then the child turns around and rolls the candy cane back to the starting line and gives the cane and pencil to the second player, who repeats these actions. The relay continues until one team finishes.

Cut ribbon relay. Two students hold a 10 foot strip of crepe paper between them. Members of their team, one after the other, run up to them, pick up (blunt-ended) scissors, cut ribbon, drop scissors, run back to line, and tag the next child who repeats these actions. (The two students continue holding crepe paper ribbon between them, regardless of its length.) The game is over when one team has had every member use the scissors.

December Puppet

You will need assorted colors of felt scraps, 1/4" diameter moveable eyes, pink, rose and red felt-tipped markers, absorbent cotton; scraps of lace, yarn and ribbon; white glue; silver glitter; stout needles and thread. Study the puppet illustrations. Cut two basic head shapes from felt and glue these together, matching the edges. When appropriate, cut out one felt hat and glue atop each head. Cut out noses and mouths, and glue them onto the heads. Use felt tip pens to color in the cheeks. Glue on eyes and collar, Santa's cotton pom pom, hat trim, beard, and mustache. Sew tiny bell to reindeer's collar. Angel's hair can be a frayed piece of thick yarn or a fur scrap glued in place. A small scrap of lace for the collar and ribbon glued beneath the head complete her.

Each square = 1 inch.

Holiday Parties

Avoid chaos by being especially well-organized this month.

Entertainment. Hand out to each child a paper on which the same sprig of holly has been mimeographed. Children make up original pictures incorporating the holly outline in any way they like; paper may be used in any direction. The class might enjoy sharing and comparing the variety of results.

Present relay. Children stand in two or more lines. Each child must run to a chair or table on which there is a "gift." He must un-tie, unwrap, re-wrap, and re-tie the gift. Then he runs back to his line, tagging second player who repeats above activity.

A Mexican-inspired piñata. A piñata made from a heavy duty, double-thickness brown paper bag works well and it is quick to make. Its only drawback is that it usually rips when struck, rather than bursting apart.

Older children especially like the feeling of striking a more solid piñata. A corrugated cardboard box can be made into an animal piñata which offers a bit more resistance to the "swinger." Put a trap door in the bottom of a cardboard box. After filling the cavity with small inexpensive wrapped gifts, candy and gum, tape trap door shut. This door should fall open after a couple of direct hits by the blindfolded child. Box can be decorated to resemble a bird or animal. Rolled newspaper serves as a base for neck, legs, wings, or arms; use staple or masking-tape to fasten these in place. Fold crepe or tissue paper (10-12 layers) and cut long strips. Along edge of each strip cut many short vertical snips. Pull strips apart; glue them two at a time about body of piñata, overlapping cut edge atop uncut edge to achieve a feathered effect.

Spread blanket on the playground under a basketball hoop. Piñata, firmly tied to a rope, is strung over the basketball hoop. Class stands behind edge of blanket out of range of blindfolded child who attempts to break the dangling pinata which you lower and raise by slackening and pulling on rope. When, after several tries, he is not successful, a new child is blindfolded and given the bat (or broomstick) with which he strikes at the piñata. Once smashed, the piñata spills its contents and the children rush forward to collect them.

Party place mats. These also make an interesting border design (for above chalkboard) in January when you return and the room is bare. So have the children make two: one for the party and one for the border.

Each child folds one segment of recycled paper or paper toweling in half and thoroughly moistens it with water. Excess water is carefully squeezed out. Towel is opened out flat. It is folded in half crosswise and then in half lengthwise. Then it is folded into a triangle as shown:

Design is begun at pointed end.

With water colors children paint different types of lines across folded paper. Dots, stars, hearts, crosses may be added. Undo 1 fold and check to see if paint is sinking through. If the lines are too faint, they are carefully retraced afresh. Undo a second fold and repeat process of re-painting, if necessary. Towel is opened out flat and allowed to dry.

Refreshments. The children would probably enjoy preparing their own refreshments (see Classroom Cookery, e.g., Nut Log) and this activity could take the place of exchanging purchased gifts. The money that would have been spent in that way could be collected and used for a charitable cause. (Save the Children Federation: 48 Witton Rd., West-port, CT 06880.) This is in keeping with the meaning of Christmas.

- *First Appearance of Sherlock Holmes, 1887*   [25]

How to take fingerprints: You will need a clean drinking glass, baby powder, Scotch Tape, and a sheet of black paper.

Hold the glass between your fingers. Now shake a little baby powder onto the glass where you were holding it. Blow lightly on the powder. Press a piece of tape onto the glass to pick up the prints. Carefully peel the tape off the glass and press it on the black paper and there you have the prints!

- *Iowa Admitted to the Union, 1846*   [28]

Etymology

Iowa takes its name from the river which was named for the Ioway Indian Tribe. The meaning of the Indian word "Iowa" is uncertain and it has been said at various times to mean "beautiful land," "this is the place," "gray snow" and "sleepy ones."

- *Texas admitted to the Union, 1845.*   [29]

Etymology

Texia was the Indian name for the group of tribes who originally lived in the eastern portion of the state. The Spanish form of this word "Tejas" (tay-haws) means "friends," "allies."

January

*In the midst of winter I finally learned
that there was in me an invincible summer.
Life is a journey, not a destination.*
—*Albert Camus*

†† Chinese New Year (a moveable feast—may occur in December or January)

1 New Year's Day

On this day in 1863, President Lincoln issued the Emancipation Proclamation, freeing the slaves in those areas adhering to the Confederate States of America.

On this day in 1975, after a 13-week trial, a federal jury found four major Nixon Administration officials (Haldeman, Colson, Ehrlichman, Mitchell) guilty of Watergate-connected crimes.

2 Betsy Ross Day commemorates the raising of first U.S. flag by the Continental Army, 1776.

Isaac Asimov, scientist, sci-fi-writer, was born on this day in Petrovichi, Russia in 1920.

3 U.S. Congress meets today, unless it has voted otherwise.

Terms of newly elected Senators and Representatives begin to-day.

Alaska, 49th state, was admitted to the Union, 1959.

4   Sir Isaac Newton, scientist, discoverer of the law of gravity, was born on this day in 1642.

Quotation of the Day: Nature and nature's laws lay hid in night: God said Let Newton be! and all was light.—Alexander Pope

J. R. R. Tolkien, writer, was born in Bloemfontein, South Africa in 1892.

Utah, 45th state of the Union, was admitted, 1896.

5   George Washington Carver Day honors the American Black scientist on the anniversary of his death in 1943.

First woman governor, Mrs. Nellie Tayloe Ross, installed as governor of Wyoming, 1925.

6   New Mexico, 47th state, was admitted to the Union, 1912.

7   First voting under the new U.S. Constitution took place during the first U.S. Presidential election (George Washington was elected), 1789.

Millard Fillmore, 13th U.S. President, was born in a log cabin in Cayuga County, New York, 1800.

Charles Addams, cartoonist, was born in Westfield, New Jersey on this day in 1912.

8   On this day in 1815, Gen. Andrew Jackson defeated the British at New Orleans, killing 700, wounding 1,400 and capturing 500. The American casualties were 8 dead, 13 wounded. This was the last battle of the War of 1812. Actually a peace settlement had been signed in Belgium two weeks earlier but no one in America knew this, as mail traveled so slowly in those days.

Elvis Presley, singer, was born in Tupelo, Mississippi in 1935.

On this day in 1959, the Cuban Revolution, led by Fidel Castro, was successful.

9   Richard Milhous Nixon, 37th U.S. President, was born in Yorba Linda, California, in 1913.

Quotation of the Day: Unlimited power is apt to corrupt the minds of those who possess it . . . where law ends, tyranny begins.—*William Pitt, the Elder, Jan. 9, 1770*

10 Thomas Paine published "Common Sense," 1776.

Ethan Allen, colonial soldier, was born in Litchfield, Connecticut, 1738.

Robinson Jeffers, poet, was born in Pittsburgh, Pennsylvania in 1887.

11 First woman to fly solo across the Pacific, Amelia Earhart Putnam, began her 18 hour flight from Honolulu to Oakland, 1935.

12 Johann H. Pestalozzi, educator, was born in Zurich, Switzerland, 1746.

First U.S. Museum was established in Charleston, S.C., 1773.

James Farmer, Black leader, was born in Marshall, Texas, 1920.

First woman was elected to the U.S. Senate, Mrs. Hattie W. Caraway (D. Ark.), 1932. (She served until 1945.)

13 Stephen Foster Memorial Day commemorates the death of the composer in 1864 in Bellevue Hospital, N.Y. (In his pockets were found his worldly goods: 34 cents and a slip of paper on which he'd written: "Dear friends and gentle hearts".)

First Black cabinet member, Robert C. Weaver, became Secretary of Housing and Urban Development, 1966.

14 Berthe Morisot, artist, was born in Bourges, France, 1841.

John Dos Passos, writer, was born in Chicago in 1896.

First assembly-line was put into operation by Henry Ford, 1914. (In 1913 it took 12-1/2 hours to put a car together, and as of this date, complete assembly of a car took 93 minutes!)

15 Human Relations Day commemorates the birth of Dr. Martin Luther King, Jr. (1929-April 4, 1968).

First cartoon showing a donkey as the symbol of the Democratic Party was drawn by Thomas Nast, 1870. (It was captioned "A Live Jackass Kicking a Dead Lion" and referred to Democractic press abuse of the late President Lincoln's Secretary of War, Stanton.)

Edward Teller, scientist, was born in Budapest, Hungary, 1908.

17 Robert Hutchins, educator, was born in Brooklyn, New York, 1899.

18 On this day in 1535, Lima, Peru was founded by Francisco Pizarro.

19 Robert E. Lee's Birthday, a legal holiday in 12 Southern states. The confederate general was born in Stratford, Virginia, in 1807.

20 Inauguration Day: the day on which, once every four years, the President of the United States is sworn into office.

First basketball game was played under the supervision of its inventor, Dr. James Naismith, in Springfield, Massachusetts, 1892.

Edwin (Buzz) Aldrin, U.S. astronaut, was born in Montclair, New Jersey in 1930.

21 Thomas "Stonewall" Jackson, Confederate general, was born in Clarksburg, Virginia, 1824.

22 First American novel was published in Boston in 1789. It was entitled "The Power of Sympathy" and was written by Philenia, a pseudonym for Mrs. Sarah Wentworth Morton. (Its plot dealt with scandal, suicide and illicit love affairs.)

Red Sunday in St. Petersburg, Russia, when the Czar's soldiers fired on 15,000 Russian workingmen as they marched to beg the Czar for better living and working conditions. Hundreds were killed and 5,000 were arrested, many being sent to Siberian labor camps, 1905.

On this day in 1973, Lyndon Baines Johnson, 36th U.S. President, died at his ranch in Texas. He was 65 years of age.

23 First American woman to become a physician, Elizabeth Blackwell, earned her M.D. on this day in 1849 at Geneva, New York.

On this day in 1950, Israel proclaimed Jerusalem its capital.

25 Robert Burns Day commemorates the birth of the poet in 1759 in Alloway, Scotland.

Shay's Rebellion took place on this day in 1787. Daniel Shay, a captain in the Revolutionary Army, led 2,000 impoverished men in a vain march on the Federal Arsenal at Springfield, Mass., hoping to overthrow the government. (Soon after, the state legislature did pass relief measures.)

Virginia Woolf, writer, was born in England in 1882.

On this day in 1890, Nellie Bly, daring young reporter for the "New York World" returned to New York, completing her amazingly fast trip around the world in the record time of 72 days, 6 hours, 11 minutes.

26   Michigan, 26th state to join the Union, 1837.

27   First tape recorder, the Wireway, was built in 1948.

On this day in 1967, three U.S. astronauts (Virgil Grissom, Edward White, Roger Chaffee) were killed by fire in their Apollo spaceship at Cape Kennedy, Florida.

28   First appointment of an American Jew to the U.S. Supreme Court, Louis D. Brandeis, was made on this day in 1916.

On this day in 1973 the Vietnam War cease fire was signed, ending the eleven year "limited war" in Vietnam.

29   Kansas was admitted to the Union as our 34th state, 1861.

William McKinley, 25th U.S. President, was born in Niles, Ohio, in 1843.

On this day in 1900, baseball's American League was organized. It was composed of eight teams: Buffalo, Chicago, Cleveland, Detroit, Indianapolis, Kansas City, Milwaukee and Minneapolis.

30   On this day in 1815, the Library of Congress, destroyed in 1814 by the British, was replaced by the U.S. government when it bought the 7,000 volume library of Thomas Jefferson for the sum of $25,000.

Franklin Delano Roosevelt, 32nd U.S. President (and only U.S. President to be elected to more than two terms of office), was born in Hyde Park, New York, in 1882.

On this day in 1933, the Nazi era in Germany began as Adolph Hitler became the German Chancelor.

On this day in 1948, Mahatma Gandhi, Indian leader and pacifist, was assassinated in New Delhi, India.

31   On this day in 1709, Alexander Selkirk, a real-life prototype of Robinson Crusoe, was rescued after being marooned for four years on Juan Fernando Island in the Pacific Ocean.

Charles Fremont, explorer, was born in Savannah, Georgia, in 1813.

Jackie Robinson, the first black major league baseball player, was born in Cairo, Georgia, in 1919.

First U.S. earth satellite, Explorer I, was launched, 1958.

January

The name comes from Latin *Januarius*, after Janus the two-faced Roman god who was able to look back into the past and at the same time, into the future. Janus also busied himself with the beginnings of all undertakings. The Romans dedicated this month to Janus by offerings of meal, wine, salt and frankincense, each of which was new. The Anglo-Saxons called January "Wulfmonath" because this was the month in which hunger drove the wolves down into the villages.

JANUARY QUOTATIONS

1   Every beginning is a consequence—every beginning ends something.—*Paul Valéry*

". . . good resolutions are easier made than executed."
—*Benjamin Franklin 1770*

"Well," said Red Jacket (to someone who complained that he had not enough time), "I suppose you have all there is."
—Samuel Johnson

2   A person gets from a symbol the meaning he puts into it.
—The United States Supreme Court

7   May God save the country, for it is evident that the people will not.
—Millard Fillmore, Nov. 11, 1844

9   In all my years of public life I have never obstructed justice. . . . Your President is no crook!*—Richard Nixon*

No public man can be just a little crooked.*—Herbert Hoover*

10   Government, even in its best state, is but a necessary evil; in its worst state, an intolerable one.
—Thomas Paine (Common Sense, *Ch. 1*)

17   My idea of education is to unsettle the minds of the young and inflame their intellects.*—Robert Hutchins*

19   The war being at an end, the Southern states having laid down their arms, and the questions at issue between them and the Northern states having been decided, I believe it to be the duty of everyone to unite in the restoration of the country and the reestablishment of peace and harmony.*—Robert E. Lee, 1865*

22   [Of Lyndon Johnson] When all the returns are in, perhaps President Johnson will have to settle for being recognized as the greatest American President for the poor and for the Negroes, but that as I see it is a very great honor indeed.
—Ralph Ellison

25   The whole world is a work of art; we are parts of the work of art. . . . But there is no Shakespeare, there is no Beethoven; certainly and emphatically there is no God; we are the words; we are the music, we are the thing, itself. And I see this when I have a shock.*—Virginia Woolf*

30   We have learned that we cannot live alone in peace; that our own well-being is dependent on the well-being of other nations, far away. . . . We have learned to be citizens of the world, members of the human community.
—Franklin Delano Roosevelt
Fourth Inaugurual Address, 1945

Hate the sin and love the sinner.

(Asked on his arrival in Europe, what he thought of Western civilization) I think it would be an excellent idea.

—*Mohandas Gandhi*

31 Jackie Robinson became America's first black major league baseball player after Branch Rickey told him: "I'm looking for a ball player with guts enough not to fight back."

At the beginning of the World Series of 1947, I experienced a completely new emotion when the National Anthem was played. This time I thought it is being played for me as much as for anyone else. This is organized major league baseball and I am standing here with all the others, and everything that takes place includes me.—*Jackie Robinson*

JANUARY EVENTS

• *The Four Day Chinese New Year:* occurs with the second new moon after the winter solstice.

Each year is assigned an animal in repeated 12 year zodiacal cycles:

Rat	*Ox*	*Tiger*	*Hare (Rabbit)*	*Dragon*	*Snake*
1936	1937	1938	1939	1940	1941
1948	1949	1950	1951	1952	1953
1960	1961	1962	1963	1964	1965
1972	1973	1974	1975	1976	1977

Horse	*Sheep (Goat)*	*Monkey*	*Rooster*	*Dog*	*Pig*
1942	1943	1944	1945	1946	1947
1954	1955	1956	1957	1958	1959
1966	1967	1968	1969	1970	1971
1978	1979	1980	1981	1982	1983

Have each child look up their year of birth and match it with the personality characteristics below. Make sure that there are dictionaries available so the students can find the meaning of any adjectives with which they are not familiar.

Rooster : calculating, ambitious, stable, self-disciplined.

Dog : humanitarian, independent, intellectual, idealistic, unconventional.

Pig : impressionable, devoted, self-sacrificing, dreamy, compassionate, emotional.

Rat : strong-willed, brave, aggressive, quick to act, assertive.

Ox : practical, stubborn, possessive, stable, enjoys luxury.

Tiger : talkative, versatile, flexible, restless, changing.

Hare : sensitive, protective, emotional, enjoys home and family.

Dragon : assertive, confident, creative, impressive, expressive.

Snake : critical, careful thinker, clean, enjoys having things in order.

Horse : easy-going, idealistic, just, stable, enjoys beauty.

Sheep : secretive, intense, purposeful, jealous.

Monkey : versatile, broad-minded, philosophical, optimistic, expansive.

Traditionally, this method of fortune-telling dates back to 2637 B.C. but it is actually probably not more than two hundred years old.

[IT'S A FACT: There is scarcely any difference between the Chinese and Aztec Zodiacs!]

Show students how to make a set of tangrams—an old Chinese game—by cutting the indicated shapes from cardboard, or from flat-sided plastic bottles, according to the following pattern and scale. Use the 7 pieces to make up your own designs or try to figure out and repeat the following patterns. A set of tangrams make a good gift for a puzzling friend.

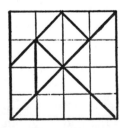

Child makes a 16 square grid and cuts on the heavy lines.

Then children try to make these, using all 7 pieces in each figure.

• *New Year's Day* [1]

Help young students to get acquainted with the new year by playing this calendar game. Give each student a duplicate sheet of the month of January as it appears on the calendar along with this list of questions:

1. On what day of the week does this month begin?
2. How many school days before ——————— (Inauguration Day, January 20)?
3. How many Sundays in this month?
4. How many days does this month have in all?
5. On what day does ——————— (January 14th) fall?
6. How many even-numbered days does this month have?
7. On what day of the week does this month end?
8. How many days until the last day of this month?

[NOTE: Such a calendar page and list of questions (with items in parentheses in numbers 2 and 5 adjusted) might be given out to students on the first day of each new month.]

Riddles about Time:

• What part of a clock is never new? (The second hand.)
• What time is it when a pie is cut up for 4 hungry kids? (A quarter to [each] one.)
• If you smash a clock, aren't you afraid people will say you *killed* time? (Not if the clock struck first.)
• A little wooden man stands on top of a very fine old clock. Every time he hears the clock strike once, he jumps twice. The clock strikes every hour. How many times does the little man jump in 24 hours? (None. A *wooden* man is never able to *hear* a clock strike.)

• *Birth of Paul Revere, 1735* [1]

Paul Revere was a silversmith. His silver work is prized by museums today.

Paul Revere was a patriot. He loved and worked for his country. He did many kinds of work in his lifetime. He published music. He printed money, and he designed the first seal for the colonies. (The seal he made for Massachusetts is still used today.) He was a dentist for awhile. He was a political cartoonist. He worked with metals, engraving them, making them into bells, and nuts and bolts. (The hardware used on the U.S.S. Constitution was made by Paul Revere.) Although he is most often remembered for his midnight ride, Paul Revere was in his own right, a Renaissance Man!

Making an engraving in the classroom

Paul made many *copper etchings*. Today we can make etchings using materials unknown in 1776. An aluminum (soda) can is opened out *flat*. It's washed with soap and dried. A sharp pointed object° is used to scratch a picture or design into the inside surface of the can. Drawings should be detailed. An oil-base blockprinting ink is applied with a (gelatin) brayer to the surface of the etching. A lightweight paper (newsprint) is carefully laid atop the inked surface and held in place with one hand. The other hand gently presses paper onto ink. The paper is carefully removed and with luck *should* now contain an etching not too dissimilar from those made by Paul Revere.

[IT'S A FACT: On the night that Revere made his famous ride, at least four other men°° also rode out to warn the colonists that British troops were coming. Paul's ride has become the most famous because 100 years later, the poet Longfellow made him into a hero in his colorful poem, "The Ride of Paul Revere."]

Incidentally, Paul had warned Concord's citizens earlier that they might be attacked and that they should begin storing food and bullets and that's lucky, because on his historic ride, he never actually reached Concord to shout a warning! British troops captured him on the way to town!

- *Birth of Sir Isaac Newton, 1642*   [4]

In the Seventeenth Century, Kepler, Galileo and Isaac Newton discovered the laws which govern the movements of the earth. They showed that these laws apply to the other planets, and we have since learned that they apply equally to the sun itself and to most of the stars. Newton did not call the earth a gyroscope because the name had not been invented in his time, but the rules by which gyroscopic instruments are designed today are based on the laws expounded by Isaac Newton.

°Utility knife, nail file, old dentistry tool. Ask your dentist to save old tools for you; they often come in handy.

°°Solomon Brown, Joseph Hall, William Dawes & Ebenezer Door.

Etymology

A *gyroscope* is a spinning mass mounted in such a way that it will keep its original plane of rotation no matter which way the ring holding it is turned. The word "gyroscope" was given to the world by the French scientist, Leon Foucault, in 1851. Foucault made his first gyroscope for the special purpose of demonstrating the rotation of the earth. The derivation of its name comes from two Greek words— "Gyros," meaning "revolution," and "Sklopein," meaning "to view." Combined they form the term that means "to view the revolution (of the earth)."

Bring a gyroscope to class. Accompany it with a copy of the very informative booklet *The Gyroscope Through the Ages*, obtainable free of charge from:

> Sperry Flight Systems
> P.O. Box 21111
> Phoenix, AZ 85036.

A magnificent collage time-line, featuring Newton and titled "Men of Modern Mathematics: 100-1950," is available free from:

> IBM
> Rte. 22
> Armonk, NY 10504

The collage designed by Charles Eames) is very detailed and older students can make up "treasure hunt" clues to help one another become familiar with the details of this beautiful chart.

Some students may want to develop a parallel chart, such as "Women in Modern Science, Mathematics" (using the help of *Women in America* Vol. I-III, which should be in the reference room of your library). Students can use magazine cut-outs or drawings as illustrations for their chart.

Many of Newton's mathematical discoveries were obtained, in part or completely, while he slept. He was not unique in this sense. Elias Howe perfected the sewing machine in a dream. Chemist Friedrich Kekule also had a vivid dream about snakes which he knew to be atoms and they were making rings by taking the tails of one another in their mouths. This dream led to Kekule's revolutionary closed chain theory of the benzene molecule!

Otto Loewi had a dream which explained how the nerves control the muscles, but on awakening, he could not remember some important parts of the explanation. Sometime later, Loewi had the very same dream *again* and this time he wrote it all down. He tested the ideas and this work led to his Nobel Prize in medicine!

Daydreaming Solutions

You can ask very young students to close their eyes, be still for a bit, and have "a *day*-dream"! Then, ask anyone who is willing, to share his/her "dream" with the class. A classroom *Book of Dreams* (real and "imagined") could be the outcome of language experience charts obtained by printing the stories on large sheets of paper as the children dictate them to you.

Ask students to "daydream" a solution or invention suited for some social or ecological problem.

Talk about the function of dreams: problem-solving, wish-fulfillment, affording practice in facing dangerous situations, and so on.

A dream uninterpreted is like a letter unopened.—Babylonian Talmud

● *Utah was admitted to the Union, 1896.*   [4]

Etymology

This state takes its name from the Ute Indians who first lived in this region.

● *Death of George Washington Carver, 1946.*   [5]

Carver was born of slave parents on a farm in Missouri. We do not know the date of his birth. He and his mother were stolen when he was a baby. Later his owner recognized his special intelligence and set him free. He worked his way through college, and as an agricultural chemist, he earned international fame. As a result of his experiments, he discovered how to use the sweet potato to make flour, shoe polish, and candy. He made starch and gum from cotton stalks, dyes from clay, and synthetic marble from wood shavings. Carver succeeded in making 300 different products from the peanut, ranging from instant coffee to ink, soap, and cosmetics! At his death in 1946, he left his life savings to be used for continued research in the field of agriculture.

The National Peanut Council offers an outstanding packet of materials for teaching about George Washington Carver and peanuts. "The Great Goober Fun-Fact Folder," a set of mimeo-master sheets of games, quizzes and recipes is available. Write, requesting it, to:

> National Peanut Council
> Communications Division
> 111 E. Wacker Dr.
> Chicago, ILL. 60601

"Growing Peanuts in a Home Garden" and "The Lion Who Liked Peanut Butter", as well as fact and recipe sheets, are also available free from:

> The Oklahoma Peanut Commission
> P.O. Box D
> Madill, OK 73446

• *American Red Cross, 1905* [5]

On this day in 1905, the American Red Cross, inspired by the work of Florence Nightingale during the Crimean War (1854-1856), was granted a Congressional Charter stating that this would be a private organization with semi-governmental status, financed by voluntary contributions and membership fees. To learn more about the Red Cross and how your class may be of service, write

> The American National Red Cross
> National Headquarters
> Washington, DC 20006

and request the classroom educational materials and the current "Editor's Kit" with materials about "The Good Neighbor."

• *New Mexico Admitted to the Union, 1912* [6]

Etymology

This state was named Nuevo Mejico by Fray Jacinto de San Francisco in about 1561. It was hoped that New Mexico would hold wealth like that found by Cortez in (Old) Mexico! "Mexico" comes from "Mexita" and means "the place of the Aztec god of war"!

- *Birth of Robinson Jeffers, 1887*   [10]

Read some of Jeffers' works to your class or make duplicate sheets of some of his poetry so that the students can become acquainted with this fine American poet.

- *Stephen Foster Memorial Day*   [13]

Born July 4, 1826, Foster wrote 200 songs in his lifetime, a dozen of which are universally known today, including *Swanee River, Oh! Susanna, My Old Kentucky Home, Camptown Races, Beautiful Dreamer,* and *Old Folks at Home.* Foster died penniless, in New York City, a victim of alcoholism at the age of 38.

You can obtain "Songs of Stephen Foster," a large book with 40 of Foster's songs and music from:

Fletcher Hodges, Jr., Curator
Foster Hall Collection
University of Pittsburgh
Pittsburgh, PA 15260

(Please enclose 25 cents with your request.)

- *Birth of Berthe Morisot, 1841*   [14]

The great granddaughter of the French master Fragonard, Morisot grew up to marry Eugene Manet, brother of the great French painter Edouard Manet. Morisot exhibited with the Impressionists and always signed her work with her maiden name. Her paintings are famous for their beautiful color and sense of light. Her body of work includes one hundred canvasses and 300 watercolors and they stand as concrete proof of her artistic mastery.

- *Inauguration Day*   [20]

Etymology

In the ancient Roman republic, election to public office was the highest honor that could come to a man. Elaborate ceremonies accompanied the oath of office rites. Seers watched flights of birds in order to determine the most auspicious time for official ceremonies to take place. This practice of taking omens (auguries) influenced the English language of later centuries when the verb 'to inaugurate' came to indicate the act of induction into public office.

- *Gold Was Discovered in California, 1848* [24]

You can obtain free literature about prospecting for gold (as well as information about caves, volcanoes, the Great Ice Age and our changing continent) by writing the:

> U.S. Department of the Interior
> Geological Survey
> 1200 South Eaas St.
> Arlington, VA 22202

Your class might enjoy experimenting with Treasure Gold Metallic Wax Colours. The eight brilliant metallic colors can be used on almost any surface and, once dry, will polish to a high lustre. Children will love using Treasure Gold next month, when they're making valentines.

Write requesting information and current price list to:

> Connoisseur Studio, Inc.
> P.O. Box 7187
> Dept. 1-12
> Louisville, KY 40207

- *Michigan Was Admitted to the Union, 1837* [26]

Etymology

Michigan may come from the Chippewa Indian word for the lake there: "Mishawiguma" which means "big waste area" as the lake has few islands on it.

- *Birth of Lewis Carroll (Charles Lutwige Dodgson)* [27]

Carroll was an English mathematician who wrote "Alice's Adventures in Wonderland" and "Through the Looking Glass." He also invented the game called "Doublets," which some of your students may enjoy.

Take two words of the same length. Change one to the other by a series of intermediate words, each differing by only one letter from the word preceding.

For example—PIG can be changed to STY as follows:

PIG WAY
WIG SAY
WAG STY

Encourage the children to make up their own Doublets and then exchange them among themselves.

● **Kansas Was Admitted to the Union, 1861   [29]**

Etymology

This state was named for the Kansa tribe of Siouan Indians who originally lived in what is today northeastern Kansas and other lands beyond.

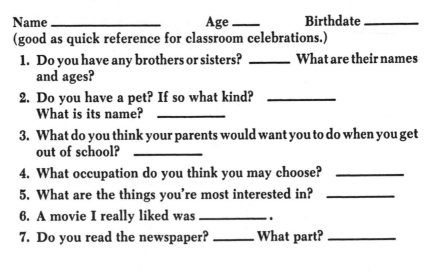

JANUARY ACTIVITIES

Now is the time of year to take stock of your relations with your students. You know each student quite well, but it's very enlightening sometimes to listen to a child talk about himself/herself. Give the following Interest Inventory to each of your students either by "interviewing" each personally or by having older students fill out mimeosheet themselves. Not all of these questions need be included. You can edit this Inventory to suit your needs.

Name _____   Age ____   Birthdate _____
(good as quick reference for classroom celebrations.)

1. Do you have any brothers or sisters? _____ What are their names and ages?

2. Do you have a pet? If so what kind? _____
   What is its name? _____

3. What do you think your parents would want you to do when you get out of school? _____

4. What occupation do you think you may choose? _____

5. What are the things you're most interested in? _____

6. A movie I really liked was _____ .

7. Do you read the newspaper? _____ What part? _____

8. What sport do you like best or would you like to learn? _____

9. Two people I'd like to know more about are _____
   and _____ .

10. If you knew how to do these things which 3 would you choose
    to do? (Number 1-2-3)
    cook _____ read comics _____ work on puzzles _____ act in
    a play _____ paint a picture _____ learn magic tricks _____
    listen to records _____ take photographs _____ play an in-
    strument _____ watch movies _____ .

11. If you were going to take a trip where would you rather go?
    (Number 1-2-3)
    camping _____ the zoo _____ a big city _____ the
    ocean _____ Disneyland _____ the mountains _____ a
    forest _____ .

Here's a board game that will give you insight into your class and it will help older students to understand one another better, too.

Ungame is a noncompetitive communication game for 2 to 6 players. While playing, the children answer such questions as What 4 things are most important in your life? If you could become invisible where would you like to go? What gives you goose bumps? The Ungame #1200 is priced at $8.50 (additional Ungame cards for students are $2.00—or the children could make up some of their own!) You can order this very thought-provoking game from:

> The Ungame Co.
> 1440 South State College Blvd.
> Bldg. 2–D
> Anaheim, CA 92806

Winning is overemphasized. The only time it is really important is in surgery and war.—*Al McGuire*

Another non-competitive game is available from:

> Family Pastimes
> RR 4
> Perth, Ontario,
> Canada K7H 3C6

They are the makers, distributors of games of cooperation: 'play together, not against each other' i.e., Games Manual (70 co-op activities), Earth Games, Our Town, Space Future.

Language Arts:

Finding your family tree: Many middle and upper grade students are fascinated by the study of personal genealogy. Such a research project can lead to improved interviewing techniques: use of notes and tape recorder and recording of statistics (some students may use a Pennsylvania Dutch format, as in the illustration below, while others will want to design their own graphic family trees).

Local reference librarians can be helpful, and students can write for helpful general information to the:

National Genealogical Society
1921 Sunderland Place, N.W.
Washington, D.C. 20036

Please enclose a self-addressed, stamped envelope with each request for information.

Roodles of riddles. One of a myriad uses of riddles in the classroom. This one is good for filling in those 5 minute pockets of time before dismissal. It may also be a godsend for the substitute teacher. Print riddles in large letters on 8″ × 24″ pieces of sturdy paper. Children read silently as you hold each card up (answer appears on back). Raised hands are recognized for guessing of answers.

The mind ought sometimes to be amused, that it may the better return to thought and to itself.—*Phaedrus (5th century B.C.)*

1. What's full of holes and yet it can hold a lot of water? *A wet sponge.*

2. What can often threaten you, but can't say a single word? *An oncoming storm, a shaking fist, or a big stick.*

3. Why is a baker like a starving man? *Because he just kneads some bread.*

4. Why can a dog run only halfway into the woods? *Because then he's running out of the woods.*

5. What is the difference between one yard and two yards? *A backyard fence!*

6. What can you put on yet never wear? *A play.*

7. Where is there a town with no people and a river with no water? *On a map.*

8. What country do you come from if you can see your breath in the morning? *Chile.*

9. What did Tennessee? *Just what Arkansas.*

10. If Miss Issippi gave Miss Ouri her New Jersey what would Dela Ware? *I don't know, Al-Ask-A!*

11. What country do babies like best? *Lapland.*

12. What country does a gentleman in a suit need? *Thai land.*

13. From what country do fish come? *Fin land.*

14. Two Ns, two Os, L & D: What city can you spell with these? *London.*

15. When is a thief called a jail *bird? When he's been a -robbin'!*

16. What is the least dangerous kind of robbery? *"Safe" Robbery.*

17. Why did the mouse want to eat the letter G when he was in Switzerland? *He'd heard that Swiss Gs was good.*

18. Why was the pirate F tired after building his secret island fort? *Because it was such a big F fort (effort).*

19. Why did the pirate's parrot hate to say "Polly wants a cracker"? *Because his name was Sam.*

20. How are handcuffs like postcards? *They are made for the two wrists (tourists).*

21. What always shoots off and never looks back? *A bullet.*

22. If I'm young, I stay young, if I'm old, I stay old, what am I? *Your photograph or a portrait.*

23. When is a dress like a chair? *When it's sat-in.*

24. Who wears 36 coats and yet never buys any clothes? *An onion.*

25. Why is silk like a crying baby? *Because it has no nap.*

26. What makes a pair of shoes? *Two shoes make a pair of shoes.*

27. What kind of cloth should an artist always wear? *Canvas.*

28. What kind of cloth should a banker always wear? *Checks, or cash-mere.*

29. What kind of cloth should a dairyman wear? *Cheesecloth.*

30. What kind of cloth should an inventor wear? *Patent leather.*

31. What kind of cloth should a fisherman wear? *Net.*

32. What kind of cloth should a sea captain wear? *Sailcloth.*

33. What kind of cloth should a mechanic wear? *Oilcloth.*

34. What always goes around a button? *A goat goes around a-buttin'.*

35. What often overtakes you and yet you never see it? *Sleep or old age.*

36. If a 1,000 lb. elephant fell into a 3 foot well, how would he come out? *Wet.*

37. Why is gum like an umbrella? *It must get wet to be any good to you.*

38. Does a young prune have wrinkles? *No, not unless he stays in the bathtub too long.*

39. What is not clean but never needs a bath? *Muddy water.*

40. What 2 things can you never have for breakfast? *Lunch and dinner.*

41. What has no beginning and no end and nothing in the middle? *A donut.*

42. What floats on the river as light as a feather, but 1000 men can't lift it? *The wind.*

43. When do elephants have 8 legs? *When there are two of them.*

44. What has 4 legs, a back and 2 arms, but no body? *A chair.*

45. What is it that when it loses 1 eye, it has nothing left but a nose? *The word "noise".*

46. Strike me on the head just once and I'll die. What am I? *A match.*

47. Why is a barefoot boy like an Eskimo? *Because he wears no shoes (snowshoes).*

48. Why should you never put the letter M in your refrigerator? *Because it can change ICE into MICE!*

49. Why is the letter E like the City of London? *Because it is the capitol of England.*

50. When does a blacksmith make trouble in the alphabet? *When he makes A poke-R and shove-L.*

51. What's the difference between a glass of water and a glass of Coke? *About fifty cents* (and 300 calories!)

52. If a papa bull eats all the tall grass and the baby bull eats all the short grass, what will the mama bull eat? *Nothing. There are no mama bulls!*

53. What kind of rocks are found in the Mississippi River? *Wet ones.*

54. A nickel and a dime crossed a bridge. The nickel fell off into the water. Why didn't the dime fall too? *It had more sense (more cents).*

What state should you go to if you:

55. need to write a letter? *PENnyslvania.*

56. want to meet a native American? *INDIANa.*

57. are hungry for a sandwich? *New HAMpshire.*

58. have a Band-Aid? *ConnectiCUT.*

59. want to get golden brown? *MonTANa.*

60. need a dime? *TENnessee.*

61. were a miner? *OREgon.*

62. What goes with a farmer's wagon, stops with a farmer's wagon and yet the wagon *can't* go without it? *A squeak.*

63. What goes all over the pasture in the daytime and sits on a shelf at night? *Milk.*

64. What goes down the road, into the creek, with water over its head and yet it doesn't take a drink? *A horseshoe.*

65. A farmer ate two eggs every day for breakfast. He had no chickens. No one gave him any eggs. He never bought, borrowed or stole any eggs. WHERE did he get the eggs? *From his farm: they were duck eggs!*

66. When you plant corn, what's the first thing to come up? *Crows, to dig up the seeds.*

67. Guess this: You throw away the outside, cook the inside, eat the outside, and throw away the inside. What is this? *An ear of corn.*

68. How can a farmer turn potatoes into pork? *He can feed 'em to his hogs.*

69. What farm animal eats and drinks with its tail? *They all do. None of them take off their tail to eat or drink.*

70. What should a cowboy always drink? *Brand-y.*

71. With which hand should you stir hot soup? *You can use either hand, but it's best to stir hot soup with a spoon!*

72. What has five eyes and can't see: *The Mississippi River.*

73. Why are Panama Hats like statues? *No matter how hard we try, we can't make them here (hear).*

74. If you had a sixth sense, why would it just get in your way? *Because it would be a real nuisance (new-sense)!*

75. What has a head, four legs, but only one foot? *A bed.*

76. What has 100 legs but cannot walk? *50 pair of pants.*

77. What has 4 legs and flies through the air? *Two birds.*

78. What has 8 legs and sings real loud. *A men's quartet.*

79. What did the big toe say to the little toe? *Hey, don't look back, but there's a real heel following us.*

80. What has no skin or bones and yet has four fingers and a thumb? *A glove.*

81. Why should doctors make good sailors? *Because they're accustomed to see sickness (sea sickness).*

82. What grows bigger if left alone and smaller if you add something to it? *A hole in your sock.*

83. When do you NOT need a license to go out flying? *When you fly a kite or a flag.*

84. What animal only likes females? *The ant-eater; he never eats uncles.*

85. What animal would you like to be on a real cold day? *A little otter (a little hotter).*

86. What's the surest way to keep water from coming into your house? *Just forget to pay the water bill!*

87. What makes the squirrel run up the tree? *Ah, nuts!*

89. What is one nut that has no shell? *A donut!*

90. What has a head but no neck? *A glass of good beer.*

91. What has a neck but no head? *A bottle.*

92. What has a head and is strong, but can't think? *A cabbage.*

93. Dogs have fleas, what do sheep have? *Fleece, too.*

94. What is yellow, pink, green, purple, blue, brown and white? *A box of crayons!*

95. What's harder to catch, the faster you run? *Your breath.*

96. What is *dark* but is made by light? *A shadow.*

97. Name five days of the week without saying: Monday, Tuesday, Wednesday, Thursday or Friday? *The day before yesterday, yesterday, today, tomorrow, and the day after tomorrow!*

98. What doesn't get any wetter no matter how much it rains? *The sea.*

99. Spell "pound" with two letters. *lb.*

100. What can you make that I can't see? *Noise, a sound.*

101. What can you serve, but never eat? *A tennis ball, a volleyball, a badminton shuttlecock.*

102. What do you drop when you need it, and take back when you don't? *An anchor.*

103. What can a bird do that a grown man can't do? *Clean his feathers, take a complete bath in a tea cup, and lay an egg.*

104. What flies when it's on and floats when it's off? *A feather.*

105. If a miser sits on gold, who sits on silver? *The Lone Ranger.*

106. What baby is born with whiskers? *A kitten.*

107. If you dropped a tomato on your foot, would it hurt a lot? *Not unless it was in a can!*

108. Almost everyone needs it, asks for it, gets it, gives it, but hardly anyone takes it. What is it? *Advice!*

109. What can you hold without using your hands? *Your temper, your breath and "your horses"!*

110. What has 50 heads and 50 tails? *Fifty pennies!*

Hard Riddles:

1. What suit always lasts longer than a person wants it to? *A lawsuit.*

2. A farmer had a goose, a fox and a bag of corn. He had to take them across a wide river in a boat that could only carry himself and one thing at a time. If he took the fox across first, the goose would eat the

corn, if he took the corn, the fox would eat the goose. How did the farmer finally get all 3 across?

He took the goose across first as the fox wouldn't eat the corn. Then he took the fox across and brought the goose back. He left the goose and took over the corn and at last went back for the goose!

3. If "joy" is the opposite of "sorrow," what is the opposite of "woe"? *Gidda-yup!*

4. When is a couch like a convalescent? *When it is recovered.*

5. What letters are like a Roman Emperor? *The Cs are (Caesar).*

6. A blind man, a naked man and an armless man were running down the street. The blind man saw a fish, the armless man picked it up and the naked man put it in his pocket. What is that? *A very big lie!*

7. What does a pet cat have that even God doesn't have? *An owner.*

8. I came to town and met 3 people. They were neither men nor women nor children. What were they? *One man, one woman, one child.*

9. What is the longest sentence in the world? *"You must go to prison for life."*

10. What has eyes and can't see and ears and can't hear and can jump as high as the Empire State Building? *A dead cat. What? A dead cat can't jump! Neither can the Empire State Building!*

11. This is a place where you'll see lifeless men and women and animals. In peacetime it's deserted, but when there's a war, then everyone is busy and full of excitement. Where is this? *On a chessboard.*

12. How should you get down off an elephant? *You can't. You get down off a duck or a goose!*

13. What is better, real happiness or a cheese sandwich? *A cheese sandwich: Nothing is better than real happiness and a cheese sandwich is better than nothing. . . .*

14. Why doesn't the biggest animal in the world have feet? *Because the biggest animal is the blue whale!*

15. Why should you feel really sorry for a farmer lifting a slab of bacon off a high hook? *Because he's a pork reacher (poor creature).*

16. When is it correct to say "I is?" *"I" is the letter after "H" in the alphabet!*

17. How do we know that Adam was a *good* jogger? *Everybody knows Adam was first in the human race.*

18. What 10 letter word starts with g-a-s? *A-u-t-o-m-o-b-i-l-e.*

19. What doesn't exist, but has a name? *Nothing, a void, a vacuum.*

20. A man named Joe and his St. Bernard are going down the road. The man rides, yet walks. What is the dog's name? *Yet.*

21. This man was driving his big black truck. His lights weren't on. The moon wasn't shining. A woman was crossing the street. How did the guy *see* her? *It was a sunny day.*

22. What relation is a loaf of brown bread to a color T.V.? *It is its mother, because you know bread is a necessity, a T.V. set is an invention and "Necessity is the mother of invention."*

23. What ghost is said to have haunted King George of England in the 18th century? *The Spirit of '76!!*

24. What announces the beginning of eternity, is the end of all time and space, in fact, it's the beginning of the end and the end of every race? *The letter E.*

January Science

Children can learn a good deal by watching the day-to-day growth of plants in their classroom; plants grow from different beginnings— seeds, cuttings, tubers, bulbs; but plants follow a definite pattern of growth. Baby plants will grow to be like the adult plants. Plants have different temperatures and require various amounts of water, sunshine, warmth and different types of soil. You can stock your classroom nursery with a variety of plants and at no expense; here's how.

Apple seeds. Seeds are not ready to be planted directly from the fruit. Put the seeds in a jar with damp moss. Refrigerate for 6 weeks (mark removal date on your classroom calendar). Turn them over periodically until they begin to sprout. Then fill a small pot with potting compost. Plant seed 1/2" down in compost. Keep in light, warm room. Keep moist.

Avocado pit. Place pit, round end down, in a small jar. Fill jar with water so that round end only is submerged. Then wait (for perhaps even 2-3 months). Keep adding water as it evaporates. When pit looks slimy and even moldy, do not despair; roots should appear any time. When root is 1/2" long, plant pit in a medium sized pot. Water it well when it is dry and give it food tablets from time to time.

Birdseed. Sprinkle on top of rich soil and cover with 1/4" more of soil. Keep it moist!

Beet. Cut to within 1" of its top, retaining leaves. Trim foliage back. Plant beet top in sandy soil. Keep moist, not wet.

Broadbeans. Soak 2-3 hours until they swell. Cut and roll a piece of blotting paper and line a 1-2 lb. jam jar up to the mouth with the paper. Place bean about 1/2 way down between jar and paper. Pour 1" of water into jar. See that blotter remains WET. Place jar in dark cupboard until beans germinate, then bring jar into the light. (If you use two jars, placing one in cupboard and leaving one in the light, children will see which grows faster. Do they know why?) Lay sprouting beans on soil. Keep it moist.

Carrot. Cut, retaining 1" of foliage and 1" of root; set in a shallow dish filled with 1/2" of water. Add tiny pieces of charcoal to keep water sweet, or trim foliage; cut root 2" from top and hollow out center; hang upside down like a basket. Keep filled with water.

Corn. As a child in Illinois, my mother was taught to plant corn in this manner: "When sowing corn, plant 5 grains: 1 for the blackbird, 1 for the crow, 1 for the meal worm, and 1 won't grow."

Date Seeds (unpasteurized). These need lots of room. Plant seed in sandy soil. When roots outgrow pot, break out bottom of pot and plant in a bigger pot.

Grapes. Dry seeds. Put 1/2" of clean pebbles in the bottom of a pot. Mix one part humus, two parts potting soil and a handful of vermiculite. Put in pot. Water, allowing soil to settle. Plant 12 seeds 1/2" deep. Keep soil damp. Place pot where it will get just 1-2 hrs. of direct sun each day—until vine is 7" tall. Put a re-enforcing stick beside vine for it to climb.

Grapefruit seeds. These do best if planted in February. You can use the grapefruit shell filled with potting soil and sand as the seed's initial holder. Soak seed overnight before planting. Sink soil down close about seed. Later transfer young plant to a sturdier container. The plant may grow for years. Keep earth moist by spraying with water every day. Also water twice a week.

Kumquats. (See lemon seeds.)

Lemon seeds. Cover with 1/2" sand and potting soil, after having soaked the seeds overnight. Keep earth moist (as described for *grapefruit*).

Lentils. Spread in single layer in a saucer. Moisten, but don't float lentils. Keep moist and in the sun. In 10 days they sprout and can be planted like beans.

Mango seeds. These are difficult to start as they, like the avocado, are slow in sprouting. Press seed into soil flat side down. Keep soil moist.

Oats. Can be started in the following way: Line the bottom of a pie tin with small stones. Add a layer of rich earth, then lay oats on top of earth. Cover oats with layer of fine soil. Cover entire top of pan with thin cloth (gauze); set in a sunny window. Sprinkle cloth with water each day. Oats should sprout on third day. Remove cloth at this time. Keep soil moist.

Onion. Place pointed end up, in a small-mouthed jar. Cover 1/2 of onion with water. Add small amounts of charcoal to water.

Orange seeds. (See apple seeds.)

Peach seeds. (See apple seeds.)

Pepper seeds. These seeds, from tiny red peppers in pickling spice, are spread out to dry on a paper towel. Punch small holes for drainage in the bottom of cottage cheese container. Fill container with soil. Barely cover seeds with soil. Keep soil moist.

Pineapple. Cut off 1-1/2–2″ from top of plant. Retain spiky foliage. Allow pineapple to dry for three days, then place in sandy soil. Water lightly. Keep as warm as possible. In about 2 weeks (if roots have grown), re-pot in good sterilized soil. Keep soil damp, warm and near light. Your plant won't bear, but it will be attractive.

Potato Porcupine. Slice off the top of an Irish potato. Carve out a hole, leaving plenty of meat on the walls. Insert 4 toothpicks as legs. Make eyes by attaching two small white paper circles with black map tacks. Fill cavity with earth (or moist cotton) sprinkled with grass seed. Keep watered for 10 days until Porky's spines sprout.

Plum. (See apple seeds.)

Pumpkin. (See pepper seeds.)

Sweet potato. Some are heat-dried and won't grow, so ask grocer for a *fresh* one. If possible choose one with a few whiskers. Cut potato in 1/2. Insert toothpicks around potato below cut surface. Place potato, tapered end down, in a jar, suspended by means of toothpicks. Fill jar with water. Put jar in closet until roots sprout, then bring plant into the light. Plant will sustain itself on water for a long while, or you may plant the potato in soil, allowing green sprouts to remain above earth.

Squash. Follow directions for pepper seeds, except press squash seeds down 3/4″ into soil.

Watermelon seeds. Plant directly in soil. Sprinkle lightly and often with water. Seeds sprout quickly and plant has abundant foliage. Continue watering as mentioned.

White potato. Cut into sections, each section containing an eye or two. Plant in rich earth and keep moistened. Let it have lots of sun.

Yam. Choose one that has purple eyes. Then follow directions for sweet potato.

For free seed catalogs to help children become better acquainted with a variety of plants, send for information to:

Burpee Seed Co.
Warminster, PA 18891

Older children may enjoy learning about herbs and plants that are less common. Free catalogs are available from:

Nichols Herbs and Rare Seeds
1190 North Pacific Highway
Albany, OR 97321

Meadowbrook Herbs and Things, Inc.
Whispering Pines Rd.
Wyoming, RI 02898

You might be interested in purchasing the "Plant Discovery Kit," which includes light filters, hormones and chemicals to make plants react in various ways. Write, requesting information about Item #71412 to:

Edmund Scientific Co.
555 Edscorp. Building
Barrington, NJ 08007

(You can also ask for a copy of their fascinating catalog.)

January Art:

Printmaking. The most basic types of prints are made by applying ink to a flat surface (i.e., a carrot sliced crosswise) and then pulling a print. Children could compile Print Samplers, experimenting and searching for unusual surface possibilities.

Rubbings. These are easy to execute. Tape or firmly hold a piece of lightweight strong paper atop a rough surface. Rub the entire piece of paper with a carpenter's pencil, crayon, or liquid shoe polish on a cotton wad inserted into the toe of a child's sock.

[VARIATION: Apply a rich wash of diluted poster paint atop a crayon rubbing.]

[VARIATION: Cut several rubbings into pieces. Make a collage of these pieces. Colored construction paper might also be used in this collage.]

Monoprints. Prepare the materials for making monoprints and then hand out the following mimeos: (Let the children read these to themselves.)

"Clear off the desk (table) in front of you. Be sure you have enough room in which to work. Lay down a large piece of plastic wrap° and tape it smoothly to the desk. Get some starch°° and pour 1/3 cup onto the plastic wrap. Return the starch. Decide on the color of paint you wish to use and *carefully* sprinkle a bit of dry powder paint onto your starch. Return the paint. Take some sheets of white paper to your desk.

Roll up your sleeves to the elbow. With *one* hand mix the starch and paint together. Try drawing in it. Use different parts of your hand and see what kinds of effects you can get. When you are happy with what you've done, take a sheet of paper (with your *dry* hand, of course) and lay it carefully on top of the starch-drawing. Pick up one corner of the paper and pull it smoothly toward the opposite corner and off the starch. Turn the paper over and look at your results. Lay this print on the floor against the wall (where the newspapers are laid) at the back of the room. Try taking another print off the same starch by rubbing your hand in the starch and making a *new* picture or design. Or, pull several prints off the same starch pattern.

When you're ready to clean up, untape the plastic wrap, roll it into a ball and place it in the waste can. Carefully wipe off the desk (and floor?) with a paper towel. Wash your hands and then read quietly or write a short story about an adventure that one of your monoprints might illustrate."

Lineoleum block prints. (For older students.) Make an outline of linoleum block on tracing paper; draw your design within it. Turn your design over onto the linoleum surface of the block. Trace over the lines, pressing heavily so that the reverse of your design appears on block. Carve out all areas of block which you *do not* want to show on your finished print. *REMEMBER:* Only the raised areas will take ink. Squeeze block-printing ink onto a small pane of glass. Roll brayer°°° back and forth through the ink until brayer is well coated. Roll brayer across face of block so that your design is fully inked. Carefully place paper on block; rub paper with spoonback or heel of hand to print

---

° Plastic produce bags, free at markets, may be slit, opened out flat and used in place of costly plastic wrap.

°° This may be commercial liquid starch (shake bottle WELL). Or you may prepare it at home the previous evening (from cornstarch) and bring it to class in plastic containers. (Keep starch quite dilute.)

°°° A brayer is a small hand roller used to spread ink thinly and evenly over surface of block.

design. Keep paper from moving. Starting at one corner, slowly peel the paper off toward the diagonally opposite corner. Allow ink to dry completely.

Prints from styro-foam meat trays. These are made by cutting or scratching design into foam tray. Ink is supplied and print taken as described above.

Veneer print-making. Described on page 27.

Felt block-printing. Children draw a basic design on paper. This is cut out and rubber-cemented firmly to a piece of felt (from an old hat or such) and when dry, is carefully cut out with scissors. Trace around this basic design on the top of a scrap block of wood. (Lumber yards are often happy to save such hand-sized blocks of scrap wood for you.) Apply rubber cement to *entire* paper-side of felt; apply glue or rubber cement to *entire* inner area of design draw-on wood block. When both rubber-cemented surfaces are dry, press felt to top of wood. Firmly attach felt to wood. Using a large (stencil) brush, apply poster-paint to felt design. Place paper to be printed atop a pad of newspapers. Then, holding paper in place, firmly press felt onto paper.

Foam-tape block-printing. Follow above instructions except use adhesive-backed foam-tape (used for weather-stripping). Child draws outline of a simple design on face of block; tape is pressed directly onto outline. Pour poster paint into flat cooky sheet; dip foam into paint and then stamp design onto paper. Child experiments with repetition of design and use of more than one color of paint at a time.

Silkscreen prints. Can be made by very young children in the following way: Purchase small (4-6″ in diameter) embroidery hoops. Cut old nylon hose into pieces and stretch these taut in hoops. Each child either cuts from newsprint a simple shape smaller than the hoop itself or, with wax crayon, draws directly onto the nylon, being sure to press firmly enough so as to fill the mesh with crayon. A tiny scraper or "squeegee" (that can easily fit within hoop), is cut from a heavy cardboard. Thick poster-paint (or a liquid starch and powdered tempera mixture) is applied to the screen with a spoon. Use the squeegee to firmly scrape the paint over the crayon drawing and through the mesh of the nylon. If a cut-out paper shape is used, place it between the nylon and the paper to be printed. The paint, when applied with the squeegee, will adhere the cut-out to the screen, producing a negative image on the paper.

Older children can use this more advanced type of screen: Cut a window in a cardboard box lid or base. Stretch and staple slightly dampened cotton organdy or an old marquisette curtain over the outside. Keep material taut, placing 1 staple in the center of each side before stapling all around. On the inside of the box, tape the edge of the window to the material. Seal all the edges with masking or paper tape. Coat all sides of the box with the shellac. Child makes a design no bigger than the window, then he/she places the screen over the design. Child proceeds to block out with a wax crayon all areas that are not to receive paint: this is done by thoroughly filling in the fabric's mesh. (Or, he may place a dampened cut-out of newsprint under the screen as described in the preceding paragraph.) Child places his screen on paper to be printed. At top of screen pour a generous amount of finger paint. Using a cardboard squeegee (slightly smaller than the window) held at a 45° angle, the child draws the paint firmly across the full length of the screen. For a 2-color print, mark guide lines on the paper being printed for registering the second screen. Then prepare a second screen, identical in size to the first. From a sheet of newsprint the size of the window, he cuts away that part of the design to be printed a second color. Screen is registered over first print, and second color (which holds newsprint to screen) is applied.

January Physical Education:

Younger children will enjoy playing these games (while they wait for the bell to ring).

Finger shapes. Student uses his/her fingers to make a letter of the alphabet and others try to guess it. Or a student draws a letter (number) in the air and others try to guess it.

Pantomime. "I am thinking of something that . . . and then child pantomimes the action and other children try to guess the object by first child's actions.

Five things in an envelope. Five different objects are put into an envelope, which is then sealed (a set of envelopes may be used). Children feel the envelope and try to guess the contents. Finally, a student uses a crayon and rubs lightly on top of envelope to make the objects "appear."

Five things in a sack (pillowcase). Child, without looking in sack, removes one object and class discusses its origin and use. This is repeated with each thing in the sack, and then objects are put back into sack. It is brought out another day when children will feel objects in sack and try to "remember" what each one is.

"**What would happen if. . . .**" A student uses this phrase to propose an outlandish situation and other students come up with different possible situations that might develop as a consequence of the situation.

Is this animal, vegetable or mineral? Each student tries to stump the class by nominating an object (such as a pencil, which is vegetable AND mineral).

Snow ice cream. Help students catch a *big* pot of snow. Then have them beat an egg until it's light and frothy and gently stir it into the snow. Add 1/2 cup half and half, (sifted) powdered sugar to taste and 1/2 tsp. vanilla. Eat at once (or freeze in small paper cups with a plastic spoon stuck in each.)

February

If February give much snow,
A fine summer, it doth foreshow.
—English weather rhyme.

††   National Childrens' Dental Health Week, beginning with the first Sunday in the month (American Dental Association, 211 East Chicago Avenue, Chicago, IL 60611).

1   National Freedom Day commemorates President Lincoln's 1865 proposal of anti-slavery amendment (13th) to the U.S. Constitution.

     Langston Hughes, writer, was born in Joplin, Missouri in 1902.

     On this day in 1958, President Nasser of Egypt announced the merger of Egypt and Syria into the United Arab Republic.

2   Groundhog Day, on which legend says the groundhog emerges from hibernation, and if he sees his shadow, he retreats back into his hole, for the shadow foretells six more weeks of winter.

     On this day in 1848, the Treaty of Guadalupe Hidalgo was signed, in which Mexico agreed to cede Texas, New Mexico, California and parts of Arizona to the United States upon payment of $15,000,000.

On this day in 1876, Baseball's National League was organized. It included 8 teams: Chicago, Philadelphia, New York, Boston, Cincinnati, Hartford, St. Louis and Louisville.

3   First American paper money was issued by Massachusetts to pay soldiers fighting in the war of Quebec, 1690.

Gertrude Stein, writer, was born in Allegheny, Pennsylvania in 1874.

4   On this day in 1789, the Electoral College named George Washington as the President of the United States.

Mark Hopkins, educator, was born in Stockbridge, Massachusetts in 1802.

On this day in 1861, the Confederate States of America was organized in Montgomery, Alabama. It included six seceding Southern states: South Carolina, Georgia, Florida, Alabama, Mississippi and Louisiana.

Gernand Legér, painter, was born in Argentan, France, in 1881.

5   Hank Aaron, baseball player, was born in Mobile, Alabama, in 1934.

6   Queen Anne of England was born in England, in 1665.

On this day in 1952, King George VI of Great Britain died and was succeeded by his daughter, Queen Elizabeth II.

7   Sinclair Lewis, writer, first American to win the Nobel Prize for literature, was born in Sauk Center, Minnesota, in 1885.

8   On this day in 1587, Mary, Queen of Scots, accused of plotting the murder of Britain's Queen Elizabeth I, was beheaded at Fotheringhay Castle, England.

William Tecumseh Sherman, General in the Union Army, was born in Lancaster, Ohio, in 1820.

9   William Henry Harrison, 9th U.S. President, was born in Berkeley, Virginia, in 1773.

On this day in 1825, the House of Representatives elected John Quincy Adams President of the United States, following the national election in which none of the candidates received an electoral majority.

10 On this day in 1763, the French and Indian War was ended by the signing of the Treaty of Paris, which gave all Canada as well as all French holdings east of the Mississippi (except New Orleans) to Spain, ending French power in North America.

On this day in 1936, Gestapo, Nazi secret police, were authorized to imprison Germans without trial, making Hitler's dictatorship in Germany absolute.

11 National Science Youth Day is observed on the birthday of Thomas A. Edison as part of National Electrical Week (Nat. Electrical Week Committee, Suite 600, 1 Memorial Dr., St. Louis, MO 63102).

Thomas Alva Edison was born in Milan, Ohio, in 1847. During his lifetime (84 years) he created 1,097 inventions!

12 First puppet show was given in America, 1738.

Abraham Lincoln, 16th U.S. President, was born in a log cabin in Hardin County, Kentucky in 1809.

On this day in 1870, all the women in the Territory of Utah were granted full suffrage.

On this day in 1912, China became a republic as the Manchu Dynasty was overthrown in a rebellion led by Dr. Sun Yat-sen.

13 First public school in America, The Boston Latin School, was established in Boston in 1635.

On this day in 1689, William and Mary were proclaimed King and Queen of England by Parliament.

First magazine to be published in America, *The American Magazine,* was issued in Philadelphia, 1747.

14   Valentine's Day

Frederick Douglass, Black leader, was born in Tuckahoe, Maryland in 1817.

Oregon, 33rd state, was admitted to the Union, 1859.

Arizona became the 48th state admitted to the Union, 1912.

15   Galileo Galilei, Italian scientist, was born in 1564.

On this day in 1764, Auguste Chouteau founded St. Louis, Missouri.

Susan B. Anthony, pioneer crusader for women's rights, was born in Adams, Massachusetts in 1820.

On this day in 1879, President Rutherford B. Hayes signed into law a bill admitting women to practice law before the U.S. Supreme Court.

††   National Wildlife Week: beginning with the third Sunday in February.

17   On this day in 1801, Thomas Jefferson was elected President by the House of Representatives on their 36th ballot.

First meeting of the National Congress of Parents and Teachers was held in Washington, D.C. in 1897.

Modern art was introduced to the public of the United States at the Armory Show in New York City in 1913.

18   Andrés Segovia, guitarist, was born in Linares, Spain, in 1894.

20   John Glenn Day commemorates the United States astronaut's orbiting of the earth in 1962. (Launched from Cape Canaveral, Florida, he circled the earth three times in his space capsule and then landed safely in the Atlantic).

On this day in 1972, President Nixon began his week-long official visit to the Republic of China for talks with Mao Tse-Tung.

On this day in 1965, the Ranger 8 spacecraft crashed into its target area on the moon after relaying back to earth some 7,000 pictures of the lunar surface.

21   First woman dentist to be graduated, Lucy B. Hobbs, took her degree from Ohio College of Dental Surgery in Cincinnati, in 1866.

First U.S. telephone book was circulated, 1878.

22   George Washington, first U.S. President, and "The Father of Our Country" was born on his parents' plantation near Fredericksburg, Virginia in 1732.°

On this day in 1819, Florida was ceded to the United States by Spain.

Edna St. Vincent Millay, poet, was born in Rockland, Maine in 1892.

23   Samuel Pepys, author of the most famous diary in the world, was born in Cambridge, England in 1633. Pepys had no idea that his diary would ever be read by the public. He wrote it in a shorthand that was not deciphered until long after his death. The diary was kept by Pepys for 9 years and 5 months.

W. E. B. Dubois, black scholar, was born in Great Barrington, Massachusetts in 1868.

24   On this day in 1868, the only impeachment proceedings ever instituted against a U.S. President were begun by the House of Representatives when it voted to impeach President Andrew Johnson for "high crimes and misdeameanors." The President had dismissed Secretary of War Stanton and was accused of declaring several laws unconstitutional. On May 28, 1868 he was acquitted by a one-vote margin.

25   First Black member of the U.S. Senate, Hiram H. Revels of Mississippi, won his seat in Congress, 1870.

On this day in 1820, Congressman Felix Walker of North Carolina whose district included Buncombe County, refused to let the

---

°His birthday is now observed as a holiday on the third Monday of February.

House vote on the Missouri Bill until he made another of his long-winded speeches about his beloved Buncombe County. We get our word "bunk" from Walker's repeated speeches about his Buncombe County. Bunk means "nonsense" or "hot air."

26   On this day in 1815, Napoleon escaped from Elba and began his second brief war in Europe.

27   N. Scott Momaday, American Indian writer, was born in Lawton, Oklahoma, in 1934.

On this day in 1973, members of the American Indian Movement occupied the trading post and church at Wounded Knee, South Dakota (site of the 1890 Massacre of Sioux Indians by the U.S. Army) to draw attention to grievances of contemporary American Indians.

28   Waslaw Nijinsky, legendary dancer, was born in Kiev, Russia in 1890.

Linus Pauling, chemist, two-time winner of the Nobel Peace Prize, in 1954 and in 1962, was born in Portland, Oregon in 1901.

29   Leap Year Day occurs only in years in which the last two digits are divisible by the number "four." This extra day comes every four years because it takes the earth 365-1/4 days to revolve around the sun and those four one-quarter days make a whole day every four years.

FEBRUARY QUOTATIONS

1   In giving freedom to the slave, we assure freedom to the free—honorable alike in what we give and what we preserve.
                                      —*Abraham Lincoln, speech on Dec. 1, 1862*

3   In the United States there is more space where nobody is than where anybody is. That is what makes America what it is.
                                      —*Gertrude Stein*

8   I am tired and sick of war. Its glory is all moonshine. . . . War is hell.—*William T. Sherman, 1879*

11   Every child should have mudpies, grasshoppers, waterbugs, tad-
     poles, frogs, mud turtles, elderberries, wild strawberries,
     acorns, chestnuts, trees to climb, animals to pet, hay fields,
     pinecones, rocks to roll, sand, snakes, huckleberries and
     hornets—and any child who has been deprived of these has
     been deprived of the best part of his education.
                                                 —*Luther Burbank*

     Recognition and approbation for work which is imaginative and
     accurate, and apathy or criticism for the trivial and inaccurate
     . . . tends to make honest, vigorous, conscientious, hardworking
     scholars out of people who have human tendencies of slothful-
     ness and no more rectitude than the law requires.
                                        —*Editorial in "Science," 1963*

12   He has the right to criticize who has the heart to help.

     Folks are generally as happy as they make up their minds to be.

     The ballot is stronger than the bullet.
                                                 —*Abraham Lincoln*

14   Hail, Bishop Valentine, whose day this is
     All the air is thy Diocese—*John Donne, 1600*

     May you live all the days of your life.—*Jonathan Swift*

     Love demands infinitely less than friendship.
                                             —*George Jean Nathan*

     True friendship is like sound health, the value of it is seldom
     known until it's lost.—*Charles Colton, 1832*

     We cannot tell the precise moment when friendship is formed. As
     in filling a vessel drop by drop, there is at last a drop which
     makes it run over, so in a series of kindnesses there is at last one
     which makes the heart run over.—*James Boswell, from* The
     Life of Dr. Johnson, Everyman

15   It is surely harmful to souls to make it a heresy to believe what is
     proved.—*Galileo Galilei* (After having been forced to recant
     the doctrine that the earth moves around the sun.)

     On being asked to censor the works of Teilhard de Chardin, Pope
     Pius XII (1876-1958) is said to have answered: "One Galileo in
     two thousand years is enough."

     Modern invention has banished the spinning wheel and the same
     law of progress makes the woman of today different from her
     grandmother.—*Susan B. Anthony*

22   The time is now near at hand which must probably determine
      whether Americans are to be free men or slaves.—*George
      Washington, before the Battle of Long Island, July, 1776*

      It is our true policy to steer clear of permanent alliance with any
      portion of the foreign world.—*George Washington, Farewell
      Address, Sept. 1, 1796*

      I often say of George Washington that he was one of the few in the
      whole history of the world who was not carried away by
      power.—*Robert Frost*

> *I like Americans.*
> *You may say what you will, they*
>   *are the nicest people in the world.*
> *They sleep with their windows open.*
> *Their bathtubs are never dry.*
>   *—Edna St. Vincent Millay*

23   And so to bed. (Diary, April 20, 1660)
      Final entry: And so I betake myself to that course, which is
      almost as much as to see myself go into my grave; for which and
      all the discomforts that will accompany my being blind, the
      good God prepare me.—*Samuel Pepys*

February

**Named for the Latin word "februare" which means 'to purify' as
this was the month in which the Romans purified themselves in
preparation for the festivals at the start of their new year.**

FEBRUARY EVENTS

● *National Freedom Day*   [1]

   Eloquent as it may be, Lincoln's immortal Emancipation
Proclamation did not, in fact, free the slaves. On September 23, 1862,
President Lincoln warned the Confederate states that any which did not

rejoin the Union before January first, 1863, would have all of its slaves freed. This proclamation was directed against the Confederate states and didn't mention slaves held in the Union states. When the states in secession did not comply with the President's demands, no action was taken, as Lincoln's proclamation actually could not be enforced.

Many slaves were freed by Union officers as they won control of Confederate territory, but these liberations were not directly linked to Lincoln's Emancipation Proclamation.

● *Groundhog Day*   [2]

The woodchuck, or groundhog, is a small, blackish-gray North American rodent. It was given this name by the Pilgrims when they arrived in America, as it lived in the woods and reminded them of the hedgehogs back in England. They also gave the groundhog the responsibility of the hedgehog on February 2nd—that of predicting the date of spring. Tradition dictates that on the morning of February second the groundhog comes up out of his hole and looks about. If the day is cold and cloudy, he decides that spring will be here soon and he emerges from his hole. If, however, it is a bright clear day, the sun will cause his shadow to be cast—and one look at his shadow sends the groundhog back into his hole and continued hibernation for six more weeks, at the end of which time it really *will* be spring.

Discuss briefly with your class: How do traditions like this get started? What are some probable reasons for such a tradition?

Science Fact. Does the groundhog really come out on February second? Research done at Pennsylvania State University over a period of 5 years and involving 4,000 groundhogs showed that a great number of groundhogs *were* seen out of their burrows on January thirty-first, and February first, second and third. Other scientists state that February second is the middle of winter for a groundhog and his hibernation should be at the deepest point. If he is seen aboveground, it must be accidental, or he may have awakened to relieve himself. Scientists disagree on the answer, which indicates that more research on hibernation is in order.

You can receive a free chart "How's Your Weather IQ?" from:

Taylor Instrument
Consumer Products Division
Sybron Corporation
Arden, NC 28704

Designed for use with a barometer, this chart has ten areas for recording such things as temperature, barometric pressure, forecast and actual weather.

A Student-Made Barometer

As a rule when you are having good weather, the air pressure is high. When the air pressure falls, this is a sign of change, often a warning of bad weather to come.

This barometer records air pressure. Paste a strip of paper on the outside of a bottle. Fill bottle three quarters full of water. Tightly cover the bottle's mouth as you invert the bottle in a water-filled pan. Stand the bottle upside down. Don't uncover the bottle's mouth until the bottle is completely submerged beneath the water.

Since changes in temperature will make air (in the bottle) expand or contract, you must keep the bottle in a place where the temperature is quite stable (e.g., in a closet). As the water climbs or falls, mark its level on the paper. In this way, the strip becomes a barometric gauge.

Weather Riddles

- What can you measure, but it has no length, width, breadth or thickness? Wind velocity, the temperature.
- What goes out black and comes in white? A black cow in a snow storm.
- What is born in winter, dies in summer and grows with its roots over its head? An icicle.
- What does a farmer plow, but never plant? Snow.
- What's black when you buy it, red when you use it, and grey when you throw it away? Coal.

I puff my breast, I swell my neck,
I have a head, I have a back,
My tail is high, my beak is hard.
High-necked two sides have I,
A midmost rod.
In my home over heads of men
When the tree-mover moves me,
With wretchedness I cope.
Rain in my high place beats me,
Hail hits me, hoarfrost
Coats me, cold snow rides me,
Belly-pierced.

What am I? (*A weathercock vane*)

—18th century riddle

● *First Issue of American Paper Money, 1690*   [3]

Etymology

Our word 'money' comes from the Latin word for "mint": *moneta*. A moneta was a place where money was coined or minted and it, in turn, got *its* name from Moneta, the surname of Juno, in whose temple all Roman money was minted!

Any numismatists (coin collectors) among your students? If so, have them write for free information to:

> Federal Reserve Bank of Atlanta
> Atlanta GA 30303
> (Request booklets called
> "Counterfeit" and
> "Fundamental Facts About
> U.S. Money")

> American Numismatic Association
> 818 N. Cascade
> Colorado Springs, CO 80903

● *Birth of Gertrude Stein, 1874*   [3]

After 1903 Gertrude Stein lived primarily in Paris. Her circle of friends included the most *avant garde* authors, composers and painters—Matisse, Picasso and Cocteau among them. In 1926, she published "The Making of Americans," which evoked heated literary controversy. She wrote a dozen more books. Some critics found her writing dull, silly and trivial, while it was hailed by others as unique, innovative and the work of genius.

Your students may be interested in reading Stein's work for themselves. Try duplicating copies of some of her poetry and have your class read it silently. Don't give any personal opinions—wait to hear their comments. Some students may even be interested in trying to use words in a way similar to Stein's.

• *William Henry Harrison (1773-1841), 9th President** [9]

He rose to fame as a soldier in the War of 1812, leading the U.S. forces against the Indians at Tippecanoe; since his vice presidential running mate was John Tyler, their campaign slogan was "Tippecanoe & Tyler, too!"

Harrison was honest and sincere. He took his duties as manager of the White House very seriously, insisting on doing the early morning marketing himself. One chill March day, he went marketing without his coat. He caught cold and it developed into pneumonia. Harrison was the first U.S. President to die in office, serving the shortest term in U.S. history—only 30 days.

• *Birth of Thomas A. Edison* [11]

Thomas Alva Edison was an inventor. He worked in his workshop. He worked in his laboratory. He worked in his mind. When he got an idea he looked at it from all sides. He never said, "That can't be done." When he was searching for the right material to burn in a light bulb, he tried 6,000 different things before he found the one he wanted! In addition to the electric light bulb, he invented the phonograph and motion pictures! Thomas Edison changed the world!

Etymology

Phonograph is a Greek derivative meaning "sound-writing." ("Phonograph; *n.* A vibrating toy that restores life to dead noises." Ambrose Bierce, from his *Devil's Dictionary.)*

Riddle:

What did the little light bulb say to its mother?
"I wuv you *watts* and *watts!"*

---

* His grandson, Benjamin Harrison became our 23rd U.S. President!

• *Birth of Abraham Lincoln, 1809*   [12]

Lincoln, six feet one in his stocking feet,
The lank man, knotty and tough as a hickory nail,
Whose hands were always too big for white-kid gloves,
Whose wit was a coonskin sack of dry, tall tales.
Whose weathered face was homely as a plowed field.
                                               —*S.V. Benet*

Etymology

Ancient Roman law prescribed a ceremony for the purchase of slaves: the new master laid his hand upon the slave's head. This was to fulfill the law of *mancipium: "possession by the hand."* Since *e* in Latin means "away," and *capio* means "taken," our word *emancipation* means "the master takes his hand off the emancipated slave."

"Freedom" comes from Old English and is related to a Norse word for "love and peace."

Here's the story *behind* Lincoln's murder° and those who paid for it. Did you know that nine people were tried for Lincoln's murder? Did you know that four were hanged and one was a *woman?*

John Wilkes Booth, a ham actor, was furious when the South lost the war. He decided to 'get even' by killing President Lincoln.

Booth got several men together who felt the way he did. They met in a boardinghouse and plotted to kill President Lincoln, Vice President Johnson and the Secretary of State. These murders were to take place on the same night: April 14th, 1865.

That night came, but only one of the men—John Wilkes Booth—succeeded in his part of the plot. After he shot Lincoln, Booth fled with one of his helpers, David Herold. A week later they were trapped in a barn in Virginia by U.S. soliders. David Herold gave up, but Booth did not. He was shot to death by a solider who fired against orders.

In the next few days the other seven men who had plotted with Booth were captured. After standing trial, four men got life terms in prison, one was freed. On July 7, three men and the woman who owned the boardinghouse were all hanged. Some people said they did not think a woman *should* be hanged, but the new President Johnson said, "She kept the nest where the murder was plotted!" And so *this* is the story behind the murder of President Lincoln.

°A story written with a low vocabulary for easy use in class.

- ### *St. Valentine's Day*   [14]

Valentinus was a Christian priest during the days of the Roman Emperor Claudius II. It was a crime at that time to give aid or comfort to Christians. Valentinus was a good and kindly man, helping anyone in need, including Christians. He was jailed by the Emperor and sentenced to death. Valentinus is credited with restoring the sight of the jailer's blind daughter, and according to legend and history, on the eve of his execution, Valentinus sent a farewell note to the little girl. He signed it "From your Valentine." He was executed February 14, 270 A.D. The practice of sending valentines grew out of an old belief extant even in Chaucer's day that birds began to mate on February 14 and so this was an appropriate day for sending lovers' tokens. It is from Roman mythology that we have little Dan Cupid with his arrows dipped in love potion.

> 'Muse, bid the morn awake,
> Sad winter now declines,
> Each bird doth choose a mate,
> This day St. Valentine's:
> For that good Bishop's sake
> Get up, and let us see
> What beauty it shall be
> That fortune us assigns.'
>   —Drayton

Bulletin Boards

Use magazine pictures to illustrate this display: *Some Facts About Animals in LOVE!!*

What animals kiss? Snails do. So do many fish. One fish, known as the "kissing gourami" has been observed kissing for as long as 25 minutes! Manatees hug one another and kiss too.

What animal brings gifts to his sweetheart? Male spiders offer the female delicacies such as a fly wrapped in a web. This is done for self-preservation in that the present keeps the female's attention long enough to give the male time to get away before the female tries to *eat him.*

How do elephants show affection? They wrap their trunks around each other and swish their tails back and forth.

How do elephants fend off unwanted romantic advances? With a slap of the trunk.

Which is the most family-oriented animal? The wolf. Wolves usually mate for life, and they even make a point of controlling their population! Generally, a "pack" of wolves consists of a father, mother and their offspring. Only two in each pack mate, but older brothers and sisters all help raise the newborn.

Which animal is best at playing hard to get? The lady porcupine who, if not interested, will threaten the male by raising her quills!

Which are the least romantic animals? Zebras, wild horses and the male orangutan (he is a real brute).

Which animals are most romantic? Gorillas, elephants and lions all show affection and are very tender lovers to their mates.

A Valentine Crossword Puzzle for Young Students:

Across°

3. It covers a bottle or a pen
5. I *am*, he *is*, we _____
7. The kind of card we send today
9. A book, _____ apple
10. This is how you say 'yes' in German
11. The opposite of DON'T
13. To move along
14. Beavers do this to a stream
16. The opposite of STAY
17. Not down
18. You chew this

Down°

1. A real friend, a good buddy
2. 3: like in a 3-cornered hat
3. A sweet treat
4. You write with it
5. He *did eat*, or he _____.
6. To really like something
7. Virginia (abbr.)
8. Each (abbr.)
12. Fourth note in musical scale
14. It makes a good pet
15. To keep quiet
19. You and me (or the country we live in: abbr.)

Valentines for 'Special People'

Ask each child to design a very special Valentine greeting for a famous historical person, a storybook character, a mythical hero, a T.V. star, a prehistoric monster, a best (animal) friend, a favorite sports star or someone you don't really know, but who you'd *like to get to know*. Encourage the use of a variety of materials and emphasize originality in wording the sentiment. (Finished valentines could be the basis of a very striking bulletin board display.)

Etymology

Cupid is from Latin *cupido* (desire, passion). Our words *friend* and *free* probably both stem from one Indo-European base which means "to be fond of, hold dear," as the basic sense of *free* is probably *dear to* (i.e., akin to) *the chief* and therefore, *not enslaved*. The word *flirt* dates back to the 16th century! The early Frisian word for a *giddy girl* was *flirtje*. It is also strongly influenced by the French word *fleureter* which means *to touch lightly; to move from flower to flower*.

Valentines

My Valentine
I will make you brooches and toys
for your delight

°Before handing out these puzzles be certain every child understands the meaning of (abbr.) and 'opposite'.

Younger children make and collect flat materials that interest them (tiny paper cutouts, sequins, glitter, tinfoil, feathers, leaves, bits of fabric, lace, string). These are arranged in a pleasing manner on a piece of wax paper. A second piece of wax paper is put on top and the two sheets are pressed together with a warm iron. Children cut a large heart-shaped piece out of a card. Then an area of their wax paper collage, chosen to go behind the heart-shaped hole, is cut and glued in place.

Individual folders to hold (and in which to carry home) their cards could be made in this way, too.

Traditionally, valentines had a lacy, almost fragile look. Besides using the commercially made white or gold paper doilies, the children can cut handmade doilies in the following ways:

(1) Fold square paper on the dotted lines. Cut shapes out of the folded square and open to form a doily.

Paste doily onto card of a sharply contrasting color. Children may want to slip tiny pieces of foil or colored tissue beneath cutout areas before doily is glued in place. This gives a more collage-like freedom to the valentine.

(2) Fold a rectangular piece of paper in half lengthwise and then in half crosswise. Cut as shown; then fold diagonally and cut as shown:

(3) Fold rectangular paper as described in #2. Cut as shown. Then open out and fold over each corner and cut as shown below.

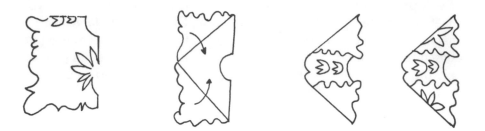

Doilies are opened out flat and carefully glued in place atop a folded card. The oval area in the centers of #2 and #3 provides a perfect frame for a snapshot of the child, or for a tiny heart that opens revealing a secret, or as a space in which to print a message.

Valentine's Day Party Suggestion

Invite an elderly person(s) to tea. This might be a grandparent of one of the students or a helpful person in the neighborhood, e.g., the crosswalk guard. The students help prepare the snack and tea (or champagne, recipe follows). (See recipe section at back of book for other snack suggestions, e.g., Biscochitos, Make-believe Fudge, Yogi tea and so on.) Children serve guests and show them some examples of their recent artwork. A short puppet show or magic act could be given. Finally, a big class-made valentine could be presented to each guest as he or she is preparing to leave.

Kids' Champagne

Add 3-4 bottles of soda water to 2 large cans of frozen unsweetened apple juice. Keep this "champagne" in tightly capped (wine) bottles to insure retention of fizz. This is a good substitute

for sugary soft drinks. (It might be served in plastic champagne glasses—the ones with the (hollow) detachable stems if such a detail would not be offensive to any classroom parents.)

A Valentine's Day Puzzle

This could be duplicated on small sheets of red construction paper and "delivered" to each young student as a little valentine from you to each of them.

Dear Valentine,
Here is a little puzzle for you to do today. Cut out the pieces and try to mend this broken heart!

Love,
Your Teacher

Valentine Riddles

- What does the valentine envelope say when you lick it? (Nothing. It just shuts right up.)
- What did the girl rodent say to the boy rodent? ("Wow, I really *gopher* you!")
- What kind of fall makes you unconscious, but is good for you? (Falling in love, falling asleep.)
- You'll find me from two to six feet above the ground. I'm not vegetable, mineral or animal. I'm not male or female. I can't be weighed or measured. I'm mentioned in the Bible and you can see me in the movies. I am used as a sign of love, or as a sign of *death*. What am I? (A kiss.)

[NOTE: Make sure that students understand how each part of this riddle relates to the answer.]

● *Oregon Was Admitted to the Union, 1859*   [14]

Etymology

First known use of the word "Oregon" was as the name for the river we call the Columbia. It was next used to speak of the territory drained by the river and was finally given to the state itself.

● *Arizona was Admitted to the Union, 1912*   [14]

Etymology

The name Arizona probably comes from the Panago Indian place name "Arizonac" which means "place of little springs."

● *Birth of Susan B. Anthony, 1820*   [15]

Susan Brownell Anthony was a pioneer in the Women's Movement. Born of Quaker parents she became involved in antislavery activities while a young schoolteacher. In 1852, she declared herself in favor of suffrage for women. She spent 50 years—all the rest of her life—working for equal rights for women.

Here are two good sources for non-sexist teaching materials:

> The Feminist Press
> Box 334
> Old Westbury, NY 11568

> Council on Interracial Books
> CIBC Resource Center
> 1841 Broadway
> New York, NY 10023

• *National Wildlife Week*   [Third full week of March]

Your students may be interested in writing letters in order to receive information about wildlife.

Here is a book for teachers about how to bring ecology home to city children and it includes a chapter called "Wildlife in Parks and Parking Lots." *Ecology for City Kids* costs $2.50 a copy and may be ordered from:

> Ecology for City Kids
> 13 Columbus Ave.
> San Francisco, CA 94111

• *John Glenn Day*   [20]

This day honors the American astronaut who orbited the earth in 1962. Glenn circled the earth 3 times in his space capsule and then landed safely in the Atlantic.

Students may be interested to learn how astronauts are chosen, the rigorous training they undertake in preparation for their duties, and may want answers to questions about women astronauts and Russian cosmonauts. Any of these subjects can be researched by looking in an encyclopedia or by requesting NASA literature. Ask the students to prepare a presentation of their information in the form of a card or board game or as a dramatic play.

Older students might like to read Glenn's autobiography and learn about Glenn's life since his safe return to Earth. They could read about other astronauts' physical and emotional problems, which may have developed as a consequence of their extra-terrestial experiences.

The students can write for a notebook-sized chart titled, "America's Twentieth Century Space Travelers," which is free from:

> McDonnell Douglas
> Box 516
> Saint Louis, MO 63166

• *Birth of George Washington*   [22]

We learn from his biographers that Washington was a Virginia gentleman who wore dentures made of wood, wire and elks' teeth; he kept detailed records of the money he spent; known occasionally to swear, Washington was not noted for a sense of humor. But it is not for these oddities that he is called the Father of Our Country. His was the strength and perseverance that kept our men fighting in a Revolutionary War that practically demanded surrender. Without Washington's leadership during the formative years of our country, America might never have existed.

George Washington's Fruit Cake*

Here is the recipe for Washington's favorite fruitcake. His wife Martha made it for him. In fact they first received it from Martha's mother on the day of their marriage!

2 cups butter	4 cups flour
3 cups sugar	1 cup currants, floured
5 eggs, separated and beaten	3/4 cup raisins, chopped and floured
	a handful of citron, chopped and floured
1 cup milk	cinnamon to suit
3 tsp. baking powder	nutmeg to suit

Cream the butter and sugar in a big wooden mixing bowl. Lightly stir in the separately beaten egg whites and yolks. Then blend in the milk. Sift the baking powder into the flour and stir this in.

After these ingredients are mixed, stir in all the fruits and spices.

Pour the batter into deep loaf pans, or long shallow pans lined with well-buttered papers. Fruitcake takes longer to bake than plain cake: bake at 275°–300° for at least two hours.

● *Birth of Samuel Pepys, 1633*   [23]

Samuel Pepys (Peeps) kept a unique diary (begun in January, 1660 and ending May 31st, 1669, when his sight began to fail). Written from day to day in an unusual type of code, Pepys' diary was not deciphered until nearly two hundred years had passed! A complete translation did not appear until 1925!

The diary tells of the life of a young man in his twenties and thirties who held an important public office during an exciting period of British history, the time of the restoration of the Stuarts to the throne of England. Pepys wrote with complete frankness, including every detail of his personal, family and official life. His diary portrays a curious pic-

---

ture of past manners, and of the gossip and politics of an historical period three centuries ago!

Codes and How to Crack Them

(Introduce only one code at a time—more would probably prove to be confusing). Let the kids try to invent their own codes. Use codes to communicate a daily message or riddle to the class.

1. Divi deth emes sage upin togr oups offo urle tter seac hand spac eitl iket his! (Divide the ...)
2. Siht ekil sdrawkcab egassem eht etirw. (Message backwards.)
3. Number corresponds to letter's position in the alphabet. a=1, b=2, c=3.
4. Reverse the position of the letters and number accordingly. a=26, b=25, c=24
5. Reverse the position of the letters in the alphabet. a=z, b=y, c=x.
6. Assign a symbol to each vowel: a = △
   e = ▢
   i = ◆
   o = ♥
   u = ▽
   y = ●

7. Jst lv t ll th vwls n th sntnc. (Leave vowels out)
8. L--v- --t th- v w ls nd sh w th-- r p-s-t--ns. (Indicate vowels with hyphen.)
9. Under/Over writing, where the position of the words on the line equals the words 'over' or 'under'. For example:

<pre>
                YOU
I STAND WHY CHARGE COVER AGENTS AS THEY TIP.
  CAN   THE   ALWAYS
</pre>

[NOTE: This Over/Under writing can be combined with code #3 to create an even more difficult puzzle.]

Here is a quick reference to Under/Over words.

UNDER—charge, cover, current, cut, dog, estimate, feed, foot, go, ground, handed, line, neath, pass, pay, privileged, rate, stand, stood, water, weight, world.

OVER—alls, board, cast, charge, coat, come, crowd, do, dose, draw, due, eat, feed, flow, grown, haul, head, heard, heat, look, pass, pay, shoe, shoot, time, turn, weight.

● *Leap Year Day*   [29]

Of unknown origin is the custom that in leap years women may take the initiative and propose marriage. In 1288 an act of Scottish Parliament permitted a woman during leap year to propose to a man and if the woman were rejected (unless he could prove that he was already engaged), the man had to pay her 100 pounds. In a few years a similar law was passed in France; in the 15th century, the tradition was legalized in Italy. By 1600 the custom was a part of common law in England.

Riddles:

1. **How many months have 28 days? (ALL of them!)**

2. **What month has the fewest beautiful sunsets? (February—because it has the fewest sunsets, PERIOD!)**

FEBRUARY ACTIVITIES

Language Arts

"**A letter to my teacher.**" Set aside a time during which the children will each write you a letter. Ask them to carefully plan the things they would like to ask or tell you. Explain that these letters are strictly personal and will not be read aloud or displayed. You might answer each of their letters separately, or you may post an open letter to the class in reply to their missives.

Haiku. This verse form has been written since the 13th century. It is a little Japanese poem of 3 lines. The first and last lines always have 5 syllables; the middle line has 7 syllables. Haiku are usually nature poems describing the season or explaining the feelings of the poet. A haiku does not rhyme. It paints a small, often exquisite picture in your mind.

The patting of rain
Mist gently on my window
Then a pounding! Hail.°

Have your class read this haiku aloud together, clapping in unison at each syllable. Ask the students to describe the mental images they had while reading this poem. Then give the children the first two lines of a haiku such as:

At this time of year
I am always thinking how

. . . . .

Let them supply the third line. Discuss their responses. Now with the aid of Webster and Roget (the thesaurus helps immensely in finding a synonym with the right number of syllables), let your class begin composing their own haiku.

Spelling. Help students discover how each of them learns most easily. Set up a spelling practice course on two long tables. Include a cookie sheet on which they can write a word in finger paint and then erase and try it again, file cards on which words are printed in Elmer's Glue and sprinkled with sand or glitter, a tape recorder which each student can use to dictate words to himself/herself, magnetic letters and metalboard, unusual writing instruments (thick felt tip pens, Sumi brush and ink, a very fine-pointed pen) with large newsprint sheets to write on, and a cut-down cardboard box with an inch of sand in it, in which words can be written and then "erased." Let students use any of these techniques they wish. Discuss which materials seemed most helpful for each of them, and talk about WHY that might have been the case.

°Used with permission of the author, Elisabeth Tracy.

Math

Mathematical memory questions (a math sheet to duplicate).

Without using a ruler, try to just imagine the size of each of these common objects. Then write the (decimal and/or metric) measurement you guess next to each object.

1. The length of your first finger _____
2. The width of your foot _____
3. The width of your desk top _____
4. The length of your math book _____
5. The diameter of a quarter; a nickel; a penny _____ ; _____ ; _____
6. The length and width of a 15 cent stamp _____
7. The height your desk is from the floor _____
8. The length of your pencil (pen); a ruler; a yardstick _____ ; _____ ; _____
9. The diameter of a kickball (basketball) _____
10. The length of your nose _____

Now take a (metric) ruler and really measure each of the things listed above. How did you do? What did this show you about the way you think about measurements?

[NOTE: Make sure you have quarters, nickels, pennies, string, rulers and 15 cent stamps ready for checking answers on these sheets.]

February Science

At this time of year most birds, insects and wild animals are not in evidence.

Many older students will be interested in animals that are disappearing permanently and in learning what, if anything, can be done to help these endangered species.

Have each student choose one of the vanishing mammals and write about it as if *it* were speaking. These stories can be written as appeals, complaints, reminiscences, hopes, or dreams, and they can take the form of letters, journal entries, or first-hand reports.

Below is a list of some of the world's vanishing animals, but you should check with a reference librarian for an up-to-date list of the endangered species:

Dolphin	Tapir
Orangutan	Puma
Siberian Tiger	Leopard
Polar Bear	White-tailed Gnu
Stellar's Sea-Cow	Brown Hyena
Manatee	Bactrian Camel
Southern Sea Otter	Giant Panda
Atlantic Walrus	Koala Bear
Blue Whale	(Hairy-nosed) Wombat
Cheetah	Wallaby
Mountain Gorilla	Yak
Dorcas Gazelle	Rhinoceros: Black, White,
Asiatic Lion	Javan, Sumatran and Great Indian
Pronghorn	Snow Leopard
Chinchilla	Okapi
Wolf	Pigmy Hippopotamus
Giant Armadillo	Mountain Zebra
Vicuña	

Finished papers could become an informative bulletin board display.

Students can write for free Whale People-to-People Petition, and Dolphin or Harp Seal Petition Packages. They can also send for *Whales* (5 cents), *Wolves* (5 cents), *What is an Endangered Species?* (5 cents) or a "Wildlife Under Attack" 25" × 35" poster of the 10 most threatened North American species, which indicates how they are killed and what you can do to help ($3.00). To obtain any of these materials, write to:

Animal Protection Institute of America
5894 South Land Park Drive
P. O. Box 22505
Sacramento, CA 95822

February Art

Bubble-blowing (a fascinating non-permanent art form). Cover the floor and table with sheets of plastic—a shower curtain works well, however, newspaper can be used in place of plastic. Keep several bath towels handy.

In a jar, mix 8 tablespoons dishwashing soap with a quart of warm water. Add a tablespoon of glycerine to the mixture (glycerine helps make stronger bubbles). Provide the children with plastic drinking straws, meat basters, and flat pans or cookie sheets filled with this soapy mixture. Let them experiment with blowing chains of small bubbles, hemispheres, and bubbles within bubbles. Add more glycerine as necessary.

Have the children ask themselves: Are the colors separate from one another, or layered one on top of the other? If food coloring is added to the soapy water, does this affect the color of the bubble? Is the color on the surface of the bubble changed?

Try looking at the bubbles through colored plastic, sheets of colored cellophane and polarized sunglasses. Which of these affect the color on the bubbles?

Airborne bubbles. These can be produced by the use of tin cans that have been opened at both ends, rolled up tubes of plastic, and bent coat hangers. A large extended tube can be made by taping three of these tin cans together end to end. Dip the tube into the soap mixture so that a film forms across the opening. Take a deep breath. Place your face against the can opening and blow gently so that a bubble forms at the other end. Now twist the can sharply and release the bubble into the air.

Giant airborne bubbles. These can be produced, but it takes a little practice. Thread (three feet of) light string through two drinking straws and tie the ends of the strings together. Wet your hands all over with the soap mixture. Hold a straw in each hand and pull them apart to form a string rectangle. Lower strings into soapy water. Lift out slowly with film across the string shape. Hold the string shape at arm's length, below your waist. Pull the string form firmly but gently upwards. A big bubble is formed. Bring the two straws together as you lift the form up. The bubble can be closed off and allowed to float free. This takes a little practice—but what rewards! It is possible, if conditions are correct, to actually create bubbles large enough to encase the student! Long strings, a strong bubble solution, patience and a long flowing gesture *can* create such a bubble. Vary lengths of straws, strings. Twist rectangle to produce twin bubbles. Try blowing gently beneath airborne bubble to keep it aloft.

Geometric shapes. These can be achieved by bending copper wire into spirals, knots, and curves and dipping these into the soapy mixture.

Another method is to make geometric structures from (paper) drinking straws. Two or three paper clips attached to one another are used to join the straws together forming angles. Dip straw structure into soapy water forming film on each side and lift structure out slowly.

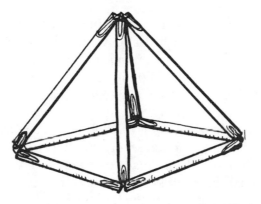

Let the students experiment, making other geometric shapes by using the straw-string method described in Giant Airborne Bubbles. Additional strings can be added to shapes and other experimental combinations can be tested.

February Music

The following information concerning the orchestra can be the basis for a student-created bulletin board. It could also be presented in four separate sessions, one on each family of instruments, illustrating each instrument by playing appropriate recordings. For example, you could use "Overture" from *Mignon* as an excellent example of French Horn, "Dawn" or "Calm" of the *William Tell Overture* for woodwinds, and "Dance of the Mirlitons" from *Nutcracker Suite* for the flute.

The Orchestra

A large orchestra may have 90-100 instruments in it. Each orchestra is made up of four families of instruments: the *strings, woodwinds, brass* and *percussion*.

The instruments of the **String Family** make music with their strings.

Violins (vi-o-lins) were first made in Italy. They were made of a special kind of wood found in Italy. A special kind of varnish and a specific type of glue were used. For years and years, one family made violins. This family was called Stradivarius. They made the finest and sweetest-toned violins that have ever been created.

Today, anyone who owns a Stradivarius has a very costly and rare instrument. The older the violin, the better it becomes, for the wood grows more mellow and the tone more sweet as time passes.

The *violin* has four strings made of catgut and its tone is made by drawing a horsehair bow across these strings. It is called "the child" of the string family because it has the highest-toned voice.

Sometimes you hear people talking about first and second violins. These are not different instruments. The first violin plays the tune, while the second violin plays a second part that is like an alto in choral work.

The *viola* (veeōla) is a little longer than the violin and has a deeper voice. It is played in the same position as the violin and is called "the big brother" of the family.

The *cello* (chellō) is still larger than the viola and is called "the mother" of the string family. It is shaped like the violin, but it stands on the floor, while the player holds it between his/her knees and rests the neck on his/her shoulder. Because it is larger, its voice is deeper and more mellow. It plays the soft tender passages of a musical piece. The bow is short. Can you guess why?

The *double bass* (dubl bās) is "the father" of the strings. Its voice is deep and not a bit tuneful when it is played alone. But it adds a lot to the music as a whole when it is played along with the other instruments. The double bass is tall—the player must stand as he/she plays. Its bow is quite short. Often, the player plucks the strings instead of bowing.

When four members of the string family (first and second violins, viola, and cello) play together, we call it a *string quartet*. Some of the world's loveliest music has been written for string quartets.

The instruments of the **Woodwind Family** were originally all made of wood. Air is blown through a woodwind to make music.

The *piccolo* (pik-u-lō) has a shrill high tone so it is called "the child" of the woodwind family. The piccolo is used for very high tones. Its voice is an octave higher than the flute.

The *flute* (flōōt) is the instrument on which the player blows *across* not *into* the mouthpiece. The flute's voice is high and dainty and is used to express the happier passages of music. The flute is a very old instrument. We read of it being used by shepherd boys as far back as Biblical times. The flute was first made from reeds, but now most flutes are made of metal, as this allows them to hold their tone longer.

The *clarinet* (klair-u-net) has a soft mellow voice. Its mouthpiece is flat, like a whistle.

The *bassoon* (ba-sōōn) is called "the father of the woodwind family." It is the "clown" instrument. It is given the comical parts to play because its voice is deep. Its mouthpiece is different from all others: a small metal rod with reeds extends from the *side* and this is where you put your mouth.

The *oboe* (ō-bō) has a nasal twang. Because of the double-reed mouthpiece, a player can play only short passages at a time. Why would this be so?

The *Woodwind Family* gives a soft, mellow tone to the orchestra. When woodwinds play with the strings some very lovely effects can be heard.

The instruments of the **Brass Family** are made of brass. We blow air through brass instruments to make music.

The *trumpet* (trum-pet) or *cornet* (kor-net) has the soprano voice. It is a very old instrument. It was first used by herdsmen to call their animals. At that time, it was made of the horns and tusks of animals. Although it looks small, the trumpet is really several feet long! It is just wound around to make it easier to handle. It has a loud clear voice and is used for commanding passages.

The *French horn* is the alto of the choir. It has a soft deep voice and is used to play the mellow parts of a score. It is usually played slowly, because its voice is tender and beautiful. (Do you think it is longer or shorter than the trumpet?)

The *trombone* (trom-bōn) is the tenor of the choir. Its long tube is really about 3 *yards* long but is bent back on itself several times so that it can be more easily handled. Instead of using *stops* to change the length of the air passage, the player *slides* the trombone. Its tone is pretty but not as mellow as the French horn nor as brilliant as the trumpet.

The *tuba* (tōo-bu) is "the father" because its voice is deep and it is the biggest of all the family. If stretched out to full length, it would be *18 feet* long!!! When played alone, it does not have a very pleasing tone, but it is important to the orchestra as it gives it depth.

The instruments of the **Percussion Family** are struck to make their music. They keep time for the other instruments of the orchestra. Not all percussion instruments are used in every performance.

The *tympani* (tim-panee) or kettle drums (there are usually two) are *tuned* drums. The sticks are padded and give a dull soft thud. The tympani are used to give a feeling of fear and suspense to the music. A good tympani player is paid well, as his/her part is very important to the orchestra.

Snare and *bass drums* are used for thunder effects, to show excitement, and to keep the other instruments together on the beat.

Tambourines (tam-bu-reens) and *castanets* (cas-tu-nets) are used for dancing parts (Spanish).

Cymbals (sim-bls) are brass plates that are struck together for loud parts.

A *celesta* (su-les-tu) is like a small organ with a high bell-like tone.

The *triangle* (trī-angl) gives a high-pitched tinkling sound when struck. The triangle is a steel rod bent into the shape of a triangle with one angle left open, allowing it to ring.

The *xylophone* (zī-lō-fon) is made of a series of metal bars, graduated in length so they give the notes of the scale when they are hit with little (wooden) hammers.

Orchestra bells, *chimes*, *gongs* and even *tom-toms* can also be included in the percussion section of an orchestra.

February Physical Education

The Zephyros Education Exchange (1201 Stanyan St., San Francisco, CA 94117) offers an extraordinary source of teaching ideas. For example, their Deschool Primer No. 14 highlights people games, machine games (What to do After You Hit Return), outdoor tournaments and games on freedom and madness: *New Games and Tournaments for Classroom Earth*, 104 pages (12 × 15) $2.50. Send for their Zephyros Catalog, it's extra-ordinary!

Purim

Hamentashen are the delicious, filled pastries that are part of the celebration of Purim, the festival marking the salvation of the Jews from the massacre planned for them by Haman, advisor to the king of Persia. Here's how they are made.

Hamentashen*

4 eggs	2 tsp. vanilla
1 c. oil	3 tsp. baking powder
1-1/4 c. sugar	1/2 tsp. salt
5-1/2 c. flour (approx.)	

Beat eggs, beat in oil, sugar, vanilla, baking powder, salt. Add flour gradually, mix thoroughly. Knead till smooth enough to roll on floured board. Roll out. Cut dough into 3"- 4" rounds. Place desired filling on each round. Pinch together sides of lower half of circles to form triangles.

Place Hamantashen on a lightly greased baking sheet or pan and bake at 350° for 1/2 hour, or until golden brown.

Fillings: The fillings are usually cooked prunes or mohn (poppyseeds). The prune filling may be made from (2 cups) cooked dried prunes with (1/2 cup) ground nuts and (1 T.) grated orange rind added. Prepared pureed prune baby food may also be used; or the mashed prune filling called lekva.

(Thank you, Janie Stein Romero!)

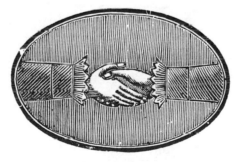

Hamen's hat pastries are made in a tri-cornered hat shape. This recipe is from "Guide for the Jewish Homemaker" by Shonie B. Levi & Sylvia R. Kaplan (National Women's League of the United Synagogue of America, 1964).

arch

March comes in like a lion
And goes out like a lamb
—English proverb
17th century

†† Red Cross Month (American Red Cross, 17th and D Streets, N.W., Washington, DC 20006).

†† Youth Art Month (Crayon, Watercolor and Craft Institute, Eden Hill Rd., Newtown, CT 16470).

1 National Weights and Measures Week (Weights and Measures Associates, 1 Thomas Circle, N.W., Washington, DC 20005).

On this day in 1781 the American colonies adopted the Articles of Confederation, paving the way for a federal union.

Ohio, 17th State, was admitted into the Union, 1803.

Nebraska, 37th State, was admitted into the Union, 1867.

2   On this day in 1877, Rutherford B. Hayes was declared elected President by a special Electoral Commission in the disputed contest with Samuel Tilden.

3   Florida, 27th State, entered the Union in 1845.

Alexander Graham Bell, chief inventor of the telephone, was born in Edinburgh, Scotland in 1847.

"The Star Spangled Banner" officially became the national anthem of the United States, 1931.

4   On this day in 1681, William Penn received the charter to Pennsylvania from England's King Charles II.

On this day in 1789, the U.S. Constitution went into effect.

Vermont, 14th State, was admitted to the Union, 1791.

Theodor Geisel (Dr. Seuss) was born in Springfield, Massachusetts, in 1904.

5   The Boston Massacre occurred when British troops fired into a crowd of unruly Bostonians, killing five men (including a Black, Crispus Attucks) in this early prelude to the Revolutionary War, 1770.

Quotation of the Day: Not the Battle of Lexington, nor the surrender of Burgoyne or Cornwallis, were more important events in American history than the Battle of King Street on March 5, 1770.—*John Adams, 46 years later.*

6   Alamo Day commemorates the end of the Battle of the Alamo. For 13 days, a tiny courageous band of Texans tried to defend their compound in San Antonio against the large Mexican Army. On this day, in 1836 Davy Crockett was killed as well as the 186 other Americans who had fought along with him.

Gordon Cooper, U.S. astronaut, was born in Shawnee, Oklahoma, in 1927.

7 Burbank Day honors the birth of horticulturist, Luther Burbank, in Lancaster, Massachusetts in 1849.

8 On this day in 1917, riots and strikes in St. Petersburg mark the beginning of the Russian Revolution.

9 *Quotation of the Day:* My movements to the chair of government will be accompanied by feelings not unlike those of a culprit who is going to the place of his execution.—*George Washington to Benjamin Harrison in 1789, referring to his forthcoming Presidential Inauguration.*

First battle between the ironclad warships, the Union's *Monitor* and the Confederate *Merrimac*, lasted for four hours off Hampton Roads, Virginia, 1862. Many historians claim the engagement ended in a draw as both ships suffered damages.

Yuri Gagarin, Soviet cosmonaut, was born in Smolensk, Russia, in 1934.

10 On this day in 1775, Daniel Boone and a group of frontiersmen were hired by the Transylvania Company to cut a road through the wilderness to the Kentucky River.

Lillian D. Wald, social worker, was born in Cincinnati, Ohio, in 1867.

First words heard over a telephone were spoken by Alexander Graham Bell to his assistant Thomas Watson, "Come here, Watson, I want you," in Boston in 1876.

11 On this day in 1810, Emperor Napoleon was married by proxy to eighteen-year-old Princess Marie Louise of Austria.

12 Walter Schirra, U.S. astronaut was born in Hackensack, New Jersey in 1923.

Quotation of the Day: Curiosity is one of the permanent and certain characteristics of a vigorous mind.—*Samuel Johnson on this day in 1751.*

13 Juan Gris, painter, was born in Madrid, Spain, in 1887.

On this day in 1971, the *Explorer 43* satellite was launched.

14 First town meeting, which was to become famous as a New England institution, was held at Faneuil Hall, Boston, in 1743.

Albert Einstein, physicist and originator of the theory of relativity was born in Ulm, Germany, in 1879.

Eugene A. Gernan, U.S. astronaut, was born in Chicago, Illinois in 1934.

15   Andrew Jackson, 7th U.S. President, was born in Waxhaw, South Carolina, in 1767.

Maine, the 23rd State, was admitted into the Union in 1820.

16   James Madison, 4th U.S. President, was born in Port Conway, Virginia, 1751

George Ohm, scientist, was born in Erlangen, Germany, in 1787.

R. Walter Cunningham, U.S. astronaut, was born in Creston, Ohio, in 1932.

First docking of one space craft with another took place on this day in 1966 when U.S. astronauts Neil Armstrong and David Scott succeeded in docking their crafts with one another.

17   St. Patrick's Day honors the patron saint of Ireland, who died about 461 A.D. in Eire.

Kate Greenaway, artist-illustrator, was born in London in 1846.

First baseball league of importance, National Association of Baseball Players, was established, 1871.

First practical submarine, developed by John P. Holland, was submerged off Staten Island, New York, for almost an hour and three quarters in 1898.

18   Grover Cleveland, 22nd and 24th U.S. President, was born in Caldwell, New Jersey in 1837.

Nicholas Rimsky-Korsakov, composer, was born in Novgorod, Russia in 1844.

First person to walk in space, U.S.S.R. cosmonaut Aleksei Lenov remained outside his spacecraft for 20 minutes secured only by a long lifeline.

19   Sergei Diaghilev, dancer, was born in Novgorod, Russia in 1872.

20   Henrik Ibsen, writer, was born in Skien, Norway, 1828.

21   First day of Spring (Spring Equinox).

International Children's Poetry Day (The Centre International
   Poesie-Enfance, Avenue des Ortolans, 95, 1170 Bruxelles,
   Belgium).

Benito Juarez, patriot and President of Mexico, was born in
   Guelatas, Mexico in 1806.

On this day in 1621, Governor John Carver and Chief Massasoit
   signed a nonaggression treaty at Plymouth, Massachusetts.

††   Pesach or Passover, is a moveable Jewish feast day, occurring in
   the spring.

22   On this day in 1775, Patrick Henry spoke out in favor of arming
   Virginia in case of war against England.

Quotation of the Day: Is life so dear, or peace so sweet, as to be
   purchased at the price of chains and slavery? . . . I know not
   what course others may take, but as for me, give me liberty or
   give me death!—*Patrick Henry*

On this day in 1943, the Danes bravely defied the Germans who
   were occupying their nation, by going to the polls to vote for or
   against Democracy. Ninety-nine percent of the ballots were
   cast for Democracy and one percent favored the New Order of
   Germany.

First spacemen to shift their orbit by manual control, U.S.
   astronauts Virgil Grissom and John Young, aboard the spaceship "Molly Brown" in 1965.

24   On this day in 1882, Robert Koch announced his discovery of the
   TB bacillus.

On this day in 1965, the Reverend Martin Luther King, Jr., led
   25,000 Blacks, and white sympathizers as they converged on
   Montgomery, the capitol of Alabama, after their five-day, 54-
   mile march from Selma, to protest Alabama's denial of equal
   voting rights to Blacks.

Quotation of the Day: Walk together, children. Don't you get
   weary, and it will lead to the promised land. And Alabama will
   be a new Alabama and America will be a new America.
   —*Martin Luther King, Jr., speaking to the marchers as they left
   Selma on March 21st.*

25   Flannery O'Connor, writer, was born in Savannah, Georgia in
   1925.

James A. Lovell, U.S. astronaut, was born in Cleveland, Ohio in 1928.

26 Tennessee Williams, playwright, was born in Columbus, Mississippi in 1911.

27 On this day in 1634, Leonard and George Calvert, English colonists, bought some 30 acres on the St. Charles River and established the first settlement in what is now Maryland.

29 First Swedish settlement in America was established at what is now Wilmington, Delaware, 1638.

John Tyler, 10th U.S. President, was born in Greenway, Virginia, in 1790

30 First pencil with an eraser attached to it was patented by Hyman L. Lipman of Philadelphia, 1858.

On this day in 1867, Secretary of State William H. Seward and the Russian minister to the U.S. reached an agreement on the purchase of Alaska by the U.S. for $7,200,000 in gold. Seward was bitterly criticized for buying Alaska and it was called "Seward's Folly" and "Seward's Ice Box".

31 On this day in 1776, Abigail Adams wrote her husband, John Adams, a member of the Continental Congress: "In the new code of laws, which I suppose it will be necessary for you to make, I desire you would remember the ladies and be more generous and favorable to them than your ancestors."

John LaFarge, writer, was born in New York City in 1835.

On this day in 1889, the Eiffel Tower was opened officially in Paris despite vigorous protests of one hundred leading writers, artists and composers.

First Negro is selected for training as an astronaut, Edward J. Dwight, Jr. of California, 1963.

arch

In the Roman calendar, March was the first month of the year. This was the season for the waging of war and so the Romans named this month after Mars, the god of war. In 45 B.C. Caesar reformed the calendar and March became the third month. The expression "mad as a March hare"evolved since "March is the mating season for hares and during this month they are supposedly 'full of whimsy.' "

MARCH QUOTATIONS

†† *Youth Art Month*

Excite new ways of seeing, feeling and being, in order to preserve the innate creative potential of every one of us.
—Ann Wiseman: Making Things

Art flourishes where there is a sense of adventure.
—Alfred North Whitehead

With an apple I will astonish Paris.*—Paul Cezanne*

I invent nothing—I rediscover.

Nothing is a waste of time if you use the experience wisely.
—Auguste Rodin

All knowledge has its origins in our perceptions.
—Leonardo da Vinci

My life has been nothing but a failure.*—Claude Monet*

People will forgive anything but beauty and talent. So I am doubly unpardonable *—James Whistler*

Lord, grant that I may always desire more than I can accomplish.
—Michelangelo

If Heaven had only granted me five more years I could have become a real painter. *—Katsushika Hokusai (at age 89)*

4   I expect to pass through life but once. If, therefore, there be any kindness I can show, or any good thing I can do to any fellow being, let me do it now, and not deter or neglect it, as I shall not pass this way again. *—William Penn*

14   Imagination is more important than knowledge.
—Albert Einstein

15   Our Federal Union! It must and shall be preserved!
—Andrew Jackson (Toast at Jefferson birthday banquet, 1830)

17   *For the great Gaels of Ireland*
     Are the men that God made mad,
     For all their wars are merry,
     And all their songs are sad.
—G. K. Chesterton

18   Though the people support the government, the government should not support the people.

I believe our great Maker is preparing the world, in His own good time, to become one nation, speaking one language.
—*Inaugural Address, 1893*
Grover Cleveland

21   Spring—an experience in immortality.—*Henry Thoreau*

Every second we live is a new and unique moment of the universe, a moment that never was before and never will be again. And what do we teach our children in school? We teach them that 2 and 2 makes 4 and that Paris is the capital of France. When will we also teach them what they are? We should say to each of them: Do you know what you are? You are a marvel. You are unique. In all the world there is no other child exactly like you. In the millions of years that have passed there has never been a child like you. And look at your body what a wonder it is! Your legs, your arms, your cunning fingers, the way you move! You may become a Shakespeare, a Michelangelo, a Beethoven. You have the capacity for anything. Yes, you are a marvel. And when you grow up can you then harm another who is, like you, a marvel? You must cherish one another. You must work—we must all work—to make this world worthy of its children.
—*Pablo Casals*

March Riddles:

• What is the worst month for a solider? (A *long* March.)

• What can pass before the sun without leaving a shadow? (The winds of March!)

• What day is a command to move on? (March fourth.)

MARCH EVENTS

- *National Weights and Measures Week*   [1-7]

What better way to note the importance of this week than by emphasizing metric weights and measures? Get a free copy of An Educator's Guide to Teaching Metrication from:

> Consumer Information Services—D/703
> Sears, Roebuck & Co.
> Sears Tower
> Chicago, IL 60684

It contains a teacher's guide, Learning Experience and Group Project suggestions and multi-disciplinary project ideas as well as a good bibliography of other places to write for additional metric aids and ideas.

- *Ohio Was Admitted to the Union, 1803*   [1]

Etymology

Its name probably means "great river" from the Iroquoian word: O-he-yo.

- *Nebraska Joined the Union, 1867*   [1]

Etymology

Nebraska is the Otoe Indian name for The Platte River. It means "flat water" and was first used by the French explorer Bourgmont in 1714.

- *Florida Entered the Union, 1845*   [3]

Etymology

Ponce de Leon first landed in this region during the feast of flowers (Pascua Florida) in the spring of 1513. Florida is a Spanish word meaning "flowery."

- *Vermont Was Admitted to the Union, 1791*   [4[

Etymology

Vermont was probably named by Samuel de Champlain from the French words "vert" (green) and "mont" (mountain).

- *The Boston Massacre, 1770*   [5]

On this day in 1770, British soldiers fired into a crowd in Boston, killing several Americans. Paul Revere made an engraving of this street fight and it is called "Bloody Massacre." *How* he made this print, as well as a reproduction of it, appears in the *Revolutionary Times, America 1750-1759* of *The School Picture Set*, put out by the Metropolitan Museum of Art in New York City. This extensive series covers American History and World History, as well as random topics such as *Animals That Never Were* and *The Artist's Workshop*. Each little book (4"x6") has 20 perforated pages, one of background information and 19 illustrated examples with short descriptive passages. These little study books can be used to make review card games, as the basis of activity card sets, and as an enrichment source (students can use water-colors to fill in the black and white museum reproductions).

The School Picture Set (about 50 cents each) may be ordered from the:

> Metropolitan Museum of Art
> Education Department
> 255 Gracie Station
> New York, NY 10028

Write, asking for a price-list.

- *Luther Burbank Day Commemorates the Birth of Luther Burbank, 1849* [7]

Educated in the public schools, Burbank, as a boy, worked for the Ames Plow Co. in Worcester, Massachusetts. There he showed remarkable inventive abilities and he soon began some small seed raising experiments. By 1873, he had developed the Burbank Potato. Two years later, he moved to Santa Rosa, California and began his life-long work of creating new fruits, vegetables, grains and grasses.

Burbank had a special sympathy for plants. This, coupled with 50 years of practical daily plant study, allowed Burbank to make connections and visualize growth outcomes that no other person could. Luther Burbank became the most famous plant originator in the world.

[IT'S A FACT: Special hormones (auxims) in a plant cause the stem to grow up and the roots to grow down. If they did not have such hormones, plants would be growing every which way and it would be impossible to have agriculture.]

Some Classroom Plants

A hanging garden. Use a needle and thread to thread a sponge on a long string. Children wet the sponge and sprinkle parsley seeds on it. The sponge is then hung in a sunny window. Children keep sponge wet by spraying it daily with an atomizer.

Green unprocessed coffee beans, fig seeds, grape seeds can all sprout indoors.

Gingerroot (fresh) grows a lovely green foliage with delicately scented white blossoms: place root horizontally in shallow dish with water 2/3 covering the root. Change water to keep it fresh. Eyes of the root will sprout, and green leaves, vine-like growths develop, but it takes time.

A Pineapple top should be cut off just under the green growth. Place it in water by a *sunny* window. Roots will develop after *several* weeks. Always keep water fresh. Plant in soil, and water once a week. This can develop into a BIG plant. (For another approach to growing a pineapple plant see page 189.)

Perhaps your class or school would be interested in constructing a hydroponic mini-garden or greenhouse. For more information write:

Hydroponic Mini-Gardens
1419 Eubank, NE
Albuquerque, NM 87112

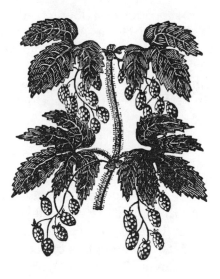

Plant Riddles:

- What berry is red when it's green? (*black*berry)
- What berry is a bird? (*goose*berry)
- What berry is used in a barn? (*straw*berry)
- What berry is not happy? (*blue*berry)
- What berry is the oldest in the world? (*elder*berry)

- *Albert Einstein Was Born, 1879*   [14]

Middle and upper grade teachers who are interested in keeping apace with the latest in science, mathematics and environmental education should find ERIC publications very useful. Write and ask to be put on their (Informational Bulletins) mailing list:

> ERIC (Clearinghouse for Science, Mathematics
> and Environmental Education)
> The Ohio State University
> 1200 Chambers Rd., 3d Floor
> Columbus, OH 43212

- *St. Patrick's Day*   [17]

Born in Britain, Patrick, at the age of 16, was kidnapped by Irish pirates and enslaved in Ireland. For six miserable years he tended sheep on the cold hills of Ballymena. He escaped finally aboard a ship to France (then known as Gaul). There he studied for the priesthood and in 431 A.D. was named a bishop. The next year he was sent by the Pope to teach the gospel to the people of Hibernia—the same wild Irish tribesmen who had kidnapped him as a boy. Patrick spent nearly 30 years trudging up and down the Emerald Isle, teaching Christianity. Few people today actually know who he was, or what he did. The Irishmen who knew him when he was alive must have loved him dearly, for they have transmitted their affection for him to their descendants for 1,500 years.

Etymology

In Irish "seamrog" is the diminutive of "seamar," a clover. So shamrock is "a little clover." Because of its 3 leaves, it was used by St. Patrick to illustrate the Trinity, and in this way it became the symbol of Ireland. The potato is a native of Peru. The Spanish conquistadores discovered it in the Andes Mts. and brought it back to Europe. The potato was introduced to American in 1719 by a group of Irishmen and so we have the "Irish potato."

- **First Baseball League of Importance, 1871**   [17]

Interested students may write for a free copy of the Famous Slugger Yearbook (65 pages of photos and baseball information):

Hillerich and Bradby Co.
P.O. Box 18177
Louisville, KY 40218

- **First Submersion of a Practical Submarine, 1898**   [17]

A submarine uses a periscope to check the surface of the sea before actually rising up to the ocean surface.

Etymology

"Peri" is Greek for around and "scope" is from the Greek "Skopos" a spy, a watcher which comes from "skopein," to see.

How to Make a Periscope

You will need a narrow box not over 3 feet long such as a shoebox, 2 (metal) mirrors (sold at sporting goods stores) and masking tape, scissors, and glue.

1. Put a mirror near the bottom of one side of the box. Trace around it. Do the same near the top of the other side of the box (a).

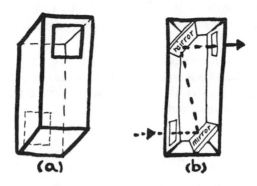

2. Glue the mirrors in place (b).

3. Adjust the mirrors until you can see out of the top hole by looking through the bottom hole.

4. Replace the lid on the top of box. Seal the lid edges to the box with masking tape.

Ask the students to experiment with their periscopes and then write a few paragraphs on one of these topics:

1. **How the Periscope Has Changed My Life.**

2. **The Adventures of a Detective and his/her Periscope.**

3. **How a _____ Could Be Improved by Equipping It with a Periscope.**

● *First Day of Spring*　[21]

On this day there are just 12 hours from sunrise to sunset and 12 hours from sunset to sunrise. This is called the day of the "equinox" because that word means equal (day and night). In Greek mythology, Demeter and Zeus had a daughter named Persephone. One day Hades, the ruler of the underworld, kidnapped Persephone and married her. When Persephone left the Earth, the flowers died and the wheat withered. Demeter begged the gods to send her daughter back; the gods agreed to let her return for 2/3 of each year. When Persephone returned to Earth, life began anew. She corresponds to the Corn Spirit (of the American Indians) which dies and is reborn each year.

[NOTE: As children have a tendency to grow restless at this time of year, plan a class walk to see pollywogs, pussywillows and to *look* at spring's arrival. If your school is in a city, what signs of spring *can* be seen and heard?]

Spring Science:

An experiment with air pressure. You will need a strip of paper, a small square of paper, a spool, a water glass, a file card, water and a plastic dishpan.

Make certain that young students know that air is the invisible mixture of gases that covers the earth, and that pressure is pressing or an action/force pushing against another force.

To show that air is all around us: Use a strip of paper to show what happens when air is taken away from one place. (Have a child hold the strip of paper close to his mouth and draw in his breath.) Have another child use a spool and small piece of paper to demonstrate the same principle as above.

In both of the previous examples, air has been taken from one side. The air pressure on the opposite side then presses toward the object.

[NOTE: In order to get the feel for doing the following experiment, practice it yourself, prior to showing it to the class.]

Perform this experiment over the plastic dishpan. Fill a drinking glass *to the top* with water. Place a card that is larger than the opening of the glass on the top of the glass, and turn it upside down as you hold your hand on the card.

Gently press upward and then release hand—the card *should* stay on the glass.

Demonstrate that air is pressing in all directions by turning glass sideways, and at angles. Let some students try this experiment.

Conclusion: the air is pressing harder than gravity is pulling. Air presses in all directions. The card remains stable when the glass is turned. (What effect does air pressure have on our weather?)

Honeybee study. An observation beehive ($25) that can be filled with bees direct from the package bee shipping cage° is offered by the A.I. Root Co. of Texas—Box 9153, San Antonio, TX 78204-Phone: (512) 223-2948 (ask for catalog). It is a 1½ inch frame hive that comes with foundation, frames, hardware, plastic tube and feeder and side panels to keep out light and protect glass. (Dimensions are 22½" × 16½".) Glass is not included. An observation hive is fascinating to most children. However such a hive is not appropriate for use in every school. Ask your principal's advice before installing such a hive in your classroom.

A color wall chart (30" × 40") *The Honeybee* ($5.50) is also available. It illustrates the anatomy of different bees, explains their functions and shows development of bee from egg to adulthood.

Youth Art Month

Creativity is so delicate a flower that praise tends to make it bloom, while discouragement often nips it in the bud. Any of us will put out more and better ideas if our efforts are appreciated.

Crayon-resist batik paintings. Have the children use crayons to make a spring drawing or design on butcher paper, such as trees blowing in the wind, blossoms on bushes, trees, new flowers, clouds or rain, or flocks of birds returning. Some areas on the paper should not be filled in with crayon.

Next, children soak their papers in water and then crumple up their drawings. Then the papers are smoothed out and blotted dry.

°One pound package of bees to stock hive. Order 1 lb. package directly from Stover Apiaries, Mayhew, Miss. 39573. Be sure to specify for filling Root Observation Hive. 1 lb. package for $20.00.

Finally, the entire surface of each paper is painted with diluted tempera paint. The paint will soak into the uncolored areas and resist those that have a crayon coating. A weblike batik pattern should appear.

Gesso. Mix commercial dry ground gesso according to the directions on the can or mix whiting and shellac to the consistency of thick cream. Young children may apply areas of gesso to a paper plate or a piece of illustration board. These areas might be a figure, landscape or animals. They could decorate around the edge of the plate too. Allow gesso to *dry*.

Older students can make hanging plates by painting 2 or 3 paper plates on both sides with the gesso. Press the plates together while still wet. Make certain the edges fit tightly. Allow plates to dry. Additional coats of gesso are added until cracks and nicks are filled and desired thickness has been produced. (Allow to dry thoroughly.) Sandpaper plate smooth. Paint entire surface of gesso with base tempera color, details are then added in contrasting colors. A protective coat of varnish, shellac, or plastic spray is then applied. A strong stick-on wall hanging attachment can be adhered to back of the finished gesso piece.

Encaustic painting. This usually refers to an ancient method of painting with heated wax in which colored pigments are suspended. Here's a way to adapt encaustic painting to the classroom:

Heat 1 oz. of beeswax and use an ice cream stick to stir in 2 tsp. dry tempera for each color. A different color of beeswax can be made in each compartment of a large muffin-tin. In this way, all colors can be kept warm on a small electric hot plate.

Students use stiff natural-bristled brushes to paint directly onto paper, tagboard, or wood. Very unusual textures and tonality are possible. Brushes should be cleaned at once after paintings are finished: Pour boiling water over bristles. Wipe on rags. Lather bristles with liquid detergent. Rinse well. Dry.

Quickie idea. Ask kids to cut a hole any place in a piece of paper. Then say, "Now make a picture around the hole. Make the hole become *a part* of your drawing."

String painting. Coat a long piece of string with glue. Immediately wrap string around a wooden block in such a way that an interesting pattern is formed. Tightly knot ends of string together (on side of block). Smooth a little tempera paint onto a piece of cardboard. Stamp block into paint and then onto a piece of (white) paper. Try overlapping designs. See how many prints you can get from each paint application. (Students may print first impression on a piece of scrap paper in order to eliminate excess paint.)

[VARIATION: Coat a small wooden block with a thin coat of glue. Place string on block to form a flower animal or bird. Allow to dry completely. (Use ink stamp pad or paint as described above.) Print on paper that is on top of several thicknesses of newspaper.]

Pesach or Passover

A moveable Jewish feast occurring in the spring. Passover is a celebration of the freeing of the Israelites from Egypt. A traditional dinner, the "seder" is preceded by a reading of the Haggadah, which tells the story of the flight from Egypt.

MARCH ACTIVITIES

Bulletin Board Suggestion

March was named for Mars, the Roman god of War. Mars is also the name of a planet, fourth in distance from the sun. Let's learn some more about this planet. Mars is famous for its red light. Its circumference is 4,230 miles. (The earth's is 24,830 miles at the equator.) Its year is 686.9 days.

(Ours is 365 days.) is the symbol of Mars (and also the symbol for *man*).

Spring Picnic

This might be a fine time of year for a late winter or early spring picnic! Wait for a bright clear day. Make sure the children are warmly dressed and then, if it's possible, head for an open natural setting. The students can see what evidence of wildlife they can detect, list, and collect. Food can be brought in an insulated picnic carrier, including such items as soup, stew, baked potatoes, hot dogs, and baked apples. Or the class can bring dry sticks, kindling and build a fire and roast hotdogs and marshmallows. Thermoses of hot chocolate or Yogi Tea (page 365) could serve as drinks. Play an active game while the fire gets going, then cook, eat, and clean up. Another game° or two and you can head back to class, invigorated and ready to tackle afternoon studies!

°See the games suggested at end of March Activities.

March Language Arts:

Cinquain. An unrhymed 5-line verse, Cinquain is a form of Japanese poetry. The youngest student can have success with this writing form:

The first line is 1 word, the title.	**Kitten**
The second line is 2 words and describes the subject.	**Brown cat**
The third line has 3 words, expressing action.	**Runs in circles**
The fourth line has 4 words expressing feeling, emotion.	**Good to play with**
The fifth line is 1 word, a synonym for the title word.	**Pet°**

Newspaper ads. Here's one way to help your class learn to be concise in what it writes. Discuss newspaper ads: what they are designed to do, why they must be concise. Then each child writes an appropriate newspaper ad for some inventor who has been discussed since fall (Edison, da Vinci, Watts, Bell, Carver, Franklin). These ads may be composed as though the inventor were trying to sell his patent or as if the invention had just been discovered today.

Rebus. This is a kind of puzzle, the meaning of which is indicated by *things* rather than by *words*. A rebus offers a way to occasionally "candy-coat" review information or a homework assignment for your class. A rebus helps children analyze the written word in a new way. It's fun to try to invent new rebus symbols. Here is a good start on a Rebus Dictionary for your students' use!

March Science:

Sea monkey. March may also be a time when your students would enjoy a new classroom pet! If time is no object, try your hand at raising Sea Monkeys! (Transcience Corp., P.O. Box 270, Flushing, NY 11352.) They're very inexpensive and fascinating to study, once the kids can see them. Regular sea monkeys may take 12-16 weeks to grow. Super Sea Monkeys cost more and grow in 4 weeks. Sea Monkeys are a kind of brine shrimp and grow to a length of 1/2" or more. Transcience Corporation offers an extensive array of Sea Monkey parts and supplies, all inexpensively priced. It's a thought.

°Written by a twelve-year-old student, Malcolm Garrard.

about	going	see
admire	great	someway
appear	had	start
are	I	straight
bath	learn	suddenly
before	like	that
beg	my	then
bring	nice	those
build	o'clock	time
can	often	tiny
country	or	turned
dark	pair	until
dear	picture	what
delight	safety	which
everyday	salesman	why
for	saw	will

"Seeing" the interdependence between water, land, animals and vegetation. Supply every four students with a large state map (available from your State Highway Department), tracing paper,° green, purple, black and red felt-tip markers and a mimeo of 30 cities in your state and their annual rainfalls. (This information is available from the State Weather Bureau.)

Instruct the students to lay tracing paper on top of the map and to mark the cities with dots according to the annual rainfall, the following color code:

- Mark cities with rainfalls of 0″—10″ in red.
- Mark cities with rainfalls of 10″—13″ in black.
- Mark cities with rainfalls of 13″—16″ in purple.
- Mark cities with rainfalls of 16″—26″ in green.

Next, an orange felt-tip pen is used to separate the areas of like-colored dots into specific regions.

Students then put this tracing paper on top of a Potential Natural Vegetation Map, available from your Agricultural Extension Service. Have them study how areas of rainfall and vegetation compare. Then have them put the tracing paper over a General Soil Map, available from State Soil Conservation Service, and have them see the correlations between soil, rainfall and vegetation.

Other possible comparisons: effects of soil, vegetation and rainfall on birds and reptiles (map available from National Park or State Monuments Office), animals (Endangered species information and map available from The Department of the Interior, U.S. Fish & Wildlife Service, Washington, D.C. 20240), and early peoples (obtain an archeological map from a local library). Have students mark sites on tracing paper and then slide vegetation map beneath and notice the correlations.

(This activity was shared with participants at a recent Project Learning Tree workshop, see page 55.)

March Math:

Make a stiff dough of flour, water and salt. Ask kids to make little pea-sized balls of dough and use toothpicks stuck in these balls to construct structures, such as a horse corral, a maze, or a windmill. Let

---

°Tracing paper can often be purchased from an offset printing company, at about 100 sheets for $5.00. Call a local printer and inquire.

them find which structure is the strongest: a triangle? a square? an octagon? a pentagon? What is the (tallest) structure you can make with 9 dough balls and 13 toothpicks? or 13 doughballs and 9 toothpicks?

March Penmanship:

Handwriting that is legible develops from easy flowing motions. Have students practice writing while listening to a slow gliding (ice-skating rink) record. Analyze the results with the class. Let each student compare two of his/her own samples of handwriting, one done without and one done with music. Does the penmanship improve? This exercise should be repeated at definite intervals to remain valid.

The Zaner-Bloser Co. offers large clear writing worksheets (Manuscript Writing, Transition, Cursive, Basic Letter Joinings, and Groups of Letters) free, from:

> Zaner-Bloser
> Handwriting
> 612 N. Park St.
> Colombus, OH 43215

March History:

Middle and upper grade students may be very intrigued by the concept of time. Here are two unique ways of expressing this concept:

1. "Eight hundred life spans have bridged the last 50,000 years. But of these 800 people, 650 spent their lives in caves or worse. Only the last 70 had any truly effective means of communicating with one another, only the last 6 ever saw a printed word or had any accurate means of measuring heat or cold, only the last 4 could measure time with precision; only the last 2 used electric motors, and the vast majority of the items that make up our material world were developed within the lifespan of the 800th person."
—Lesher and Houwick, NASA Report SP 5067

2. Geologic Time Compressed into One Year. The age of the earth is considered to be about 4.5 billion years old. On this basis:

- Each day = 12,000,000 years (1.23×10)
- Each hour = 513,000 years (5.13×10^5)
- Each minute = 8,550 years
- Each second = 142 years

Pre-Cambrian: Extensive periods of volcanic activity, mountain-
building, erosion, ocean and atmosphere develop-
ment; re-cycles of all these; early

ERA:	Millions of years ago:	Correspondent Date/Time	Correspondent Time Elapsed
Paleozoic			
(trilobites)			
CAMBRIAN	550	17 November	321 days
ORDOVICIAN	480	22 November	326 days
(primitive vertebrates)			
SILURIAN	435	26 November	330 days
DIVONIAN	405	28 November	332 days
CARBONIFEROUS	345	3 December	337 days
PERMIAN	275	9 December	343 days
(ancestral Appalachians)			
Mesozoic			
(dinosaurs)			
TRIASSIC	225	13 December	347 days
JURASSIC	180	16 December	350 days
(ancestral Sierra Nevada)			
CRETACIONS	130	20 December	354 days
(Rocky Mountains)			
Cenozoic			
TERITIARY	65	26 December	360 days
(Calif. Coast Ranges)			
QUATERNARY	2,000,000 years ago	31 December	8:06 p.m.
(earliest man)			

Recorded history began 6,000 years ago   11:59:18 p.m.
Christ was born—1980 years ago   11:59:46 p.m.
Columbus discovers America—472 years   3.3 seconds before midnight
Declaration of Independence—188 years ago 1.3 seconds ago

Discuss possible ways of visually expressing the above information and ideas with the students.

March Music:

These instruments may be made by the teacher, by older students for a younger group, or by the students themselves:

Bass viol. Prepare a *large* tin can (an oil can from a gas station) by removing one end with a can opener. In the middle of the remaining end punch a small hole. Take a long piece of cord and thread it through the hole. Secure it in place by tying a button to it on the outside of the can. Tie a large button to the other end of the cord. Oil cord well with a candle stub. To play, child sits in a chair, grasps can between feet, holding cord taut by button with one hand and strumming cord with remaining hand.

Bongo drums. Stretch heavy plastic taut across open mouth of coffee can. Secure plastic in place with strip of inner tube or rubber sheet. Repeat with a second coffee can. Bind the two cans side by side with rope or masking tape.

Bell sticks. Saw 3/4"-1" width dowel sticks (or an old broomstick) into 6" lengths. Nail (or staple) large jingle bell onto either end of stick.

Bottle xylophone. Fill eight identical bottles with varying amounts of water to reproduce (approximate?) the 8 notes of the musical scale. Bottles are struck with a pencil or dowel.

Cigarbox guee-tar. Stretch four rubber bands of varying widths & lengths over an open cigar box. Pick or strum bands.

Drums. Bases can be #10 cans, nail-kegs, automatic transmission fluid cans, coffee cans, or chopping bowls. Heads can be heavy oilcloth or canvas; this is coated, after attachment, with clear dope. Inner tube drumheads are more resonant; after attaching, hold tubing firmly to base by overlapping 6(1-1/2") inner tube strips. Heads are attached to metal bases by strips of inner tubing and to wooden bases by tacking the head along one edge, pulling tight on the opposite side and tacking. Repeat until tacks are placed every 1" or 2". Child may hold smaller drum under one arm to play.

Ersatz bells. Have children collect and bring in old keys to class. These or curtain rings strung on a string simulate, when shaken, the sound of bells.

Gongs. A bent metal rod or a heavy pot cover suspended from a pole is held aloft and struck with a wood spoon.

Hand bells. Cut two pieces of elastic, 8" each in length. Make a loop of each and sew its ends firmly together. Sew bells onto that section of each elastic which will cover backs of hands. (Child slips hand into loop and shakes or claps hands to play bells.)

Kazoo. Cut several small holes in the middle of a paper-toweling tube. Cover one end of tube with a large piece of wax paper taped in place. Child places fingers on varying holes and hums or sings into open end. Of course, this instrument must, by its nature, be played by just one student. If several kazoos are made, children's names can be printed on each.

Knockers. Nail a flat block of wood to a dowel handle, or drive a nail down through the center of a wooden spool (handle) into 4″ × 6″ wooden block. Make two of each knocker.

Nail chimes. Hang nails from a thick dowel and strike with a small metal pipe.

Raspers. Staple sandpaper on underside of a set of knockers, or notch the length of two thick dowel rods. These are then rubbed against one another.

Rattles. Scrub six to eight ring-shaped bones of lamb shoulder or lamb chops, dry well and string, or nail a wooden dowel handle to a frozen orange juice can, put pebbles inside and cover the top of the can with vinyl and a rubber band. Or, use small boxes or cans with snap-on lids and put rice or buttons inside. You can also papier mache *heavily* over a large used light bulb and break bulb within when thoroughly dry.

Tambourine. Make tiny slits every inch or two along the edge of the round top of a cardboard container. Insert loop of sleigh bell through slit and secure in place from behind with a safety pin. Or cut two (1/4″) circles of plywood (5″ in diameter). Enamel the edges. Mark off the edges into 1/8″ divisions. Flatten a number of soda pop bottle caps and punch a hole through each. Hammer a nail through each of the 1/8″ marks in one circle. Place four flattened caps on each nail so that they can move freely up and down. Place second circle atop nail points and hammer gently and firmly in place.

Tom-tom. Get a large hatbox or round wooden cheese box. Cut its lid in 1/2. Glue 1/2 of lid securely in place atop box. With string, secure a 3″ long flat stick to the middle of the lid as shown. Tap on free end of stick to produce a tom-tom-like beat.

Xylophone. This affords a good lesson in fractions. Have the children collect cardboard mailing tubes. You will need strong cord and two wooden lathes. The proportions are: 1, 8/9, 4/5, 3/4, 2/3, 3/5, 8/15, 1/2. Tubes are struck with a dowel that has a cork nailed to its end.

March Games:

Points (For Young Children)

Two people play this game with a small rubber ball. A small stick about the size of a pencil is placed on a line drawn at an equal distance between the two players.

One player bounces the ball to the other trying to hit the stick on the center line.

The purpose of the game is to hit the stick off the middle line by throwing the rubber ball at it. Each time the player hits the stick and pushes it from the middle line, he wins a point.

The player who first gains ten points, wins the game.

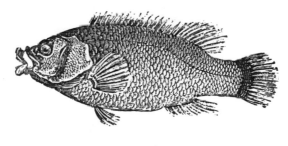

Fish in the Sea

All the children but one stand behind a line. They are the fish. The remaining child stands midway between the line of children and a "Home" line thirty feet away. He or she is the fisherman and shouts "Fish in the ocean, fish in the sea! Don't get the notion that you can pass *me!*" At the end of this signal, the fish all rush past the line and try to reach the "Home" line without being tagged by the fisherman.

Fish tagged join hands with the fisherman and become the net. They then try to help catch the fish when they leave the Home line. If the net breaks, any fish caught on that turn are set free.

[VARIATION: Only the ends of the net may catch fish.]

April

Sweet April showers
Do spring May flowers
—Thomas Tusser, 1573

††   National Automobile Month

1   

2   International Children's Book Day (The Children's Book Council, 67 Irving Pl., NY, NY 10003) marks the birthday of Hans Christian Andersen, 1805.

     On this day in 1917, President Wilson asked Congress to declare war on Germany.

     Quotation of the Day: The world must be made safe for democracy.—*Woodrow Wilson, April 2, 1917*

3   Jane van Lawick-Goodall, anthropologist, was born in London, England in 1934.

4   Exactly one month after he became President of the United States, William Harrison died in the White House following an attack of pneumonia, 1841.

On this day in 1932, Professor C.G. King isolated Vitamin C, after five years of research.

5   Sir Joseph Lister, English surgeon and founder of modern antiseptic surgery, was born in Upton, England in 1827.

6   On this day in 1896, the United States, competing unofficially, won the first modern Olympic Games in Athens, Greece.

On this day in 1909, after 23 years of effort, Robert E. Peary became the first western man to reach the North Pole.

Quotation of the Day: My dream and goal for 20 years. Mine at last! I cannot bring myself to realize it. It seems all so simple and commonplace.—*Robert Peary, diary entry of April 6, 1909*

7   Ravi Shankar, musician, was born in Benares, India, 1920.

8   First Jewish congregation in America, Shaarit Israel, consecrated their synagogue in New York City in 1730. This congregation dates back to 1655 when Sephardic Jews from Portugal settled in what was then New Amsterdam.

On this day in 1974, Hank Aaron hit his 715th home run, breaking Babe Ruth's forty-seven-year-old record.

9   First public library in America was founded by the townspeople of Peterborough, New Hampshire in 1833, to be supported by municipal taxes.

On this day in 1865, Confederate General Robert E. Lee surrendered the Army of Northern Virginia to General Ulysses S. Grant, commander-in-chief of the Union Army, at a farmhouse in Virginia.

Quotation of the Day: The whole country had been so raided by the two armies that it was doubtful whether they would be able to put in a crop to carry themselves . . . thru the next winter without the aid of the horses they were then riding. . . . I would, therefore, instruct the officers . . . to let every man of the Confederate Army who claimed to own a horse or mule take the animal to his home.—*Gen. Grant to Gen. Lee*

10 On this day in 1849, Walter Hunt received a patent for his invention, the safety pin.

Clare Booth Luce, writer and stateswoman, was born in New York City in 1903.

11 On this day in 1814, Napoleon abdicated his throne.

First secretary of the Department of Health Education and Welfare, Mrs. Oveta Culp Hobby, was sworn in and so became a member of the President's Cabinet, 1953.

12 The Civil War began as Confederates fired on Fort Sumter from the harbor of Charleston, South Carolina, 1861.

On this day in 1975, official U.S. presence in Cambodia came to an end.

13 Solar New Year

Thomas Jefferson, third U.S. President, was born in Shadwell, Virginia in 1743.

Quotation of the Day: We hold these truths to be self-evident, that all men are created equal; that they are endowed by their Creator with certain unalienable rights; that among these are Life, Liberty and the Pursuit of Happiness.
      —*Thomas Jefferson, The Declaration of Independence*

On this day in 1870, the Metropolitan Museum of Art was founded in New York City.

14 Pan American Day.

First Abolition Society, "The Society for the Relief of Free Negroes Unlawfully Held in Bondage," was organized in Philadelphia, with Benjamin Franklin as its president, 1775.

First edition of Noah Webster's dictionary was published in 1828.

15 Leonardo da Vinci, artist-inventor, was born in Italy in 1452.

On this day in 1865, President Lincoln died of the gunshot wounds he had received the day before.

16 U.S. Apollo XVI, manned by astronauts John Young, Charles Duke, Jr., and Thomas Mattingly II, began an 11-day mission, which included a record 75-hour exploration of the Moon, 1972.

17   Verrazano Day marks the discovery of New York Harbor by Giovanni de Verrazano in 1524.

Thornton Wilder, writer, was born in 1897 in Madison, Wisconsin.

On this day in 1961, the disastrous Bay of Pigs Invasion by U.S.-based anti-Castro Cuban rebels took place. Responsibility for its institution and its failure is a subject of continued controversy.

18   On this day in 1906, at 5:15 AM, San Francisco suffered the worst earthquake ever to hit the United States. Huge fires raged for 3 days following the quake and half the city was destroyed, leaving 500 dead and over a quarter of a million people homeless. (For information about the Great Earthquake and Fire Muster in San Francisco write Mr. William Koenig, San Francisco Fire Dept., 260 Golden Gate Ave., San Francisco, CA 94102.)

First crossword puzzle book was published in America, 1924.

First laundromat, which was called a "washateria" was opened in Forth Worth, Texas, 1934.

19   Patriot's Day commemorates the battles of Lexington and Concord, which marked the start of the American Revolutionary War, 1775.

Quotation of the Day: If they mean to have a war, let it begin here.—*Captain John Parker, Commander of the Minutemen, April 19, 1775*

On this day in 1783, eight years after the Battle of Lexington, Congress announced the end of the Revolutionary War.

On this day in 1967, U.S. Surveyor III, Lunar probe vehicle, made a soft landing on the Moon, and with its digging apparatus, it established surface qualities.

20   Marcus Aurelius Antoninus Roman emperor and philosopher was born in 121 AD.

On this day in 1657, Asser Levy and Jacob Barsimson won the right as Jews to full citizenship in New Amsterdam.

Juan Miro, painter, was born in Barcelona in 1893.

21   Charlotte Bronte, author of *Jane Eyre*, was born in Thornton, England, 1816.

Queen Elizabeth II was born in London in 1926.

Quotation of the Day: Remember, remember always that all of us, and you and I especially, are descended from immigrants and revolutionists.—*Franklin D. Roosevelt, April 21, 1938*

22 Earth Day and the week encompassed by it, Earth Week, celebrates the equinoxes and stands for balance and harmony on Earth.

†† Easter (a moveable feast)

†† National Library Week begins with the second or third Sunday of the month (National Book Committee, 1 Park Ave., NY, NY 10016).

†† Arbor Day. Sometimes celebrated on the 22nd but date varies from state to state.

23 On this day in 1616, William Shakespeare died on his 52nd brithday in Stratford, England.

Joseph Turner, artist, was born in London in 1775.

James Buchanan, 15th U.S. President, was born in Franklin County, Pennsylvania, in 1791.

24 First American newspaper to be printed on a regular basis, "The Boston News-Letter" began publication on this day in 1704.

On this day in 1800, the Library of Congress was established in Washington, D. C.

The launching of the first satellite by the People's Republic of China, made China the 5th nation to orbit a satellite with its own rocket. This satellite broadcasted telemetric signals and the Chinese song "The East is Red," 1970.

†† Daylight Saving Time: The Uniform Time Act of 1966 provides that standard time in each zone be advanced by one hour from 2 AM on the last Sunday in April until 2 AM on the last Sunday in October (unless State legislature provides exemption).

25 Guglielmo Marconi, inventor of the radio, was born in Bologna, Italy in 1874.

First license plates were issued by the State of New York, 1901. Exactly 954 cars were registered. Each license plate carried the initials of the owner.

26   First British colonists to establish a permanent settlement in America landed at Cape Henry, Virginia on this day in 1607.

The Great Plague began in London, 1665.

John James Audubon, artist-naturalist, was born at Les Cayes, Santo Domingo in 1785.

††   Public Schools Week (date varies from state to state).

Ulysses S. Grant, 18th U.S. President, was born in Port Pleasant, Ohio, 1822.

28   James Monroe, fifth U.S. President, was born in Westmoreland County, Virginia in 1758.

Quotation of the Day: Preparation for war is a constant stimulus to suspicion and ill will.
                                   —*President James Monroe, April 28, 1818*

Maryland, 7th U.S. State, entered the Union, 1788.

On this day in 1947, Thor Heyerdahl set sail from Peru on the raft Kon Tiki in an attempt to prove that early man could have sailed from the Americas to the islands of the South Pacific. (His expedition was successful.)

29   First patent for a "separable fastener" (our modern-day zipper) was received by Gideon Sundback of Hoboken, New Jersey in 1913.

On this day in 1945, the bodies of Benito Mussolini and his companions were hung up and displayed to the citizens of Milan, Italy.

On this day in 1945, Adolph Hitler, Nazi dictator of Germany and perpetrator of the deaths of six million Jews, gypsies and Eastern Europeans, committed suicide in his bunker 30 feet beneath the ruins of the Reich's chancellery in Berlin.

30   Louisiana Admission Day: Louisiana became the 18th State on this day in 1812.

On this day in 1975, the last one thousand Americans were removed by helicopter from South Viet Nam, ending more than twenty-five years of U.S. military involvement. (This was at a cost of 56,555 American deaths, 303,654 American wounded, and $141,000,000,000 in the last fourteen years alone.)

pril

This word probably comes from the Latin 'aperire' (to open)
referring to the opening of spring buds and flowers.

APRIL QUOTATIONS

Whanne that Aprille with his shoures sote
The droughte of Marche hath perced to the rote.

—*Canterbury Tales: Chaucer*

Lord, what fools these mortals be!
—*Shakespeare (Midsummer Night's Dream)*

2   Reading is to the mind what exercise is to the body.
—*Sir Richard Steele*

To read without reflecting is like eating without digesting.
—*Edmund Burke*

13   When asked by Alexander if he lacked anything, Diogenes
replied, "Stand a little less between me and the sun."

I'm a great believer in luck, and I find the harder I work the more I
have of it.

No man will ever bring out of the Presidency the reputation which
carries him into it . . . To myself, personally, it brings nothing
but increasing drudgery and daily loss of friends.

In questions of power, let no more be heard of confidence in man,
but bind him down from mischief by the chains of the
Constitution.—*Thomas Jefferson*

15   I have offended God and mankind because my work didn't reach
the quality it should have.—*Leonardo da Vinci*

(Said of da Vinci) He might have been a scientist if he had not
been so versatile.—*G. Vasari*

16   You will give yourself relief if you do every act of your life as if it
were the last.—*Marcus Aurelius Antoninus*

> *The people will live on*
> *The learning and blundering people will live on*
> *They will be tricked and sold and again sold*
> *And go back to the nourishing earth for rootholds.*
> —*Carl Sandburg, "The People, Yes"*

17   It goes so fast. We don't have time to look at one another. . . . Goodbye, Goodbye, world. Goodbye, . . . Mama and Papa. Goodbye to clocks ticking . . . and Mama's sunflowers. And food and coffee. And new-ironed dresses and hot baths . . . and sleeping and waking up. Oh, earth, you're too wonderful for anybody to realize. Do any human beings ever realize life while they live it?—every, every minute?—*Thornton Wilder (Our Town, Act III)*

19

> *By the rude bridge that arched the flood,*
> *Their flag to April's breeze unfurled,*
> *Here once the embattled farmers stood,*
> *And fired the shot heard round the world!*
> —*Ralph Waldo Emerson April 19, 1836*

The tree of liberty must be refreshed from time to time with the blood of patriots and tyrants. It is its natural fertilizer.
—*Thomas Jefferson*

20   The universe is change; our life is what our thoughts make it.
—*Marcus Aurelius Antoninus*

22   He plants trees to benefit another generation.
—*Caecilius Statuis*

††   (For Easter.) The hen is the egg's way of producing another egg.—*Samuel Butler*

23   All the world's a stage, and all the men and women merely players: they have their exits and their entrances; and one man in his time plays many parts. *(As You Like It, Act II)*

There is nothing either good or bad, but thinking makes it so. *(Hamlet, Act II)*

How beauteous mankind is! O brave new world, that has such people in it. *(The Tempest, Act V)*

There is a tide in the affairs of men, which taken at the flood, leads onto fortune; omitted, all the voyage of their life is bound in shallows and in miseries. *(Julius Caesar, Act IV)*
—*William Shakespeare*

If you are as happy, my dear sir, on entering this house as I am in leaving it and returning home, you are the happiest man in this country.—*James Buchanan to Abraham Lincoln*

26 But Lord! How everybody's looks and discourse in the street, is of death, and nothing else; and few people going up and down, that the town is like a place distressed and forsaken.
—*Diary of Samuel Pepys, August 30, 1665*
(Written in London during the Black Plague.)

I know no method to secure the repeal of bad or obnoxious laws so effective as their stringent execution.
—*Ulysses S. Grant (Inaugural Address, 3/4/1869)*

28 The American continents . . . are henceforth not to be considered as subjects for future colonization by any European powers.
—*James Monroe, The Monroe Doctrine,*
December, 1823

Mankind has grown strong in eternal struggles and it will only perish through eternal peace. *(Mein Kampf Vol. I)*

A majority can never replace the man—just as hundreds of fools do not make one wise man, a heroic decision is not likely to come from a hundred cowards. *(Mein Kampf, Preface)*
—*Adolf Hitler*

APRIL EVENTS

● *April Fools' Day* [1]

Traditionally, on this day Noah sent the dove from the ark and it returned, unable to find land. Some sources say that April Fools' Day is an old Celtic heathen festival. In any case, there are 18th century records of April Fools' Day celebrations being held throughout Europe. In Scotland, if you're tricked today, you're a "gowk" (Scottish for "cuckoo"); in France, you become "un poisson d'Avril" ("an April fish"). In other words, you're a person who's easily caught.

Some general suggestions. Write the date on the chalkboard: "April 1, 1943"; asterisk the date and at the foot of the board, in tiny letters, print: "April Fool." Set the clock ahead (or back) and when this is discovered, use the opportunity to emphasize time-telling. Prepare a bulletin board or a mimeographed worksheet titled: "Don't be April-fooled! Answer the question and define the word!" Beneath this appears: "Would you feel flattered if someone called you arrogant? enthralling? vociferous? facetious? eccentric? insipid? rapacious? valorous?"

Etymology

The Latin word *follis* from which we get "fool" means "a bag of wind"! Ambrose Bierce, in his *Devil's Dictionary,*° defines April Fool as: "noun. The March fool with another month added to his folly." Vocabulary enrichment words: gullible, deceptive, fraudulent, ingenuous, guile equanimity.

In the Middle Ages 'a fool' was a dessert made of stewed fruit with whipped cream. Another name for a sweet dessert was 'a trifle.' Trifle also means something unimportant so—a silly person whose ideas are unimportant is now called a fool!

A caricature is a drawing or performance that makes fun of someone by over-emphasizing their manner or some of their features. The Italian "caricare" means "to load" so caricature actually means to *over* load or exaggerate.

Jovial comes from the Latin Jovix (Jove or Jupiter). The Roman god Jove was known for his hearty good humor. To be jovial is to be gay and good humored—like Jove!

Our word "joke" comes from the Latin "jovis" which was an amusing game.

°Ambrose Bierce, *The Devil's Dictionary* (180 Varick St., New York, N.Y. 10014: Dover Publishing Co., 1958). © by Dover Pub. Co., Inc.

Fysshe Stories

April Fool Fish Stories:

Explain to the class that "fish stories" are tall tales or exaggerations of the truth.

HOW MANY of THESE FISH STORIES
DO YOU BELIEVE?
(Careful.... don't get APRIL FOOLED....!)

Just lift up the bubble to find out the answer!

There's a fish that uses a fishing pole & bait to catch OTHER FISH.

Some fish live for 100's of years: true or false?

Some fish sleep with their eyes open.

flying fish can't really fly.

There is a fish that shoots his meals with a bow and arrow.

No fish can live out of water for very long.

An angry swordfish can saw a boat in half!

There is a fish that gets new teeth every day of his life.

Fish can catch cold: yes or no?

Each fish-story on this bulletin board is printed on a bubble, which the child can lift up to learn the answer:

1. Some fish live for hundreds of years. True or false? (That's right! The carp, halibut and the pike have been known to live over *200* years!

2. It's very cold in the sea and fish sometimes *catch cold* . . . yes or no? (It's true, and a fish can get an upset stomach also!)

3. *Some* fish sleep with their eyes open: true or false! (True *and* false: All fish sleep with their eyes open because fish have no eyelids— so they can't close their eyes!)

4. No fish can live out of water for very long. What's your guess? (At least two fish can! The *walking fish* of Australia walks out of the water, climbs a tree and sits there for hours eating bugs. The *lungfish* lives in mud and when the water dries up the lungfish just dries out in the mud too. After months it can still be put back in water and it will "come back to life!"

5. An angry swordfish can saw a boat in half (true or false?) (Well, maybe not in *half*, but swordfish have often put holes in boats and have even sunk some!)

6. Flying fish can't really fly. (Right! A flying fish gets up speed, heads sharply into a wind and *soars* in an arc—that can be 25 feet high!)

7. There is a fish that uses a fishing pole and bait to catch other fish. (The angler fish, found along the eastern U.S. coast, has a rod that is one foot long! On the end of it are worm-like pieces of skin that the angler can blow up to act like a worm. When the rod and bait aren't in use, they lay down against his back so the angler can swim smoothly.)

8. There is a fish that shoots his meals with a bow and arrow! (False, but the archer fish shoots down his meals with strong streams of water squirted out of his mouth! He nearly always hits the target—even when it's as far as four feet away!)

9. There is a fish that gets new teeth every day of his life. (True: The shark is always growing new teeth to replace the worn or broken ones.)

Take a pencil and see if you can draw this fish with just one line, without going over any line twice and not crossing over any part of a line. Good Luck.

Give up? Well, here's how:

Fish Riddles:

Try these on your younger students:

- What fish can you find in a bird cage? (perch)
- What fish can you find in a shoe? (sole)
- What fish can you find in a sports shop? (skate)

Component word drawings. Give each child one of the following and ask him/her to make a small drawing, not of the word, itself, but of its two component words: These are then posted or each child holds his/her picture up and the rest of the class tries to guess the (single) word being illustrated:

1. egg plant
2. pencil point
3. horse fly
4. kitchen sink
5. milk man
6. ice skate
7. fish scale
8. tea pot
9. bull doze
10. clam bake
11. snow man
12. lip stick

13. pie pan
14. man hole
15. gun play
16. sea sick
17. tooth brush
18. flower box
19. ski jump
20. home run
21. alarm clock
22. lemon peel
23. window (pain)
24. April Fool

Riddle cards kids can make: Have each child draw a small picture of an object and write a few things about it as if the object were really alive. For example, "Daddy put the bread in the dragon's mouth. It got hot and red and after awhile smoke came out and the dragon spit the burnt bread at my Daddy! (Toaster)" Very young children may dictate the description for you to print it on tagboard. Each riddle card has description on left and a flap covering the answer picture on the right.

All I do all day is just shovel it in.
Or else I just run around and around in a circle.
I'm really glad to lay down flat at night!
Can you guess what I am?
A Spoon

Sequential Thinking: Tell the class "Here are some jokes, but the lines are out of order. Read each sequence and decide which line should come first, which second, and so on. Number each line according to where it comes in the joke:

"Jill" said the teacher, "What is a comet?"
"Now," said the teacher, "name one."
"I know," said Jill, "a star with a tail."
"Lassie?"

"Oh, the dog ate all the cookies I baked, sob-sob!"
"What's the matter, Sis? Why are you crying?"
"Don't cry. We can always get another dog!"
"Boo-hoo-hoo, sob, sob . . ."

"This book on math will do half your homework for you."
The salesman walked up to him.
Joe went into the book store.
"Great," said Joe, "I'll take two of them!"

Jack was having trouble in school.
So he said to him, "What do you expect to be when you get
   out of school?"
He never did his homework.
The teacher wanted to get to know Jack better.
Jack thought this over and finally answered, "A very
   old man . . . ."

Simple Simon Series: In each row below, the numbers form a series. Can you figure out the next two numbers in each series?

1. 1 3 5 7 9 __ __
2. 32 16 8 4 2 __ __
3. 0 1 4 9 16 __ __
4. 75 60 45 30 15 __ __
5. 0 1 1 2 3 5 8 13 __ __
6. 2 4 5 10 11 22 __ __
7. 12 2 6 14 2 7 16 __ __
8. 16 4 9 3 4 2 __ __
9. 56 8 7 30 6 5 12 4 __ __
10. 6 5 3 7 5 4 8 5 5 __ __

Answers:

1. 11,13 (odd numbers)
2. 1,1/2 (Divide by 2)
3. 25, 36 (Successive squares: $0^2=0, 1^2=1, 2^2=4, 3^2=9, 4^2=16, 5^2=25, 6^2=36$)
4. 0,−15 (subtractions of 15)

5. 21,34 (Addition of 2 preceding numbers)

6. 23,46 (Double—add one—Double)

7. 2, 8 (Divisions by 2)

8. 1, 1 (Successively lower square roots: $16=4^2, 9=3^2, 4=2^2, 1=1^2$)

9. 3, 2 (First number is product of second and third numbers and the multipliers are decreasing toward 0)

10. 9, 5 (6-53) (7-54) (8-55) (9-56 . . .)

● *International Children's Book Day.*   [2]

Children's Book Day is a day for celebrating books. For information about English posters and materials for this day, write to the Children's Book Council, 67 Irving Place, NY, NY 10003, and for information about materials in other languages write IBBY, Leonhardsgraben, 38A, CH-4051, Basel, Switzerland.

Here are some unusual ways to give a book report:

1. Collect a group of objects mentioned in your book and use these to illustrate an oral book review.

2. Make a time line to illustrate a book you've read.

3. Read about an author you admire (Use Current Biography). Report on him/her to the class.

4. Make flannel-board figures and use them to give a book review to a class at a lower grade level.

5. Make an original film strip illustrating your book (see page 104 for information about do-it-yourself film-strips.)

6. Design a miniature newspaper that could have appeared during the period in which the book's story is set. Include as many details and extensions of information given in the story as you can.

7. Choose an interesting episode in the story: it could be scary, funny or sad. Present it as a TV soap-opera or comedy. Try to make the audience want to read the book to learn what happens next.

8. Choose your favorite character in the book. Describe his/her personality. Explain why you enjoyed reading about him/her. Read an excerpt from the book to illustrate these points.

9. Take the characters in your book and extend them into a new original adventure. Try to write it in the style of the original author!

● *First Modern Olympic Games, 1896*   [6]

In ancient Greece the Olympic Games in honor of Zeus were held every four years. This was a festival of various contests including athletics, poetry and music. In modern time, the Olympics have become an international athletic competition held every four years in a different city around the world. The first modern Olympic Games were held in Athens, in 1896, and the United States won the majority of the competitions.

A large informative booklet, *The Olympic Games* is free from:

> The U.S. Olympic Committee
> 1750 East Boulder Street
> Colorado Springs, CO 80909

A good source of glossy black-and-white action sports photos can be found in the photography department of your local newspaper. Ask to speak to the sports photographer and explain that you would appreciate obtaining some outdated sports photos (from the dead photo files) for your classroom. Choose photos with young players featured or dangerous moments highlighted. These photos will be very useful as bulletin-board or creative writing stimuli.

Sports Riddles:

- ● **What's pitched but never batted? (A tent.)**
- ● **What usually has more than 2 feet? (A football field.)**

- Why did the man in the restaurant use a brush on his dish before he ate? (It was just a habit. He was an umpire and they always brush off the plate before things get started!)

- *Thomas Jefferson Was Born, 1743*   [13]

He was described by his biographer, James Parton, as "The gentleman of 32 who could calculate an eclipse, survey an estate, tie an artery, plan an edifice, try a cause, break a horse, dance a minuet and play the violin."

Jefferson himself wrote this epitaph for his grave: "Here was buried Thomas Jefferson, author of the Declaration of American Independence, of the statute of Virginia for religious freedom, and father of the University of Virginia."

- *First Edition of Noah Webster's Dictionary, 1828*   [14]

Very often, Webster's Dictionaries are not written by Webster! There are dozens of "Webster's" Dictionaries because the name cannot be copyrighted. Noah Webster named his great reference work: *The American Dictionary!*

- *Leonardo da Vinci Was Born, 1452*   [15]

Leonardo da Vinci was a pioneer in modern anatomy, inventor of a parachute and a helicopter, architect, engineer, scientist, and the man who used steam before Watt and who knew before Copernicus that the sun stood still.

- *Apollo XVI Explored the Moon for 71 Hours*   [16]

The surface of the moon is pitted with craters. Falling tektite formed some of these craters. The earth's surface has been changed, also; sometimes by violent earthquakes

- *San Francisco Earthquake*   [18]

Students can obtain the following *free* materials pertaining to earthquakes:

1. World Seismicity & Volcanic Activity in 1975
2. Volcanoes of the World (a *big* full color map)
3. Earthquake Epicenters of the World (a do-it-yourself icosahedron globe)

by writing to:

> The United States Dept. of Commerce
> Nat. Oceanic & Atmospheric Admin.
> Environmental Data Service
> Boulder, CO 80302

● *National Library Week*   [Begins with Third Sunday of April]

Have students make a group list of every type of book they can. Then show them a list of the *Dewey Decimal System* for classification of books.

000-099 General Works (encyclopedias, magazines, bibliographies)

100-199 Philosophy, Psychology, Ethics

200-299 Religion and Myths

300-399 Sociology(civics, economics, education)

400-499 Philology (language, dictionaries, grammar)

500-599 Science (math, chemistry, biology, botany)

600-699 Useful Arts (medicine, agriculture, T.V.)

700-799 Fine Arts (painting, music, photography)

800-899 Literature (novels, poetry, plays)

900-999 History, Geography, Biography

Elicit their ideas as to *why* one type of book is made to precede another. This should greatly assist them in understanding the logic behind the layout of their library!

● *Easter*   [A Moveable Feast]

The three principal events celebrated by those of Christian faith are the birth of Christ, His crucifixion and His resurrection. Easter commemorates the latter two.

Easter falls on the first Sunday following the full moon of, or after, the spring equinox (March 21). Its name and time of celebration indicate that it was originally a festival of ancient times, celebrating the death of winter and the resurrection of the sun. Early Germanic peoples honored "Ostern," the goddess of spring, at this time of year; her name was also related to the East—in which the dawn appears.

Easter eggs. From earliest times, the egg has been the symbol of the universe. It also stands for fertility; ancient Babylonians exchanged eggs at the beginning of each spring. Colored eggs symbolize rebirth; the Persians, Egyptians and ancient Chinese dyed eggs for their spring festivals. The origin of the *Easter egg hunt* is unclear. One source states that a noble woman was the first to hide colored eggs for the children.

Easter bunny. Our Easter bunny is related to the ancient Egyptian belief that the rabbit is the symbol of spring, the beginning of a new life.

Easter lily. There is also an original *American* Easter symbol! Towards the end of the last century, churches in America began having special Sunday services to help console those who had lost loved ones in the Civil War. The churches were filled with flowers, one of these being a Bermuda lily which was used in such profusion as to become associated with this season and which has since been named the Easter lily.

Vocabulary enrichment words: confections, apocalypse, resurrection, transfiguration, renaissance, crucifixion, Calvary.

Easter Riddles:

These may be presented in the form of 3-4 Easter Rabbit Riddle Books, simply illustrated with colored felt-tip pens. Each answer would appear on the back of each riddle's page. Children might read these books during their free time.

- How can you find the Easter Bunny when he gets lost? (Make a noise like a *big* carrot.)
- How can you buy eggs and be *sure* there are no baby chicks inside? (Buy duck eggs.)
- What kind of bush does the Easter Bunny hide under on a rainy day? (He hides under a wet bush.)
- What's the difference between a crazy rabbit and a phony dollar bill? (One's a mad bunny and the other's bad money.)
- There were 9 ears of corn in a field and a rabbit came each night and took away 3. How many nights did it take him to get *all* the ears? (Nine nights: each night he took his *own* ears when he left the field.)
- What goes up pink and comes down white and pink and yellow? (An Easter egg.)
- Which is correct: the yolk of an Easter egg *is* white or the yolk of an Easter egg *are* white? (Neither, because the yolk of any egg is *yellow!*)

- My father and mother were both great singers, tho' neither had any teeth. I am white and bald and I have a yellow heart.... Who am I? (an egg)

Hatching Chicks in the Classroom*

Purchase a small electric incubator and four dozen fertilized eggs. (Call a grain-feed store for advice as to where these can be found in your area.) Set up the incubator with the eggs so that they will hatch during the middle of a week. Follow the directions that come with the incubator. After eighteen days, take the incubator to class.

Put a Window in one of the Eggs!

1. Cut a small square of Saran Wrap.
2. Cut four narrow strips of adhesive tape.
3. With a pencil, draw a circle on the eggshell.
4. Cut around the circle carefully using a new clean razor blade. Score the pencil line.
5. Cut an X inside the circle.
6. Using the X for a starting point, carefully pick off the shell-bit-by-bit.
7. Put the Saran Wrap over the hole.
8. Attach the Saran Wrap to the egg with the strips of adhesive tape.
9. Position the egg in the incubator so the kids can easily watch what's happening in the egg.

Draw a large egg shape on the board and sketch in the position of the unborn chick to show how he uses its bill to break the shell. Talk about how its feet, under the bill, help turn its body and finally kick off the shell.

---

*This activity may take practice and/or patience. Some people seem to have the touch for hatching eggs and do it successfully year after year. Hopefully *you* will, as students are very intrigued by the process.

In about 20 days, the first cracked shell will probably be seen. The kids can touch the chicks as soon as the incubator is opened. Chicks don't often make good pets and after a day or so they can be given to a farmer or to the feed store.

Decorating Easter Eggs in Unusual Ways!

Dyes. Make dyes from the husks of yellow onions (lots of them) or the tops of 4 or 5 bunches of carrots, by boiling vegetation in 2 quarts of water for 1/2 hour and adding 1 Tbsp. vinegar to "set" color.

Wrapped eggs. Wrap a small flat leaf or flower or paper cut-out around the egg. Hold it in place with square of nylon stocking fastened *tightly* by a tied thread or a rubber band.

Dip in dye (in natural dyes, simmer for 20 min.) until egg is dark hue. Remove nylon, allow to dry. Rub dry egg with salad oil to make it shine and to make the design stand out.

Beaded eggs. Older children pencil floral free-form patterns on the shell (non-geometric designs). Then, each child threads a very fine needle and glues one end of the thread to the egg's midsection with rubber cement. Working horizontally, they string beads in colors to conform to the penciled designs and glue them down about one inch at a time. When the egg has been completely encircled let the cement set. Then each student continues with the same thread, and begins the next circle as a separate row—trying not to spiral. As they come to the end of a thread it is dabbed with cement and tucked between beaded rows; then a new thread is begun.

Feather-covered eggs. Students collect many lovely small down feathers (or you purchase them at a craft store). Then they coat the egg with rubber cement and let it dry. Next, the underside of each feather is coated with rubber cement and glued to the shell (one at a time), beginning at the top and working down in slightly overlapping rows.

Marbelized (tortoise-shell) eggs. Fill pan with 2″ water, put a bit of turpentine in a cup. Add some dark brown oil paint until the mixture is of a milky consistency. In a second cup, mix a bit of turpentine and gold paint to the consistency of milk. Dip brush in brown, and then spatter onto water in pan. *Don't touch the water.* Do the same with gold paint mixture. Use a stick to evenly swirl paint on water's surface. Put a Q-Tip into a hole in the egg and gently twirl egg on surface of water. Place Q-Tip in upright position in a piece of modeling clay. Let the egg dry thoroughly.

Photo-copy eggs. Wash an egg carefully with liquid detergent to remove oils from egg surface, and then dry the egg. Cut out small magazine photos and letters. Coat part of the egg with Clear Acrylic Medium. Adhere the photo, face down, to the egg. Press firmly, then peel off. Egg should now have the printed image on it.°

Eggheads with HAIR. Use half an empty egg shell. Using a spoon, each student fills a shell with soil and vermiculite. Then the child draws a face on the egg with felt-tip pens. Soil is sprinkled with grass seed and is watered lightly. Each shell is kept in a carton section of an egg carton. These hairy eggs will make unusual greetings at this Easter season!

°Some magazine photos have a very slick surface and don't reproduce well. Have kids try different kinds of photos from funny papers and various slick magazines.

- *Public Schools Week*   [Date Varies from State to State]

Some suggestions for preparation of your room: Display the children's work by subject matter but *don't* label groups as "Our Best Work" unless *all* students have papers exhibited. Every child should have several examples of his efforts on display; some papers can be taped to windows if these are at eye level.

There can be a *large* book of drawings and stories covering many subjects. Classroom plants can have little signs noting dates seeds were planted. Try emphasizing the foreign language taught (if any) by labeling all the common objects about the room with the foreign names which the children have learned. Post examples of comparative writing efforts (September and April); include one sentence that is the same, if possible (i.e., "This is my very best penmanship"), and of short paragraphs written especially for this display ("What I Love About My Parents," "The Funniest Day in (4th) Grade," "Why I Think I Want to _____ When I Grow Up"). Display many different types of artwork, labeled as to the medium used: tempera, collage, silkscreen, rubbings, etc. Have a small group of photographs taken each month, covering as many subject areas as you can. Set out the microscope with slides *they've* made.° On the Science table have an experiments display: list purpose, materials, procedure, results, conclusions; have the experiment's materials set up in the center of the table.

Have a pile of mimeographed sheets for parents to take home; these might cover: Characteristics of the (4th) Grader—physical, emotional, intellectual, and so on. Enliven presentation of learning projects, study materials and students' work with tape recordings (at a labeled "Listening Post"), or by having an automatic cartridge of slides shown in one corner of your room. Post this proverb and discuss it with your class: "Remember: it was the North Wind that made the Vikings."

For parents of older students, prepare a mimeographed sheet of objectives for each subject covered at your grade-level. Word these concisely; avoid using educational jargon, generalizations. Note areas to be covered, projects and enrichment work. For example:

Reading: Continuation of the developmental reading program. In addition to this, a study of vocabulary, root words, structural and

---

° Boxes of unprepared slides (and directions for their preparation) are available through scientific supply houses.

phonetic analysis is emphasized. Recreational reading ("reading for fun and profit") is encouraged through the library program. Subject matter reading is stimulated through assignment of projects in Science, Social Studies and other academic areas. Your child will be encouraged in many ways this year to develop a life-long interest in reading!

- *Arbor Day*   [22—but date varies from state to state]

J. Sterling Morton proposed to the Nebraska legislature the establishment of an Arbor Day to be observed on April 10, 1872. The date, in many states, is now fixed at April 22, coinciding with Morton's date of birth.

[IT'S A FACT: How does a sprouting seed, buried in the ground, know which way is up? If a plant stem can sense the warmth of the sun it will go towards this heat. If water is near, the plant's roots often grow towards *this*. If the plant cannot sense heat *or* water it will develop in response to hormones and gravity!]

Etymology

Even in pre-historic times, people were interested in plant life and its cycles. In one of the earliest Anglo-Saxon documents, written over a 1000 years ago, reference was made to a plant's "vital juice" or "saep."

In most plants, sap abounds while the plant is young and immature, so it's natural that people began to make jokes about the amount of sap in the head of some inexperienced person. Eventually any green or unsophisticated person was referrred to as "a sap."

Arbor Day Activity Suggestions:

1. Arbor Day is the day to plant a tree. You can get a small sprouting tree at a nursery and ask advice there on how best to plant it and care for it in your community.

2. If you have no room for a tree you might call the City Parks and Recreation Department and ask if the children could help plant a tree for them.

3. Research the trees in your area. Make plastic-covered labels that tell the (Latin) names of the nearby trees and a little about their history. (Use the *Tree Key*, a small-sized 280-page paperback by Herbert Edlin, published in 1978 by Charles Scribner's Sons, NY: a really handy reference book!)

For information about trees, write for free materials to:

> National Parks & Conservation Association
> 1701 Eighteenth St., NW
> Washington, D. C. 20009

The U.S. Forest Service, USDA Washington, D. C. 20250 offers an interesting book "*A Tree Hurts, Too*" and a Catalog of Forest Service Films available on free loan from your regional Forest Service office.

Math enrichment. To measure the diameter of a tree: with a tape, measure the girth of a tree. Divide this number by 3 (for an estimated measurement), or by 3.1416 (for a more exact measurement). To measure the height of a tree: with a piece of chalk, mark the trunk of the tree at 4 feet from the ground. Holding a ruler outstretched *at arm's length* before you, step back from tree. Close 1 eye and continue stepping back until the 1/2" mark on your ruler covers the area from the ground to the chalkmark on the trunk. From this exact distance measure the entire tree on your ruler. Multiply the number of 1/2" by 4 to get the height of the tree.

A Tricky Math Puzzle for Older Students on Arbor Day:

A rich man lives in a *big* house. Around his house are 8 shade trees. Around these trees are houses which he rents to others. And around these houses are 10 plum trees. The rich man wants to have all the plum trees for himself. He tells the other people that THEY can have the shade trees! How shall he build his fence so that *he* gets the plum trees and *they* get the shade trees? Answer:

Arbor Day Riddles:

1. What tree is never alone? (Pear)
2. What tree is part of the sea? (Bay)
3. What tree is always sad? (Pine)
4. What tree keeps the rich lady warm? (Fir)
5. What tree is part of each month? (Date)
6. What tree is not a good credit risk? (Willow)
7. What tree is kept in bottles? (Cork)
8. What tree do you carry in your hand? (Palm)
9. Which tree is older than others? (Elder)
10. What tree is like a sneeze? (Cashew)
11. What tree can be burned and still be itself? (Ash)
12. What tree is made of stone? (Lime)
13. What tree reminds you of a color? (Redwood)
14. What tree can you hang a picture on? (Walnut)
15. What pine has the sharpest needles? (A porcupine)

• *John James Audubon Was Born, 1785* [26]

Audubon spent his life painstakingly recording, in beautiful water-colors, the wild birds of 19th-century America. Many states celebrate Audubon's birthday (in some places Audubon Day and Arbor Day are celebrated as one).

Have the children observe birds. Help them learn to discriminate as to size (relative to the robin, starling, and sparrow), color (markings), and shape of body and bill. With experience, children will learn to make finer discriminations. (How does it fly? How does it get its food? Does it run or hop? What are its nesting habits? Of what value are these birds, ecologically?)

Some Facts About Our National Bird, the Eagle:

Today the bald eagle is shown on the Great Seal of the United States, the Presidental flag, and on U.S. coins and bills.

Early patriots had wanted a noble American bird as the national emblem. Eventually the choice was between the turkey (indigenous to the United States) and the bald (white-headed) eagle, which early Americans did not realize could be found in other parts of North America. In 1782, the eagle was chosen as the official emblem of the United States. Benjamin Franklin hated the choice and said flatly that the bald eagle ". . . is a bird of bad moral character . . . and he is generally poor and often very lousy."

For a hundred and fifty years the eagle was widely hunted. Alaska even offered a bounty for eagle feet (50 cents a pair in 1917 and $2 in 1930). Finally, in 1940, the eagle was given legal protection in 48 states. Today, if you kill an eagle you are subject to six months in prison or a large fine.

Today, when an American Indian medicineman needs eagle feathers for a religious ceremony, he is not allowed to send out scouts to find a bird. Rather, he sends an application to the U.S. Fish & Wildlife Service in Albuquerque, New Mexico. This department collects eagle feathers from downed birds and from U.S. zoos and supplies them to Native Americans for use in sacred ceremonies.

An Audubon Day Quiz:

Careful now . . . don't fowl up!

1. What bird can you get into locked places? (tur*key*)
2. What bird has a grassy place in it? (*meadow*lark)

3. What bird has stealing in it? (*ro*bin)
4. What bird is part of a chain? (bob-o-*link*)
5. What bird is worth a great deal? (*gold*finch)
6. What bird has a metal container in it? (peli*can*)
7. What 4 birds have letters of the alphabet in their names? (blue-jay ('j' and 'a'), *seagull* ('c'), *eagle* ('e'), flamingo ('o').
8. What 4 birds have colors in their names? (*blue*bird, *scarlet* tanager, *black*bird, *blue*jay)
9. What bird has a little rodent in it? (tit*mouse*)
10. What bird has a big mammal in it? (*cow*bird)
11. What bird has a boy's name? (*Jack*daw)
12. What bird could use an oar? (c*row*)
13. What bird has a measurement of length in it? (*finch*)
14. What bird has a twinkling heavenly body? (*star*ling)
15. What bird has a musician in it? (sand*piper*)
16. What bird is a monarch? (*king*fisher)
17. What bird means to lose your balance? (*fal*con)
18. What bird has an automobile in it? (*car*dinal)
19. What bird should a baker like? (dodo)
20. What bird has a cry of pain? (gro*use*)
21. What bird has a tiny insect in it? (pheas*ant*)
22. What bird has a period of Chinese history in it? (fla*ming*o)
23. What bird has a hen's baby in it? (*chick*adee)
24. What bird has the opposite of STOP in it? (fla*min*go)

Audubon Materials

The National Audubon Society offers excellent books, charts, fact-sheets, flash cards, slides and records covering topics including American Indians, ecology, and natural science as well as birds! Request their catalogs of books, natural science study aids, Conservation Fact Sheets, and their Pesticide Do and Don't sheet. (The Book Catalog has *very* interesting illustrations.) Write to:

The National Audubon Society
950 Third Avenue
NY, NY 10022

Three Good Bird Feeders To Make

Plastic-Dome Feeders offer protection from cold winds, and while the students watch birds feeding, the birds feel safe because the feeder has no blind spots.

Procedure:

1. Cut a pattern from heavy (24" × 36") paper.

2. Draw a line 32-5/8 inches long, 8-1/2 inches from lengthwise edge. Using cord and pencil as a compass, determine a point 22 inches from both ends of this line. Using a radius of 1-1/4 inches from this point, make a curved line with a cord compass and cut out tip.

3. Draw in 1-inch squares in pattern above 32-5/8-inch line as a guide in developing larger curve.

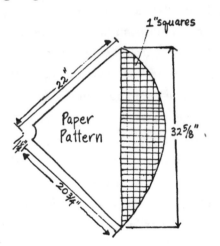

4. Use pattern to cut feeder top from sheet of .02-inch cellulose acetate. Have a parent cut the triangular platform from outdoor plywood.

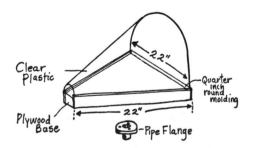

5. Fasten plastic along sides of platform with wood strips. Nail quarter-round molding across exposed side to keep feed in, and their bird feeder is ready for use!

The cherry log feeder is just that—a short log of medium thickness with several large holes bored in it and several big nails hammered in as perches. Holes are filled with suet and the log is suspended from aloft

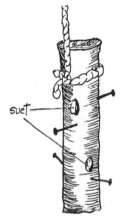

suet

The pickle jar feeder can be constructed by students. Filled with sugar water (4 tablespoons sugar to 2/3 cup water colored red with food coloring) it can provide nourishment and moisture to birds year around, as the sugar water will not freeze, not even in winter.

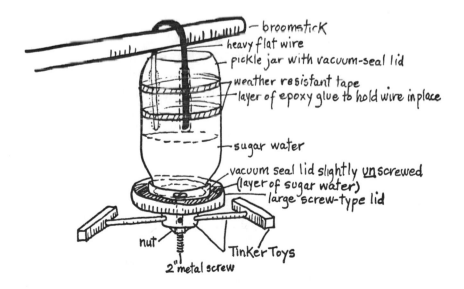

- broomstick
- heavy flat wire
- pickle jar with vacuum-seal lid
- weather resistant tape
- layer of epoxy glue to hold wire in place

- sugar water

- vacuum seal lid slightly unscrewed
- (layer of sugar water)
- large screw-type lid

nut

2" metal screw

Tinker Toys

Use a hammer and nail to make a hole in the middle of each of the two jar lids. Run the metal screw down through the two lids and the Tinker Toy; fasten them together with the nut. Be careful to leave space between the two lids so that sugar water can seep down into large screw-type lid. Insert two Tinker Toy 'perches'. Adhere wire to jar's outside surface. When glue is dry, reinforce with strapping tape. Fill jar with sugar water. *Lightly* screw on lid-feeder. Hang feeder so that students can watch it being used.

Bird Riddles:

- What can you throw up in the air and it won't fall back down? (a live bird)
- How many steps does a sparrow take in an average day? (None. A sparrow *hops.)*
- Why is a lawyer like a crow? (He likes to have his cause (caws) heard.)
- Why are birds always sad in the morning? (Because their bills are all over dew [all overdue])
- If a guy is trapped on top of a burning building with a goose in his arms, what is the wisest way for him to get down? (Start plucking that goose! . . . . that's how you get 'down'.)

- *National Automobile Month*

Etymology

In French, "auto" means "by itself" and "mobile" means "moving," so automobile means "a self-propelled machine."

In ancient Gaul the carros was a two-wheeled war chariot. This word came into French as carre and later in English became our word: *car.*

Some activity suggestions for students who are car-enthusiasts:

1. Design a crash helmet or a car decoration using fire, or a phoenix bird, or a skull.

2. Study some modern cars. Then design a fast car with air-foils.

3. Write a race car driver's life story in the form of excerpts from a diary.

4. Visit a car showroom with an adult. Get background information and literature from the salesman. Find a good way to share with the class what you have learned.

5. Read some articles in car magazines. Choose a race car driver you admire. Write a letter to him/her (in care of the magazine). Ask some good questions. (Enclose a stamped self-addressed envelope.)

6. Finish each of these sentences and use them in a paragraph. Cars are a big part of our lives. Because of them we have _____ , _____ , _____ , _____ . Because of cars, people are now able to _____ and _____ . Because of cars, we've been forced to build _____ , _____ , and _____ . Cars have caused us lots of trouble. They _____ and _____ . But cars have also made life better in these ways. They _____ and _____ .

7. As a teacher, write to the Bradley Automotive Division of

Thor Corporation
7669 Washington Ave. South
Edina, MN 55435

Say how interested you are in learning about how to build a Bradley sports car. Ask for some literature. (Enclose a self-addressed stamped envelope.)

Car Riddles:

- What comes with the car, is of *no* use to the car and yet the car can't run without it? (the noise of the engine)
- What grows less tired the more it works? (an automobile tire grows less "tired")
- What car name did the farmer say when he bought the little red hen? ("Chevrolet": "She ever lay?")
- What do you always see running along the streets of a town? (the curb)
- What makes a road broad? (the letter "b" [b-road!]
- If a car has a horn, but no engine and no wheels, how does it go? (Beep-beep!)
- How is your front door like a speeding driver? (In the end they'll both get locked up. . .)

Creative Writing Self-Starters:

1. Make a list of things that you can *not* change or control in anyway. Then tell what you think about this fact. Now write about

power: what is it, who do you know who has it, and why? What powers do you now have? What kind of power do *you* want?

2. Write your ideas about what a woman or a man is.

3. Today you will find a marvelous thing. You'll recognize its importance at once. Tell how you find it and how it changes your life.

4. Make a list of various farm chores. Make a list of misfortunes that can befall a farmer. Make a third list of very happy moments we all experience in our lives. Include these three lists to compose random diary entries covering several months or years in a pioneer's life. Include lots of details and expressions of feelings.

5. Choose an object in your house. Now choose a part of this object. "Become" that part: write about your life, why you enjoy it, how a common day goes, friendships you have, what you think will happen when you get broken or finally wear out.

6. Use a large paper cutter and cut up a newspaper at random into *little* squares. Each child gets a square and writes an elaboration on the details found in the tiny square. This may be in the form of a monologue, a reporter's adventure, a managing editor's story or a detective's notes.

7. Write 4 or 5 paragraphs with the title of "I am. . ."

8. You are reading a book about _____ when you fall asleep. You dream . . . and your dream takes you far away. Write about this dream. Where does it take place? Who is in it? Is it a funny or a frightening dream? Why? Describe the dream and what you do when you wake up.

9. If I could change the school day, I'd like to . . . . (Give 5 or 6 suggestions and tell about each of these in some detail.)

10. Choose a familiar object. Now look at it real hard. Describe small parts of it or unusual ways it might have been used from time to time. Don't tell what it is. See if a friend will recognize what the object is by just reading your description.

11. Write an imaginary biography of a famous fictional character. Give lots of details.

12. Use the exclamation "What's happened to the car?" in an original story.

13. Create an original folktale based on one of these:

- How the *(some animal or bird)* got its *(some characteristic that distinguishes that animal).*

- How *(something in nature)* came into existence.
- How the *(an animal or bird)* lost its *(something it does not actually have)*.

14. You got into a time-machine and came from the past to the present. Tell what you think about life in the present compared to the world you left. Do you return to the past? Why?

15. Create a *Witches (Warlock's) Cookbook of Hateful Recipes.* Include recipes for preparation of lizard, spider, snakes, and so on. Give menu and party suggestions. Make your cookbook *detailed* and as "unreal" as you can. (Use metric measurements.)

16. Through the centuries, books have been written on all kinds of materials: on wood, on papyrus, on beaten bark, on rolled parchments in monasteries of the Middle Ages or ancient Egypt, on stone tablets in Assyria, on silk scrolls in China, on buffalo hides by the American Indians and on cowhides by early pioneers. Design a book made of a special kind of material and then fill it with material (a ship's log, a prisoner's journal, and so on) that reflects its cover.

17. Create a character to appear in several story episodes. Will it be a woman or a man? Will they have magical powers? Superhuman strength? How old will they be? How tall? Describe the character completely. Then have them appear in several "cliffhanger" stories, such as a fire at sea, caught in the path of an on-rushing train, car, or bull, or lost in the Amazon jungle and captured by enemies, and so on.

18. I'd like to be a spy for _____ in _____: fill in these two spaces and then write about the statement.

19. Choose one of these chapter titles and use it to write an autobiographical story: "My Earliest Memory (Memories)," "The One(s) I Love the Most," "My Best Friend," "My First Day at School," "When I Got Lost," "My Happiest Day(s)."

20. In the 5th-grade classroom, money has been missing from Mrs. Romero's desk drawer. Then one day at lunch, as she is coming back from the Teacher's Room, she sees Teresa coming out of the classroom. Mrs. Romero says "hello" to her and goes into the room. When she opens her desk, she finds that the class money she had put there *just before lunch* is *gone.* What should Mrs. Romero *do?* Write your ideas and suggestions in the form of (alternative) endings to this problem situation.

May

The merry month of May.
—Richard Barnfield, 1598

†† National Radio Month (Nat. Assn. of Broadcasters, 1771 N St., N.W., Washington, D.C. 20036).

†† National Correct Posture Month (American Chiropractic Assn., 2200 Grand Avenue, Des Moines, IA 50306).

†† National Music Week, beginning with the first Sunday in May. (Nat. Federation of Music Clubs, 600 S. Michigan Ave., Chicago, IL 60605) and Be Kind to Animals Week (American Humane Asociation, P.O. Box 1266, Denver, CO 80201).

1 May Day. Traditionally a spring festival involving flowers and dancing around a Maypole.

Scott Carpenter, U.S. astronaut, was born in Boulder, Colorado in 1925.

Quotation of the Day: (On this day in 1964, President Johnson predicted the day when a woman would serve as President of the United States): "I can see the day coming when none of the great offices of the Republic will be closed to women of talent, not even the office of President—although I hope you will forgive one for hoping that day is still a few years off!

2   On this day in 1936, Prokofiev's "Peter and the Wolf" had its premiere in Moscow, U.S.S.R.

On this day in 1954, Stan Musial of the St. Louis Cardinals hit 5 home runs in one day in two games!

3   On this day in 1963, thousands of blacks staged protest marches in Birmingham, Alabama. Police dogs and powerful streams of water from fire hoses were used against the marchers. The arrests of adults and juveniles topped 2,000!

4   On this day in 1776, Rhode Island declared its independence from Great Britain.

Horace Mann, educational reformer and "Father of the Public School System," was born in 1796 in Franklin, Massachusetts.

On this day in 1970, National Guardsmen killed four students at Kent State University in Ohio after a campus protest against U.S. invasion of Cambodia.

5   Karl Marx, philosopher, was born in Treves, Prussia in 1818.

Nellie Bly, investigative reporter, was born in Cochrane Mills, Pennsylvania in 1867.

On this day in 1961, Alan Shepard, Jr., was rocketed 115 miles into space and became America's first space explorer.

6   Willie Mays, baseball player, was born in Fairfield, Alabama in 1931.

7   On this day in 1792, Capt. Robert Gray discovered the Columbia River.

8   On this day in 1541, Hernando de Soto and his men discovered the Mississippi River at a point near the present city of Memphis, Tennessee.

Harry S. Truman, 33rd U.S. President, was born in Lamar, Missouri in 1884.

9   On this day in 1502, Christopher Columbus and his 13 year old son
     set out from Cadiz, Spain on his fourth and last voyage. His ex-
     pedition included four ships and 150 men, who mutinied near
     the easternmost tip of Central America. Columbus was
     stranded for a whole year on the island of Jamaica.

     First Nazi book burning. Twenty-five thousand books were
     thrown on a huge bonfire by Hitler and Nazi leaders in Berlin in
     1933.

     On this day in 1974, the House Judiciary Committee began formal
     hearings on the impeachment of President Richard Nixon.

10   On this day in 1775, Ethan Allen and his "Green Mountain Boys"
     captured Fort Ticonderoga in New York during the
     Revolutionary War.

11   John Chapman, also known as "Johnny Appleseed," planter of
     thousands of apple trees, was born in 1768.

     Quotation of the Day: (In a eulogy given in the Senate:) Your
     labor has been a labor of love and generations yet unborn will
     rise up and call you blessed.—*General Sam Houston*

     Minnesota, 32nd state, joined the Union in 1858.

12   Florence Nightingale was born in England in 1820.

††   Mother's Day is the second Sunday of May

13   First permanent English settlement in the New World,
     Jamestown, was founded near the James River in Virginia,
     1607.

14   On this day in 1804, Captain Meriwether Lewis and William
     Clark set out from St. Louis, Missouri for the Pacific Coast in
     order to explore the Louisiana Purchase.

15   First copyright law was passed in Massachusetts in 1672.

     On this day in 1869, a group of women met in New York to form
     the National Woman Suffrage Association. Its purpose was
     mainly to secure the ballot for women. Elizabeth Cady Stanton
     was the first president.

Jasper Johns, artist, was born in Augusta, Georgia in 1930.

16   On this day in 1868, in a crucial vote in the Senate, the impeachment of President Andrew Johnson, inspired almost exclusively by political considerations, failed by one vote.

17   On this day in 872, the Kingdom of Norway was founded.

On this day in 1792, twenty-four New York brokers met under a cottonwood tree (on the present site of 68 Wall Street) and signed an agreement to fix uniform rates of commission in the sale of stocks and bonds. This was the real beginning of the New York Stock Exchange.

On this day in 1954, the U.S. Supreme Court declared racial segregation in schools to be unconstitutional.

Quotation of the Day: Separate educational facilities are inherently unequal.—*Chief Justice Earl Warren, May 17, 1954.*

18   Tsar Nicholas II was born in St. Petersburg, Russia, 1868.

Bertrand Russell, philosopher, was born in Trelleck, Wales in 1872.

First woman to fly faster than the speed of sound, Jacqueline Cochran, piloted an F-86 Sabre jet fighter plane to Edwards Air Force Base, California at an average speed of 652.337 miles an hour in 1953.

19   On this day in 1536, Anne Boleyn (mother of Elizabeth I), who had been married to King Henry VIII of England for 3 years, was beheaded on the Tower Green in London; the execution was carried out by an expert imported from France by the King.

20   Henri Rousseau, artist, was born in Laval, France in 1844.

First public viewing of motion pictures occurred in New York City, projected by the Latham family, 1895.

First solo nonstop flight across the Atlantic when Charles A. Lindbergh took off from Roosevelt Field, New York, 1927.* (Thirty-three-and-a-half hours later, he landed in Paris, greeted by a crowd of 100,000.)

---

*His plane was stocked with 451 gallons of gas and 20 gallons of oil, but had no lights, heat, radio, automatic pilot or de-icing equipment!

21   On this day in 1881, the American Red Cross was founded in Washington, D. C. by Clara Barton.

First test explosion of an airplane-borne hydrogen bomb was conducted over Bikini Island in the Pacific Ocean by the United States, 1956.

Robert Creeley, poet, was born in Arlington, Massachusetts in 1926.

22   Sir Arthur Conan Doyle, writer and creator of Sherlock Holmes, was born in Edinburgh, Scotland in 1859.

23   Carl von Linné (Linhaeus), botanist, was born in South Rashult, Sweden in 1707.

South Carolina, 8th U.S. state, entered the Union in 1788.

On this day in 1969, five U.S. satellites were launched by one rocket.

24   On this day in 1626, Peter Minuit, director of the Dutch West India Trading Co. bought the island of Manhatten from the Indians for $24 in trade beads, and then founded the colony of New Amsterdam.

Queen Victoria was born in Kensington, England, 1819.

First public telegraph message ("What hath God wrought!") was sent from Washington, D.C. (by S.F.B. Morse) to Baltimore (received by Alfred Vail), 1844.

On this day in 1962, Scott Carpenter became the second American to go into orbit as he circled the world three times.

25   Theodore Roethke, poet, was born in Saginaw, Michigan in 1908.

On this day in 1969, Thor Heyerdahl set sail from Egypt in *Ra*, a reed boat, in an attempt to prove that ancient Egyptians could have sailed to the Americas. (His expedition was successful.)

26   On this day in 1954, the funeral ship of the Egyptian Pharaoh Cheops was unearthed in a limestone chamber near the Great Pyramid in Egypt.

††   Memorial Day, last Monday in the month of May, originally a day on which to honor those killed in the Civil War, it is now observed in memory of the nation's dead in all wars.

27   Amelia Bloomer, women's rights champion, was born in Homer, New York in 1818.

Rachel Carson, writer, was born in Springdale, Pennsylvania in 1907.

28   Thomas Moore, poet, was born in Dublin in 1779.

On this day in 1959, two monkeys, Able and Baker, survived a 300 mile trip into space, while confined in the nose of a rocket and were picked up, uninjured.

On this day in 1967 Sir Francis Chichester sailed back into Plymouth, England, completing his 226-day solo round-the-world voyage.

29   On this day in 1453, Constantinople, capitol of the Byzantine Empire, was captured by the Turks, signifying the end of the Middle Ages.

Wisconsin, 30th U.S. state, entered the Union, 1848.

First party to climb Mt. Everest, Edmund P. Hillary, of New Zealand, and Tensing Norkay of Nepal, achieved the summit, 1953.

John Fitzgerald Kennedy, 37th U.S. President, was born in Brookline, Massachusetts in 1917.

30   Tsar Peter the Great, was born in Moscow in 1672.

31   First taxis in America, taximeter cabs, imported from Paris, came to New York City, 1907.

Joe Namath, football player, was born in Beaver Falls, Pennsylvania in 1943.

On this day in 1964, the longest double-header in major league baseball history was played in New York by the New York Mets and the San Francisco Giants, with the Giants winning both games. The total playing time was 10 hours, 23 minutes!

May

This month was probably named for the Roman goddess, Maia, goddess of growth.

MAY QUOTATIONS

††   The music teacher came twice each week to bridge the awful gap between Dorothy and Chopin.—*George Ade*

1   Who was the first around the moon? An atheist Russian or God-fearing Americans?—*Scott Carpenter*

4   Be ashamed to die until you have won some victory for humanity.—*Horace Mann*

5   From each according to his abilities, to each according to his needs.—*Karl Marx*

8   (Statement by Truman to reporters April 13, 1945 the day after his accession to the office of U.S. Presidency.) When they told me yesterday what had happened I felt like the moon, the stars and all the planets had fallen on me.

The Buck Stops Here. (Sign permanently posted on Truman's desk in the White House).

The release of atomic energy constitutes a new force to revolution to consider in the framework of old ideas. (Message to Congress on Atomic Energy 10/3/45)

—*Harry S. Truman*

When all the poison gases are exhausted, a man, made like all other men of flesh and blood, will in the quiet of his room invent an explosive of such potency that all the explosives in existence will seem like harmless toys beside it. And another man, made in his image and in the image of all the rest, but a little weaker than them, will steal that explosive and crawl to the center of the earth with it, and place it just where he calculates it would have the maximum effect. There will be a tremendous explosion, but no one will hear it and the earth will return to its nebulous state and go wandering through the sky, free at least from parasites and disease.—*Italo Svevo (1923) "The Confession of Zeno"*

Rest in Peace. The mistake shall not be repeated.

—*Cenotaph in Hiroshima*

12 [Of Florence Nightingale] She held that the universe—including human communities—was evolving in accordance with a divine plan; that it was (our) business to endeavor to understand this plan and guide (our) actions in sympathy with it. But to understand God's thoughts, she held we must study statistics, for these are the measure of His purpose. Thus the study of statistics was, for her, a religious study.—*Karl Pearson*

Too Kind—too kind. (When handed the insignia of the Order of Merit on her death bed.)—*Florence Nightingale*

> *The hand that rocks the cradle*
> *Is the hand that rules the world.*
> *—William R. Wallace*

18 Mathematics possesses not only truth but supreme beauty— a beauty cold and austere, like that of sculpture.

The secret of happiness is this: let your interests be as wide as possible, and let your reactions to the things and persons that interest you be as far as possible friendly rather than hostile.
—Bertrand Russell

24 I will be good .(Resolution on ascending the throne)

We are not interested in the possibilities of defeat. (to A.J. Balfour in December, 1899)

We are not amused. (January 2,1900)
—Queen Victoria

27 For all at last returns to the sea—the beginning and the end.
—Rachel Carson

Nature's laws affirm instead of prohibit. If you violate her laws, you are your own prosecuting attorney, judge, jury and hangman.—*Luther Burbank*

Any interference with nature is damnable. Not only nature, but also the people will suffer.
—Anahario, wife of Grey Owl, 19th century

29 For those to whom much is given, much is required. (1961)

Ask not what your country can do for you; ask what you can do for your country. (Inaugural Address, 1961) *—John F. Kennedy*

31   They say you can't do it, but sometimes that isn't always true.
                                                                    —*Casey Stengel*

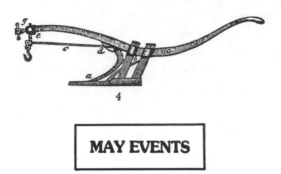

4

MAY EVENTS

• *May Day*   [1]

Although no longer as popular as it was 50 years ago, May Day remains a fine time to note the advent of spring.

This is one of our oldest holidays. Over 2000 years ago, the Romans honored Flora, the goddess of flowers on this day. The tall marble columns in Flora's temple were twined with garlands and the children danced about them praising the goddess; such is the history of *the May pole.* The Pilgrims brought from Europe the custom of giving *May baskets,* which are a secret message of friendship and celebrate the arrival of spring.

With older children, discuss the relative importance of this day in relation to other holidays; why has it lost importance through the years?

May Art

Quickie baskets: Make a slit at the center of each end of a rectangle of construction paper. Lap over ends and staple or glue. Attach handle.

Paper doily. Doily is folded in 1/2 and rolled into a cone. Glue edges together and let dry thoroughly. Attach handle of pink construction paper. *Fruit basket* can be painted, if it is wooden, with colorful stripes of poster paint. If basket is plastic, strips of a contrasting color of paper are woven in and out between slats of the basket. Staple the handle in place. *Tiny paper basket* may hold a few flowers and a haiku, or a few pieces of candy made in class. Each child folds an 8″ square of paper in 1/2 horizontally and then in 1/2 vertically. This is then folded in 1/2 along a diagonal line and cut as shown. Fold across tip. Open out and overlap each section with the one next to it. Rubber cement sections in place and add a handle.

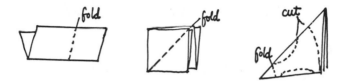

A conservationist's May basket. Using 6″ × 9″ pieces of paper, children design their own flowers to fill this basket. Once colored (or painted or cut and glued), basket of flowers is cut out and paper is formed into a circle and glued. A 1/2″ × 13″ strip of paper becomes the handle. A variety of leaf and flower shapes help this to become a very pleasant and personal May basket.

Completed baskets may hold cookies made in class (see suggested recipes at back of book) and can be "delivered" to an older person or a shut-in. Teacher might arrange in advance to give baskets to a local convalescent or rest home.

- *Rhode Island Declared Its Independence from Great Britain, 1776* [4]

Etymology

The Italian navigator, Giovanni de Verrazano, visited Narragansett Bay in 1524. He noted an island that reminded him of the Island of Rhodes in the Mediterranean Sea. This fact appeared in the ship's log and eventually led to this state being called Rhode Island.

- *Minnesota Joined the Union, 1858* [11]

Etymology

Minnesota comes from the Dakota Indian words meaning "sky-tinted waters."

- *Mother's Day* [Second Sunday in May]

President Woodrow Wilson proclaimed this day as a national observance on May 9, 1914, but it has roots far back in history. In pre-Christian times the people of Asia Minor worshipped Rhea, the great mother of the gods, as she was called. When Christianity took the place of these ancient rites, the Virgin Mary became "the Mother of the Roman Catholic Faith" and the "Mother Church" idea developed. During the Middle Ages in England this Mid-Lent Sunday was called "Mothering Sunday." It was the custom for each person to return to the place of his birth and attend his mother church. As everyone was in his home town, after church services people would go and visit their parents, bringing cakes and gifts to their mothers.

Language Arts

Have the children, as a group, dictate sentences (which you quickly record) based on their ideas and feelings about "Mothers." The teacher organizes these and prints them, in large letters, on a piece of butcher paper that nearly covers a bulletin board. A colorful paper border outlines the composition for which the class should chose a title. This is also an appropriate time for improving public relations by writing your Room Mothers notes of thanks; perhaps you might organize a small party for all the mothers of your students.

Mother's Day Cards

Pop-up card. Make by folding a piece of 8″ × 10″ paper in 1/2 lengthwise and cutting out a 3″ × 3″ notch as shown. The portion that is left jutting out from card is folded inside and pops up when card is opened. Children modify pop-up shape (oval, heart) or draw a face, a bouquet or a jack-in-the-box on it. Cover of card is designed so as to accommodate "cut-off" top left-hand corner.

Have each student compile a long list called "Some Reasons I Love My Mother!" Each item should be in the form of a complete sentence Check lists for grammar and spelling. Children can then recopy lists in their best handwriting. These lists can be folded and put into envelopes, or rolled as scrolls and tied with ribbons. They should make very pleasant reading for lots of Mothers!

Science: Find My Mother

To encourage growth in the concept of development, provide young children with two sets of pictures, one of baby animals and one of their adult counterparts. Ask children to match each baby animal with its mother. This can be set up as a manipulative bulletin board or a desktop game.

Mother's Day Gift Suggestions:

A plant can be grown in class from a seed or carrot top; class-made cookies or other sweets (see recipes at back of book).

Sesame Honey Candies:
180 balls

Purchase the little pleated paper candy-holders, used by commercial candy makers and often sold at fine candy stores. Kids love the professional look these little holders give their gifts!

1-1/4 cup butter, melted in skillet over low heat
2-1/2 cups sesame seeds   Add to the butter and stir
5 cups grated coconut   over low heat for 5 minutes

Remove pan from fire and add: 2-1/2 tsp. vanilla
                                 1-1/2 cups honey

Mix well. Then put in cool place until candy becomes stiff enough
to shape into balls (1/2 hour in a freezer).

Students roll candy into balls and place each one in a little candy
cup. Each child then puts six to eight of these in a little box or in a
circle of cardboard, which is then wrapped in colored tissue and
tied with pretty ribbon and yarn.

[NOTE: Refrigerate your candies until you've given them to
Mother.]

Dried Orange or Lemon Peel

Using a fine grater each kid grates peel from several oranges or
lemons.° (Grate peel only, not white membrane.) Place in open glass
dish and allow to dry at room temperature 1 day. Store in airtight jar.
Use as spice or to make Orange or Lemon Pepper and Orange or Lemon
Sugar.

Orange or lemon pepper. Mix two tablespoons orange or lemon
peel and 1 tablespoon coarse black pepper. Store in airtight container.
Each child makes 3-6 tablespoons and gives it in a small jar. A little note
is tied to each jar: "This is good pressed into hamburgers just before
cooking! I love your cooking—and YOU!" A small picture, decorated
with glitter, can be glued to the face of each jar lid.

Orange or lemon sugar: Mix 1/2 cup sugar with 1/4 cup orange or
lemon peel. Store in airtight container.

Each child makes this recipe (3/4 cup) and gives it to his/her
Mother in a little jar decorated with a ribbon. An accompanying note
says: "Sprinkle this on a warm cake, or pancakes or try some in hot tea! I
hope you'll like it, Mama.°° I love you."

°Fruit may be squeezed then and enjoyed by class or frozen into ice cubes and made into
Slush-Cones (see recipes at the back of the book).
°°Ask each child to write here the word that s/he calls her/his parent, e.g., Mom, Mommy,
Mama, Ma. Be sure they understand spelling of word involved.

Little Mouse Pincushions.

Each student will need a 5″ × 6″ piece of light grey (tan) felt or flannelette, a 1-1/2″ × 4″ piece of grey (tan) felt, a 2″ × 3-1/2″ piece of composition board, two tiny buttons or sequins for eyes, Elmer's glue, grey sewing thread, scissors, cotton (stuffing), a needle and black embroidery thread.

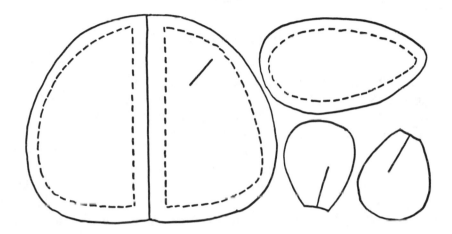

Mouse body and bottom are cut out. Tail is cut out and stitched (glued) to rear of bottom. Ears are cut out, slit and folded (glued) in place to inside of slits in head. Body sides are carefully and firmly glued together. These can be kept in a book, under pressure. Later they are filled with stuffing and carefully glued to the bottom. Extra filling can be added if necessary. Two eyes are sewn (or glued) in place. The nose and whiskers are applied by sewing with black embroidery thread or by applying black with a fine-point felt tip pen. And there is your mouse!

A few new straight pins can be stuck in the cushion before it is wrapped. Check every seam of every child's pincushion before gifts are wrapped to be certain all seams are secure.

- *Florence Nightingale Was Born, 1820*   [12]

She is regarded as the founder of modern nursing. After completing her medical studies in France and Germany, Nightingale returned to England. She volunteered her services to the British wounded in the Crimean War in the south of Russia. She was named Lady-in-Chief of 33 nurses and they were sent to the Crimea in November, 1854. When they finally arrived, almost half of the British wounded had died because of bad sanitation. Under Nightingale's direction, care of the wounded improved until less than two in every hundred wounded became a fatality.

In 1856, she contracted Crimean fever and was bedridden for 11 days, but she refused to return to England. She remained in Crimea until the peace was signed and the hospitals were closed, in the summer of 1856.

As a consequence of her experience in Crimea, Nightingale's health was broken and she was never able to practice nursing again. She spent the next 64 years writing on nursing, hospital administration and woman suffrage.

She was the first woman to receive the British Order of Merit.

- *First Permanent English Settlement in New World, 1607*   [13]

*James*town was founded near the *James* River in *Virginia* nearly 400 years ago. Both the town and the river were named in honor of King James I of England, who ruled at the time. And the state got its name from Queen Elizabeth, who named it Virginia in honor of herself, the Virgin Queen!

One of the ways we get new English words is from people's names. For example:

Fuchsia is named after the German botantist, Leonard Fuchs (1501-1566).

Nicotine comes from Jean Nicot, who introduced tobacco into France (1560).

Watt comes from James Watt, 18th century Scottish inventor.

Teddy bear comes from Theodore (Teddy) Roosevelt, who had a chubby bear-like appearance.

Chauvinism comes from Nicolas Chauvin, a solider of Napoleon's army, who was known for his bragging about the vast capabilities of the French.

Use the names of the students in your class and try to turn some of them into new words. Make up a meaning for each word, so that it has to do with the nice things about that person. Here's an example:

A noun from "Jim": "A jimmer meaning a really pleasant surprise."

A verb from "Cathy": "To cathy someone meaning to convince them to help you." Could you also make up adjectives and adverbs?

Carloslike	Marially
Benlike	Sammish
Jessicalike	Anticarlish

As an alternative homework assignment, ask the students to go through their phone books or state map and list the ten most unusual surnames or town names they can find, such as Jazz, Lovelady, Coaxum, and Scallion. Include the five most unusual women's names (Marvella, Velvet, Irish, Genie) and the five most unusual men's names (Darlo, Marketer, Bubber). If they discover any real good full names have them note these too (Melody Occhiogrosso, Etropuis Coleman, Gonzales Dubois, Alfonia Gethers).

A composite list (written as blank verse) could be executed by two or three students. The finished chart will draw a lot of attention and provide some laughs for readers.

Riddles:

- What would be a good name for waitress? (Carrie)
- What would be a good name for a woman lawyer? (Sue)
- What would be a good name for a woman gardener? (Rose or Lily)
- What would be a good name for a woman jeweler? (Pearl or Ruby or Opal)
- What would be a good name for a ballerina? (Grace)
- What would be a good name for the wife of a sailor? (Bertha)
- What would be a good name for a woman chemist? (Ann Eliza [analyzer])

- If lawyers are disbarred and clergymen defrocked, doesn't it follow that:

  electricians can be delighted

  musicians denoted

  cowboys deranged

  models deposed

  tree surgeons debarked and

  drycleaners depressed?

  —*Virginia Ostman*

- *Formation of The New York Stock Exchange, 1792*   [17]

Etymology

In early civilization, animals were the most important form of moveable wealth. Herds and flocks were measured by counting heads. In late Latin the name for cattle was taken from "head" (caput). Criminals who were guillotined and lost their heads, became known as victims of *capital* punishment. The head letter of a sentence was then called the capital letter. Business-men of the 17th century began to call the initial stock of goods a starting or head stock of goods: "capital." And so today, 400 years later, "capital" means all wealth used to initiate enterprises that are meant to make more wealth.

- *Sir Arthur Conan Doyle Was Born, 1859*   [22]

Sherlock Holmes, the great detective (whom Doyle created) often used his highly developed sense of smell in order to solve a difficult mystery.

Use the following information as the basis of a bulletin board or a learning center that makes "good scents."

[IT'S A FACT: A tester in a French perfume factory must be able to distinguish between 7,500 different scents and odors.]

How Do We Recognize the Tastes in Foods?

Our tongues have many small bumps (papillae) which are composed mainly of taste-buds. Most of the 9,000 or so individual taste buds have only 1 or 2 functions. Some signal the amount of sweetness sensed, others recognize sour or bitter or salty flavors. Our taste buds are capable of recognizing very subtle differences. With experience, you can come to tell the year a wine was bottled or even the tree from which some olives were picked!

It is not on the tongue, however, that the finer distinctions of taste are made. It is in *the nose*, in an area smaller than a dime, that some 600,000 sensory cells note and then report to the brain the more subtle of flavors as they are experienced!

Some activities involving the sense of smell:

Use a stick of scented cologne or a pump-spray room freshener° to spray a specific spot near the wall, such as in a corner. As students feel their way around the walls of the room with their eyes closed, ask them to try to find the sprayed areas. Or spray pieces of cotton and let the kids go throughout the room sniffing out the smells.

Place three scented items on a tray and have the students identify the three smells. Then, use two trays with four scented items on each. Make three of the smells identical and the other one different. Ask students to match the smells.

One student holds a paper plate to be smelled (it has been rubbed or soaked with the scent to be smelled), or post five plates with five different scents or with only one having been given scent. The correct identification can be verified by comparing plate numbers to those on a master sheet.

Use scented candles or incense and have the children sit quietly, allowing the scents to transport them to far-off places.

Have the students make collections of scents associated with different jobs: painter, housewife, mechanic, farmer, secretary, teacher. These collections could be presented by each child as little mysteries to be "solved" by the other students.

Let the children make up names for some new perfumes and then decant, dye, and label the new products.

° or pickle juice, a cut onion, lemon juice, peanut butter, bleach, or cinnamon can also be used.

Use herbs to help sensitize olfactory perception: Use dill, sweet basil, chives, rosemary, tarragon, sage, peppermint, lemon balm, oregano. Older students can learn to identify the scent or taste of many different herbs in the mint family: applemint, spearmint, pineapple, pennyroyal, peppermint, Corsican, lemon mint, Indian mint, orange mint, curlmint, and emerald or gold mint.

Set up a smell-a-rama in the classroom. Have the students determine rules and procedures. Then, invite a neighboring class to enjoy the experience. Ask any grade level class to drop by. In fact, kindergartners and first-graders would love to have second or third-graders as their guests! Serve an odiferous stew that the class has cooked, and which emphasizes smells like celery, onion, green peppers, carrots, and garlic. You might read aloud the story of *Stone Soup* retold by Marcia Brown and encourage the students to sense the smells of cabbage, carrots and potatoes, as the story unfolds.

Familiarize young students with a new taste and smell by serving little paper cups of warm camomile tea right at the end of the story of *Peter Rabbit* (Beatrix Potter) so that they may understand how Peter felt at the end of his long day.

Christopher Morley's *Smells** can be read aloud to the children. Ask that they try to clearly imagine the scents (and tastes) involved in this poem.

- *South Carolina Was Admitted to the Union, 1788*   [23]

Etymology

This territory was called Carolina in the Charter of 1629 in honor of Charles I.

- *Memorial Day*   [Last Monday in May]

This was originally called Decoration Day and had its first formal observance on May 30, 1868. In the South, after the Civil War, mourning friends and relatives of slain soldiers put flowers on the graves of both Southern and Northern soldiers. The news of this gesture traveled north and soon most of the states honored the war dead on this day.

Smells appears in the anthology 'Yesterday and Today,' edited by Louis Untermeyer, which was published in 1926 by Harcourt Brace and Co.

- *Discovery of the Funeral Ship of the Egyptian Pharaoh Cheops,*
  Near the Great Pyramid of Giza, Egypt, 1954   [26]

On this day the Pharaoh's funeral ship was unearthed in a limestone chamber. The magnificent ship and its contents—both those luxurious and those utilitarian—were meant to serve the pharoah on his journey to the Other World.° They now serve us as the contents of a special time capsule that reveals much about people who lived 3,000 years ago!

Contact the Metropolitan Museum of Art (255 Gracie Station, N.Y., NY 10028) to obtain the six-inch Hicroglyphic Computer (L7510) for three dollars. Children can use it to write their names in ancient Egyptian or to decipher a pharaoh's cartouche. It introduces the original picture alphabet of 25 signs with English pronunciation and meanings. It also includes numbers from 1 to 1,000,000.

Have the class design a contemporary time capsule. Include information about architecture, government, U.S. history, religions, transportation, art, inventions, sports, entertainment, food, and humor. How might our language be explained? How could we show what humans are like at this present moment in history?

Each student could design a personal time capsule such as "A Day In My Life" or "My Family" or "My School" or "My Hometown (City)," or they could design a time-capsule to be opened when they've grown up! Ask the children to think about what they'd like to tell that adult of the future: What do you not want to forget about being a child? How would you advise your adult self to treat children; how will you raise *your* children? What do you want to say about how *you* see adults *today*?

Once materials have been prepared and collected, obtain an airtight container: a Tupperware plastic box with lid works well. Put materials inside the container and replace the lid. Seal the box inside a heavy plastic bag. Then dig a hole and bury the time capsule. Be certain to make a clear map of where it is buried. Deposit this map in a *safe*

°Fabrics, actual flowers, sculpture, furniture, grain, baskets, jars, fans, food: fruits and seeds (mandrake, dates, grapes, melon seeds, nuts), gold, silver, jewelry were found. The funeral ship was to provide transport to Heaven. Beautifully-carved human figures were also included to serve as substitutes for the dead. In case Osoris, divine King of the dead, imposed tasks of penitence on the new arrival which were not befitting the dignity of an earthly Pharoh, the little human figures were to do penitence in his stead.

place: ask your parents to put it with their Important Documents file or
in their safety deposit box, if they have one. This way you will know exactly where to dig 20 years from now!

- *Rachel Carson Was Born in 1907*   [27]

Rachel Carson foresaw the polluted future and tried to warn us
about ecological dangers in an industrial world. She wrote a book about
the time that might come, if we do not become more conscious of the
ecological consequences of living as if there were no tomorrow. She
called her book "The Silent Spring."

A fascinating bulletin board for your school hallway can be
achieved by using the simple display called "The Changing Countryside," a mural of 7 very large fold-out pictures in full color, showing
what can happen to a countryside in a few years' time. These pictures
cover the same landscape from 1953-1972 at intervals of 3 years. The
devastation increases in a constant progression. Both students and
adults will spend long periods of time "reading" this ecological statement. Also available is Vol. II, "The Changing City," which is equally
strong. Both are the work of Swiss artist Jörg Müller and can be ordered
from:

> Antheneum Publishers
> 122 E. 42nd St.
> New York, NY 10017

They cost $10 each and are well worth it!

The Green Box offers outstanding humanistic enviromental
teaching materials. *The Green Box Kit* includes 96 Do Cards, 250 Show
Cards (activities), 5 Think Cards, 40 School Projects, 7 Activity Booklets
and Access Tracking Sheets. The complete Kid is $40.00,* but you can
write to request a three-dollar sampler, *The Seed Book*, which includes 2
Do Cards, 1 Think Card and 2 Show Cards. A very special teaching
program, *The Green Box* is available from:

> Humanistic Enviromental Education
> Humboldt County Supt. of Schools
> 555H Street
> P.O. Box 11408
> Eureka, CA 95501

(Thanks to Betty Graham!)

---

*California residents: add 6% sales tax, please.

Attributes: A Good Review Game

Discuss the meaning of game's name. *Attributes* are the qualities or characteristics of something.

Divide the class into two or three teams. Team 1 goes out of the room and chooses some element of nature such as water, heat, light, sound, air or magnetism. They discuss its many attributes. Then they return to the room and the members of the other team(s) ask each of them: What can you do? Each member of Team #1 must give a different answer, such as "I help you feel comfortable," "I help you stay alive," "I am needed to read a book," "I can keep cars driving," and so on. The other team(s) get one guess after each answer. Once a player cannot think of the answer (or once the other team has guessed the element), the identity of the element is given and another team leaves the room to choose an element of nature.

Information Sources

An excellent catalog, *A Selection of Water Conservation Program Aids* is free from:

> The Dept. of Water Resources
> P. O. Box 388
> Sacramento, CA 95802

The Center for War/Peace Studies publishes *Intercom* ($1.50 ea.) which provides resources and program ideas for the furtherance of democratic values. *Intercom* #71, "Teaching About Spaceship Earth: a Role-Playing Experience for the Middle Grades" is excellent. For information, write:

> Intercom
> 218 East 18th Street
> New York, NY 10003

● *Wisconsin Joined the Union, 1848*　　[29]

Etymology

First spelled Miskonsing, it comes from the Native American name for the main river in the region and meant "gathering of the waters."

- *Be Kind to Animals Month*

  Animals are such agreeable friends; they ask no questions, pass no criticisms.—*George Eliot*

One reason people choose to be kind to animals is that they are able to *empathize* with weaker creatures. *Empathy* is "a feeling into-ness," the ability to sense how another is feeling. Help the children to learn to be more empathetic.

Ask the kids to pretend they are each a pet. Then have each describe exactly "what things would make you happy and comfortable, and how would your master/mistress behave to keep you a happy, healthy pet."

Have the kids write stories in the first person, pretending that they are each an animal, in places like a game refuge, at a school yard, in a zoo or on the farm. Have them *anthropomorphize* these animals:

For example, a golden eagle at a game reserve waits to experience the sights and sounds of people away from their natural habitat of noisy, dirty, smelly cities. He's anxious for the younger wildfowl to observe how unfortunate the human species is not to have wings. He expects to show the young birds the shell-like metal objects people crawl into to get around, often jostling one another and honking like geese. He wants his youngsters to observe the strange eating and drinking habits of people. He tells them how humans seldom eat mice or grasshoppers, but instead consume strange mixtures out of cans or paper sacks! He plans to spend most of the afternoon feeding in the fields and creeping as close as possible to watch the people without frightening them off.

Ask each student to write about how his/her own pet may see them: in what way are they good owners and how they might improve. Or, let students talk about being "kind" to animals, why kindness is important, why we care, and how each of us can honestly help.

Information Sources:

Request: *Thank You for Helping Us* and "Fitting 'Em in . . ." (chart) from:

> Bureau of Land Management
> U.S. Dept. of Interior
> Washington, DC 20240

Request: "*A Nutrition Guide for Pet Owners*" (FDA 74-2021) from:

> U.S. Govt. Printing Office
> Supt. of Documents
> Washington, D.C. 20402

(Also check addresses listed under Cat Week and Dog Week)

Tongue-twister:

What kind of noise annoys an oyster? A noisy noise annoys an oyster!

Riddles:

- Why is a horse an odd eater? (He eats best when there isn't a bit in his mouth!)
- When is a fish the most lovable? (When it hugs the shore.)

MAY ACTIVITIES

May Social Studies:

In honor of Florence Nightingale, whose birthday is May 12, invite a nurse to visit your class. Before she actually arrives, talk over with the children types of questions that *they* would be interested in asking her. Help them to cover a wide range of topics; encourage them to take full advantage of this opportunity to interview a professional in the field of medicine. (Just for fun to help break down pre-conceptions, you might sometime invite a male nurse.)

May Poetry:

May

May be chill, may be mild,
May pour, may snow,
May be still, may be wild,
May lower, may glow,
May freeze, may burn,
May be gold, may be gray,
May do all these in turn—
May May.
    —*Justin Richardson, in "The Countryman"*°

May Reading:

A good way to learn or to review Greek myths is by use of the deck of cards called *Greek Myths and Legends* (available from Educational Products, 1310 Hill Street, Ann Arbor, Michigan 48104 for about five dollars). This a lively game based on thirteen of the best known myths and legends of the ancient Greeks. Four cards make up a "book," which tells the story. When a player has a book he/she announces the name of the myth and receives ten points, as does the first player who can tell the story and name the four cards.

May Science:

Etymology:

Entomology is the study of insects. This word comes from the Greek *entomos* which means "cut-up." Insects have segmented or "cut-up" bodies. Our word "insect" comes from the Latin *insectum* which means "cut up." It is simply the Roman word for the Greek *entomos!*

°Quoted in *New York Herald Tribune* and subsequently in *The Reader's Digest.*

Metamorphosis is from the Greek; *meta-* means "changing" and *morphe* means "form." Metamorphosis means "a change of form or shape."

Insects are incredibly strong: A weight-lifter has about 800 muscles while a caterpillar has more than *4000 muscles!*

A human weight-lifter can lift about twice his own weight in a clean and jerk overhead lift. Some beetles can lift objects 850 times their own weight!

A desert locust can fly for nine hours without a break. A monarch butterfly may fly 650 miles without eating! Insects really *are* strong!

Trapping insects. Lay a towel out or open an umbrella beneath a bush; beat the bush with a stick. At night, collect moths from about neon signs. The grills of cars sometimes afford undamaged insects. Bury a topless tin can, its upper edge flush with the soil; pour a little molasses into bottom of can. Place a large stone *over* can (but *not interfering* with access to *rim* of can); beetles should crawl toward sweet smell and be trapped in the can. Lightly bury a cookie sheet in soil; put a dead mouse or baby chick (some pet shops sell these frozen) on top of the soil-covered sheet. Scavenger insects should appear beneath the animal after a few days.

Rearing insects. Children can experiment with raising various sorts of insects:

Beetles are kept in a large gallon mayonnaise jar that is fairly high in humidity. (see De-nested and Mealworm)

Butterflies can be raised from *larvae*, from *pupae* or from *eggs*.

Crickets are raised in a one-gallon jar, the bottom of which has 2" of soil spread on it. Put a watch glass° (or plastic container lid), filled with water, on top of the soil. Mouth of jar is covered with wire mesh. Make certain that watch glass remains filled with water. Crickets eat old mashed potatoes, tiny shreds of lettuce, corn meal mush or bread soaked in milk; once in a while give them a little library paste or peanut butter for a special treat!

De-nested beetles are caught as they are attracted by a piece of cheese children have left outdoors in warm weather.°° Placed in a screen-covered jar, they are given the dried carcass of a dead mouse. Class may study *osteology* at the same time ("Osteon" is Greek for "bone") as beetles clean off carcasses, exposing skeletons beneath.

° A 1/2"-1" deep glass receptacle used in science studies.
°° Beetle cultures may be purchased from a Biological Supply House (i.e., Scientific Center, Santa Clara, Calif.). Cricket cultures are available from Wards Natural Science Estab., Inc., 316 Cannery Row, Monterey, CA 13940.

Grasshoppers are raised in a 1 gallon jar, the bottom of which has been lined with a 2″ sod of grass. This is watered from time to time and provides food and an egg-depository place for grasshoppers.

Larvae (caterpillars) are raised in a wooden crate that has its bottom knocked out and its sides covered with screening. Box is stood on end and potted "feedplant"° with larvae on it is placed in box; or line bottom of aquarium with 2″ of moist soil into which are planted "feed plants" (or jars of water with stalks of "feed plants" are placed in tank). Put larvae on "feed plant." Cover top of aquarium with "Stretch and Seal." The more airtight the larvae's cage, the longer his food supply will remain fresh and edible. There's little chance of suffocating larvae as they use very little air to live.

Mealworm beetles cultures can be obtained from a biological supply house if no one is able to find any in a seldom-used box of cereal, corn meal or flour. Fill gallon jar 1/2 full of All-Bran®, atop which you lay a piece of crumpled newspaper. Put 1/2 a potato on top of the newspaper; this affords moisture and food. Place culture in jar and cover jar's mouth with screening. Put jar in a warm place. Replace potato when it dries up.

Moths can be reared from larvae, from pupae or from eggs.

Praying Mantises are carnivorous and eat live insects; give a baby mantis aphids to eat, while an adult mantis will eat houseflies and roaches. If not fed enough the mantis will turn cannibalistic. Spear tiny piece of liver on a toothpick if no live insect food is available. Eggcases must be collected in the fall or winter°°, brought indoors and placed in a jar (as described under Roaches). Babies emerge in 2-4 weeks.

Pupae: Larvae will molt several times and then stop eating. They may go beneath soil in jar to pupate. Don't bother them. Keep pupae to watch adult emerge (or children may collect cocoons and bring them and branches of the "food plant" to class). Put 1″ soil in bottom of large jar; stick branches in the soil and with a few drops of glue attach cocoons to sticks. Cover the mouth of the jar with screening. Once a week, spray the soil and pupae with water to keep air in jar humid (but

---

°The real secret to successful rearing of larvae is to keep them well-supplied with their "food plant": each adult female lays her eggs on a specific plant which will provide the food for emerging larvae. These larvae will usually *not* eat *any other* plant and so most captive larvae in the classroom starve to death amidst heaps of grass and green leaves. It is essential to identify the "food plant" of larvae, e.g., either take note of plant on which larvae is found and get it and keep it fresh for larvae or use Frank Lutz's book: *Field Book of Insects of U.S. and Canada* (New York: G.P. Putman's Sons, 1948) to help identify food source.

°°Or you may purchase praying mantis cocoons from Bio-Control, Route 2, Box 2397, Auburn, CA 95603. Each cocoon contains *many* young insects.

never to the point of producing mold or mildew). If kept in a warm room, cocoons will produce adults in a few months; these will die if their host plants are not in leaf and available. If you wish to raise eggs and larvae from the adults, you must prevent their emergence until the spring. To do this, place the jar between a regular window and a storm window on the northern side of the school building. To make certain that you get fertile eggs, you'll need both sexes of moth from pupae. A newly emerged female attracts males, so just put her in a cheesecloth covered jar and set this outside of an evening—males should arrive any time!

Let the children study photographs to learn how bees (and other insects) are physically constructed. Then let the children make *big* insect constructions using colored paper, fuzzy pipe-cleaners and heavy plastic° for the wings. These creations could be anthropomorphized by addition of hats, glasses, scarves or ties.

Or you could let students plan and execute professional filmstrips or slides about insects. Prima Educational Products (Hudson Photographic Industries, Inc., Irvington-on-Hudson, NY, NY 10533) offers U-Film 35mm clear mounted slide blanks, set of 100 for $11, or student U-Film Master Sound Filmstrip and Slide Kit $15, or replacement roll, 25 feet-$8. The specially treated slide and filmstrip surfaces can be drawn on, written on and erased for reuse.

For information about a career in entomology (the study of insects) your students may write:

> Entomological Society of America
> 4603 Calvert Road
> College Park, MD 20740

Plant fertilization. How many kinds of plants are dependent upon bees for the preservation of their species? Honeybees are responsible for the fertilization of at least 100,000 different kinds of plants!

°Clear plastic of dry cleaning bags can be used.

In tropical regions and in the southern hemisphere birds are more important than insects in the fertilization of plants.

But if all the insects and birds in the world were suddenly to disappear, what plants, if any, could continue their growth cycles?

Many plants are never cross-pollinated by bees or birds. The wind carries out their fertilization. The pine tree, for example, depends on the wind for its pollination and each grain of pine tree pollen is like a tiny kite that is easily flown long distances by the wind. Many wind-fertilized plants release their tiny pollen grains only in early spring before most plants have leaves, as foliage could interrupt the flight of fine pollen and keep it from a correct destination.

Most plants visited by insects and birds have smooth-surfaced pollen which would not be a good flyer!

Riddles:

- What do you yell when you see a hot bunch of bees? (S'warm!)
- What are the *biggest* ants? (gi-ants!)
- What is smaller than a flea's mouth? (The food that goes in it!)

May Art:

This month freshen up your room by developing a Creative Corner in the classroom. Here, when children have free time and the inclination, they can sit quietly and experiment, inventing new toys, games, constructions, and new ways of looking at things. The Creative Corner should be functional but not elaborate, containing a table, chairs and a *few* of the following objects (as the days pass, objects can be changed; specific areas of interest shown should be noted and capitalized upon when new objects are added): tiny boxes, scraps of colored plexiglass, film-tins, a large magnifying glass, colored toothpicks, Styrofoam, geometric wooden shapes (scraps from lumber yard), Plasticene® (modeling clay), interesting buttons and seeds, a small flannel board and colorful felt scraps, scissors, a small piece of pegboard, yarns, Mexican hemp, golf tees, a broken alarm clock, sea shells, negative and positive shapes cut from cardboard (some reproductions of Arp)°, durable toys from different countries—made of different materials, small wheels of different sizes, and organic materials (i.e., blown-out egg shells). From time to time, a book might

---

°Jean Arp (1887-1966), French painter & sculptor.

also be put on the table such as a book of African masks, mythical creatures, folk art, and so on. After a while, the children can decide on a special name of their own for this corner, in which case it could be printed in large bright letters on a sign that is posted above the table. Experimentation of all types should be allowed; what might appear to be dawdling can often lead to the most inventive results, and of course, not all results will be material.

June

And what is so rare as a day in June?
Then, if ever, come perfect days.
—James R. Lowell (1819-1891)

††   Dairy Month (American Dairy Association, 20 North Wacker Dr., Chicago, IL 60606)

1   Pere Marquette, explorer, was born in Laon, France in 1637.

First commercial U.S. oil refinery, 1860.

Kentucky, 15th U.S. State, entered the Union in 1792.

Tennessee, 16th U.S. State, entered the Union in 1796.

2   On this day in 1924, Congress conferred citizenship on all American Indians.

Charles Conrad, Jr., U.S. astronaut, was born in Philadelphia in 1930.

3   Jefferson Davis, President of the Confederate States of America, was born in Fairview, Kentucky in 1808.

Raoul Dufy, artist, was born in LeHavre, France in 1877.

4   King George III was born in London in 1738.

5 World Environment Day

Federico García Lorca, Spanish poet and playwright, was born in Fuente Vaqueros, Spain in 1889.

On this day in 1967, Israel became involved in conflict with Egypt, Syria and Jordan in the Six Day War, which it won.

On this day in 1968, Senator Robert F. Kennedy was shot in Los Angeles; he died the following morning.

6 Nathan Hale, patriot, was born in Coventry, Connecticut in 1775.

Thomas Mann, writer, was born in Lubeck, Germany, 1875.

First drive-in movie theatre was opened in Camden, New Jersey in 1933.

D-Day: On this day in 1944, allies began the invasion of Nazi-held Western Europe on the beaches of Normandy, France.

7 Freedom of the Press Day (Inter-American Press Association, 141 Northeast Third St., Miami, FL 33132)

On this day in 1769, Daniel Boone began his exploration of Kentucky.

Paul Gauguin, artist, was born in Paris in 1848.

8 On this day in 1965, President Johnson authorized the U.S. military to go into combat against the Vietcong in South Vietnam.

10 Gustave Courbet, painter, was born in Ornans, France in 1819.

11 King Kamehameha, unifier of the Hawaiian Islands, was born in 1758.

Gerard Manley Hopkins, poet, was born in England in 1844.

First woman member of Congress, Jeannette Rankin, was born on this day in Missoula, Montana in 1880.

12 On this day in 1630, John Winthrop, first governor of The Massachusetts Bay Co., entered the Salem harbor in the ship, the Arbella.

On this day in 1839, according to legend, Abner Doubleday created a new ball game in Cooperstown, New York. Doubleday called his game "baseball"!

On this day in 1963, Mississippi Black leader Medgar Evers was shot and killed by a sniper in front of his home in Jackson, Mississippi.

13   On this day in 323 B.C., Alexander the Great died in Babylon.

The missile age was born as German flying bombs, V-1 and V-2 rockets, hit England in World War II in 1944.

14   Flag Day commemorates the adoption of our flag by the Continental Congress in 1777 and Flag Week includes this day.

On this day in 1846, the California Republic was established as independent of Mexico.

Margaret Bourke-White, photographer, was born in New York City in 1906.

15   On this day in 1215, King John of England, under pressure from his barons, set his seal on the Magna Carta, basic document of Anglo-Saxon law, "the cornerstone of American liberty," at Runnymede, England.

On this day in 1752, near Philadelphia, Benjamin Franklin flew his kite in an experiment that was to prove that lightning contained electricity.

Arkansas, 26th U.S. State, was admitted to the Union, 1836.

Father's Day is the third Sunday in June.

17   On this day in 1972, five men were caught trying to wiretap the Democratic National Committee Headquarters in the Watergate Building in Washington D.C. The Watergate political scandal would continue until August 9, 1974 when Richard Nixon would resign from the Presidency.

18   On this day in 1812, Congress declared war on Great Britain, for the second time in American history.

On this day in 1815, Napoleon was defeated at the Battle of Waterloo in Belgium by British and Prussian troops. Waterloo was Napoleon's final effort to conquer Europe. Four days later, Napoleon wrote his act of abdication.

19 On this day in 1867, Emperor Maximilian was executed by the rebel Benito Juarez, after France had withdrawn her military support of the Emperor.

Lou Gehrig, baseball great, was born in New York City in 1903.

20 First U.S. steamship, the S.S. *Savannah*, to cross the Atlantic, reached Liverpool from Savannah, Georgia.

West Virginia, 35th State, was admitted to the Union in 1863.

Lillian Hellman, writer, was born in New Orleans, Louisiana in 1907.

21 Summer solstice is either today or tomorrow.

New Hampshire, 9th State to join the Union, put the U.S. Constitution in effect, 1788.

First long-playing phonograph record was produced in 1948.

22 Ann Morrow Lindbergh, writer, was born in Englewood, New Jersey in 1906.

Sir Julian Huxley, biologist-writer, was born in London in 1887.

On this day in 1964, three civil rights workers, Andrew Goodman, Michael Schwerner and James E. Chaney, disappeared in Mississippi. Their bodies were discovered August 4, 1964.

23 Donn Eisele, U.S. astronaut, was born in Columbus, Ohio in 1930.

24 On this day in 1497, explorers John and Sebastian Cabot landed on a peninsula in northeastern North America today called Labrador.

First suffragette in American history, Mistress Margaret Bent, a niece of Lord Baltimore, appeared before the all-male Maryland Assembly and demanded both voice and vote for herself in that body in 1647. The Assembly was shocked.

Ambrose Bierce, writer, was born in 1842 in Horse Cave Creek, Ohio.

First reports of flying saucers came from the area of Mount Rainier, Washington, 1947.

25   George Orwell (Eric Arthur Blair), writer, was born in Motihari, India in 1903.

26   On this day in 1284, according to legend, The Pied Piper of Hamelin° who had rid Hamelin of its rats, lured the children of the village to a mountain where they all disappeared, in revenge for not receiving his fee of 1,000 guilders.

27   Helen Keller, blind and deaf author and lecturer, was born on this day in Tuscumbia, Alabama in 1880.

           Quotation of the Day: Literature is my Utopia. Here I am not disfranchised. No barrier of the senses shuts me out from the sweet, gracious discourse of my book-friends. They talk to me without embarassment or awkardness.—*Helen Keller in her book,* The Story of My Life

28   King Henry VIII, was born in Greenwich, England in 1491.

           On this day in 1778, Mary Ludwig Hays, better known as Molly Pitcher, took her mortally wounded husband's place at a cannon at the Battle of Monmouth, New Jersey. In recognition of her heroism, the valiant woman was commissioned a sergeant by General George Washington.

30   On this day in 1859, 5,000 people watched Emile Blondin, a French acrobat, dressed /in pink tights, cross Niagra Falls on a tight rope in just five minutes' time.

June

May have been named for the great goddess Juno, protectress of women, although some Romans felt that its name came from the Latin *juniores,* in which case June would be a month dedicated to the young. Some scholars believe that "June" is derived from Junius, a Latin family to which the murderers of Julius Caesar belonged.

°Pied means covered with patches, a piper plays a flute (or bag pipes), Hamelin is a city in northwestern Germany.

JUNE QUOTATIONS

3   All we ask is to be let alone.—*Jefferson Davis, Inaugural Address as President of the Confederate States of America*

5   If I were to name the three most precious resources of life, I should say books, friends and nature; and the greatest of these, at least the most constant and always at hand, is nature.
                                    —*John Burroughs*

7   I shut my eyes in order to see.—*Paul Gauguin*

24   Barometer, n. An ingenious instrument which indicates what kind of weather we're having.
                         —*Ambrose Bierce, The Devil's Dictionary*

25   All animals are equal, but some animals are more equal than others! *(Animal Farm)*

Big Brother is Watching you. *(1984)*
                             —*George Orwell*

27   Science may have found a cure for most evils; but is has found no remedy for the worst of them all—the apathy of human beings.—*Helen Keller*

JUNE EVENTS

A few words about June. Try to plan these last weeks of school so that the inevitable restlessness of the children will not be compounded. Let the children work with the encyclopedia, tracking down answers to questions the class raises as a group. Bring in large, sturdy puzzles of the U.S.A. or of the world. Bring to class a set of wildlife books for free time reading. Construction paper scraps need to be used up, so encourage the making of collages, torn paper compositions, or a scrapbook of magazine and student-made pictures for a hospital children's ward. The classroom will have to be cleaned on the last day of school. This can be facilitated by dividing older children into four groups, each assigned the responsibility of thoroughly cleaning one side of the classroom. Make sure that all things to be accomplished in each area are clearly noted, such as where to put old papers and so on, before you announce the beginning of house cleaning. The first group finished is rewarded in some small way. This may mean 5-10 minutes of noise, but at the end of that time your room should sparkle!

- *The First Commercial U.S. Oil Refinery, 1860*

This was erected near Oil Creek Valley, Pennsylvania, in June, 1860. The only product saved was the kerosene. They ran off the small amount of gasoline into Oil Creek. The kerosene was sold (in competition with whale oil) to be used in lamps.

In energy-conscious times, oil and its location and refinement are of special interest. Have older students write to the oil companies below, requesting the latest information about this natural resource.

Exxon
1251 Ave. of the Americas
New York, NY 10020

Shell Oil Co.
1 Shell Plaza
P.O. Box 2463
Houston, TX 77001

Union Oil Co.
1650 E. Golf. Rd.
Schaumburg, IL 60196

American Petroleum Institute
Publications, Distribution Section
2101 L. St., N.W.
Wash., DC 20037
(Supplementary Energy Sources
  booklet)

● *Kentucky Was Admitted to the Union, 1792*   [1]

Etymology

Kentucky is either Iroquois or Cherokee in origin and has been said to mean: "dark and bloody ground," "prairie," "meadowland," and "land of tomorrow."

● *Tennessee Was Admitted to the Union, 1796*   [1]

Etymology

Tennessee is of Greek derivation ('Tanasc') with the meaning of "old (or beloved) town." First a place, then a river name, it finally became the name of a large region.

● *World Environment Day*   [5]

Discuss with your class the implications of this day. Students may want to write to:

> The Sierra Club
> 530 Bush St.
> San Francisco, CA 94108

> Nat. Audubon Society
> 950 Third Ave.
> NY, NY 10022

and ask for their Environmental Education Pack and request Nature Center Planning information.

• *Freedom of the Press Day*   [7]

Here are some unusual ways to use up any stacks of newpapers you may have.

1. Make a collage using different styles of type and photographs to build up "a tabloid image."

2. Twist and roll a newspaper and tie it to form a rough shape that stands. Use strips of cheese cloth soaked in delayed-setting plaster to cover the form. Wrap and work in any additional plaster needed. Sculpture can be painted when dry.

3. Once the class has discussed and studied different famous people, have the children each pick one he or she especially likes. Then each prepares an article in the form of a newspaper report written as though he/she had been there when this famous person was alive. Each report should include: main idea (headline), identification of main points, conciseness in wording.

4. Ask the students to see in which part of the newspaper they would most likely find: reports of important events, personal opinions about the news, entertainment announcements, and legal notices.

5. Have them compare writing styles of editorials and news stories.

6. Give each student a page from a newspaper. Each child skims the page for a 1-5 minute time-period. Then, papers are put away and each child makes a list of as many ideas as he/she can remember having read on the page.

7. Have each child skim a newspaper story in order to answer: Who? What? When? Where? Why?

8. *Headliner.* Divide students into groups of six. Cut the words from some newspaper headlines, mix them up in a sack and have one child from each team choose 3-5 words from the sack. These words are taken back to the teams and the children try to arrange them in an order that forms some kind of plot, around which they can develop a 3-8 minute play or pantomime. An announcer gives an introduction to each presentation and the other children try to guess the 3-5 words involved.

- *Birth of Jeannette Rankin, 1880* [11]

America's first congresswoman, Jeanette Rankin, was elected in Montana and was the only Representative to vote against the United States' entry into World Wars I and II, protesting that "we have to get it into our heads once and for all that we cannot settle disputes by eliminating human beings."

She cosponsored the amendment to give women the vote and lobbied effectively as a private citizen for maternity measures, child labor laws, and, always, peace. She led the Jeanette Rankin Brigade through the streets of Washington in 1968 to protest the war in Vietnam.

Jeanette Rankin was an active feminist right up until her death at age 92 in 1973. One of her last wishes was to see a female in Congress from every district. "Maybe we wouldn't do any better than the men," she liked to say, "but we certainly couldn't do any worse."

Ask the students to write about "The Strongest Woman I ever Met," or "Why I Don't (or Do) Believe in War," or "Women who have Influenced *My* Life," or for girls only, "The Woman I Hope to be Ten (or Twenty) Years From Now."

- *Age of the Missile Began, 1944* [13]

Etymology:

The word *missile* comes from the Latin "missilis" which comes from mittere, to send or throw. The word *age* is a very old word and has its roots in Old French and Middle English.

Age Riddles:

What Age—

is a place wild animals are kept?	(c*age*)
do you turn in a book?	(p*age*)
is a place where actors work?	(st*age*)
is wise?	(s*age*)
shows anger	(r*age*)
is a salary?	(w*age*)
is a vegetable?	(cabb*age*)
is a traveler's trunk?	(bagg*age*)
will you find in a letter?	(mess*age*)

● *Flag Day*   [14]

When he taught in Wisconsin in the early years of this century, Dr. Bernard J. Cigrand, each June 14th (in honor of the anniversary of the day in 1777 when the U.S. flag was adopted), would fly the American flag over his school. In 1916, President Wilson officially designated June 14th as Flag Day.

History. Each day, as the children salute the flag, they should understand the true meaning of the words they speak. Why not (with the assistance of the children and their dictionaries) paraphrase the salute to the flag, "I promise (myself) that I'll be loyal to the American flag and to the United States, whose power belongs to the voters, a country which, believing in God, cannot be divided and offers liberty and justice to everyone."

Occasionally, set aside 5-10 minutes prior to the pledge, in which you discuss a topic such as: How Are Flags Made Commercially? Who wrote the Pledge of Allegiance? What is the Flag Code? (approved in June, 1942, by the U.S. Congress.) Who were Barbara Frietchie and Betsy Ross?°

- *Arkansas Was Admitted to the Union, 1836* [16]

Etymology

Arkansas comes from a Siouan Indian tribe the Uga Khpa, meaning "downstream people." Through the years it was pronounced and spelled in various ways, but in 1881, the present spelling and pronunciation was legalized.

- *Father's Day* [The Third Sunday in June]

Mrs. John B. Dodd and her five brothers and sisters had been raised by their father after their mother's death. One spring day in 1919, while listening to the Mother's Day sermon, Mrs. Dodd had an idea. She thought how she would like to honor her father and other men like him, so she spoke to her minister after the sermon. He agreed with Mrs. Dodd and drew up a resolution for her, proposing that June 10,1919, be set aside as Father's Day. Three years later, on the third Sunday of June, America celebrated the first national Father's Day.

Although Father's Day usually falls after the closing of school, a small gift made in advance would undoubtedly be welcomed by Daddy. (See December: Christmas Gifts, pg. 152, for suggestions, or recipes at the back of the book.)

Ask the children to finish: "My Daddy is _____" and illustrate these sentiments.

- *West Virginia Was Admitted to the Union, 1863* [20]

Etymology

West Virginia was named for the Virgin Queen, Queen Elizabeth I of England, who ruled from 1558-1603.

°For enlightening information about these two women and others read *The Female Hero in Folklore and Legend* by T. P. Griffin; a Continuum Book published in 1975 by Seabury Press, Inc., New York, NY.

- *New Hampshire Was Admitted to the Union, 1788*   [21]

Etymology

It was named for Hampshire, England in a grant in 1629 to Captain John Mason of Hampshire.

- *First Long-playing Phonograph Record, 1948*   [21]

Here are some sources for phonograph records. Request their catalogs and perhaps order some new records for "next year's class."

> Pickwick Records
> 7500 Excelsior Blvd.
> Minneapolis, MN 55426

> Weston Woods
> Weston, CT 06883

- *Summer Solstice*   [21 or 22]

In the northern hemisphere, the sun appears at its highest point in the sky on June 21 or 22. On this day, the sun's rays shine directly on the Tropic of Cancer, an imaginary line north of the equator, which encircles the globe. This line goes through Havana, Cuba; Calcutta, India; and Hong Kong, China. People living in these three cities see the sun directly overhead on June 21 or 22.

- *Birth of Anne Morrow Lindbergh*   [22]

To help facilitate quiet moments during the last hectic days of school, read some of Anne Morrow Lindbergh's peace-evoking poetry.

- *Birth of Helen Keller, 1880* [27]

Free information concerning the life and achievements of this great American are offered by:

American Foundation for the Blind
15 West 16th St.
New York, NY 10011

Also request the booklet, "Understanding Braille."

JUNE ACTIVITIES

Bulletin board lettering suggestions. Cut letters from corrugated cardboard; use these themselves, or cut letters in reverse from corrugated cardboard, paint these and while wet, stamp letters of title on a long strip of white paper.

Bulletin board idea for the last week or two of school.

Cover board with white butcher paper. Provide pins, felt tip pens and poster paints and brushes. Encourage the students to communicate through collages, drawings, paintings and prose, in illustration of the topic, "What *I'm* going (I'd like) to be doing this summer!"

Game of presidents. Write on the board or duplicate a mimeo-sheet.

What *President* was called: Tippecanoe? (Harrison); was the son of a President? (John Quincy Adams); said "I do not choose to run"? (Coolidge); was called Old Hickory? (Jackson); was called "the Sage of Monticello"? (Jefferson); outlined a foreign policy with South America? (Monroe). What two Presidents died on the same day? (Jefferson & John Adams.) What four Presidents were assassinated? (Lincoln, Garfield, McKinley, Kennedy.)

Language Arts:

At the end of the school year have the children write a class letter thanking the Room Mother. Each child designs and cuts out of colored paper a tiny bird, flower, butterfly, heart or angel and these are pasted all around the letter, in its margins. The letter is rolled up and tied with a

pretty ribbon, each tail of which each has a pasted on it.

Reading:

A wheel of fortune. This helps break the routine of drill sessions in the reading group. Pointer of tagboard wheel is spun and number designates pile of cards from which the "fortune" is chosen. This card is read aloud by the child and can indicate a small prize, a poem, a puzzle or a penalty. Reading instruction may be involved in the "deciphering" of the fortune.

On finishing a reader. Ask the children to think back over the stories they have read and choose one, giving it a different ending (beginning). Ask how each character might have behaved differently in that case.

[VARIATION: Go through the reader and choose sentences at random from different stories. On slips of tagboard print 2-3 sentences that might begin or end a story. These slips are drawn from a box by children. Each child thinks for a few moments and then tells his original story, based on these sentences, to his group. Children may enjoy trying to identify the story in the reader from which sentences were actually taken.]

Summer reading club.* At the end of the school year, there will be several children who have just "caught on" to reading. You don't want them to lose over the summer what they've spent all year achieving. Perhaps you can try this: After discussing the idea with parents, send an invitation to each child to join a summer reading club. The club would meet once a week at your house. There'd be no drill, no exercises, no word study. You would simply read for the fun of reading.

At the first meeting, each child chooses two or three library books. At following meetings, the children talk about them and select others. You can often schedule related filmstrips, role-play favorite characters, or sing songs. After refreshments, you can read them a story or two. A summer reading club will help with the children by noticeably improving reading skills and the children might then think of reading as "lots of fun!"

June Science:

Tadpoles are often plentiful in June. If you catch some of these tiny creatures and care for them, you can watch their transformation and

---

*Elizabeth Williams, first-grade teacher at Mayfield Christian School in Grand Rapids, Michigan, used this plan to keep beginners reading over the summer months.

then release the frogs or toads where you found the tadpoles. You can keep the tadpoles in a fishbowl. Clean the container once a week.

When they develop four legs, keep only 1″ of water in the bowl and add rocks onto which they can climb. Cover the bowl with screening so that they don't hop out. The tadpoles can eat little bits of egg yolks, cooked oatmeal, fish food, cooked lettuce, and sausage. The grown frogs and toads eat only moving insects. If you can't provide live insects, let the animals go right away.

Grasses and cacti. Grasses are among the most useful of all plants. They flower in summer but do not ripen until late July, August or September. Wild grasses include timothy, rye grass, meadow foxtail, cock's foot and common quaking grass. Cultivated grasses include wheat, barley and oats. The flower-head of grass is called the "ear" or "panicle." The flowers that develop are called "spikelets."

Classroom cacti may flower in June. Give them a bit of water once a week if the weather is dry.

History Culmination:

You can try preserving food, as some Native Americans still do, by drying it!

Suitable fruits are peeled and cored apples, sliced 1/8 inch thick in rings; peaches (peeled); pears (peeled); apricots and nectarines (peeled); figs; halved plums (peeled or unpeeled); pitted cherries.

To keep them from darkening badly coat fruit slices with lemon juice or ascorbic acid.

Let the children use new needles and double threads to string long lines of fruit pieces. These strings are tied to clothes hangers that are hung in a warm dry place. Some fruits, such as apricots, become bitter if they are dried in direct sunlight.

Help the children learn to draw conclusions by giving them some "problems" to discuss and answer: I think Henry David Thoreau was a great man because _____ ; If I had come on the Mayflower, I would have brought _____ ; If Franklin (Lincoln, Booker T. Washington) had never lived, the world today would be different in these ways: _____ .

(Getting Ready For) Art (Next Year):

Have older students go through old magazines (ask the city librarian if you could have any discarded National Geographics, Realities, or art magazines).

Have the children collect examples of different art forms of a given period, such as Baroque, Renaissance, or Modern, to show the correlation that exists between art, music, and poetry. Use this correlation to demonstrate that all art forms are expressions of the culture of a people. Discuss these forms with the class. How can they each affect us? Which gives the strongest impression? Why will they not affect all people in the same way?

Examples can be saved and put to good use as bulletin board illustrations next year.

Getting Ready for NEXT Year!

This summer, make a collection of materials which you will find handy in the fall. Garage sales and flea markets can offer unexpected treasure! In addition to the usual items, such as magazines, pillows, newspapers and fabric pieces, try saving some empty shoe polish or roll-on deodorant bottles with applicators to refill with paint, cooky sheets for finger painting, computer read-out sheets for interesting scrap paper, sawdust (not redwood) for clay making, a broken clock for curiosity's sake, large glass jars for terrariums, plant-cuttings, old inner tubes to inflate and have fun with, a big galvanized tub or plastic pan for sand or water play, scrap tile for math work, paper and matboard in a variety of textures and colors (may be collected from a framer's or printing shop) large old salt shakers for shaking fine sand over glue for sand paintings, jazzy old dressup clothes (hats, silk scarves, shoes, bags—both male and female attire should be accumulated), a sturdy trunk or box in which to keep all these clothes. How about raiding a soft drink machine for the bottle caps (which can be used as counting devices or for tiny rock gardens), or asking a wallpaper store to save you a sample book (this may take months to get, but it's worth the wait). Ask an architect for old blueprints, a feed store for burlap bags, loose grain, and seeds (for experiments, art projects, birds), and a doctor or dentist for used X-ray sheets and so on . . . . . . !

If you know, or can get in touch with, a home economics teacher, you may be able to get a discount on any appliance (broiler-oven, electric skillet, blender, iron) you'd like to purchase for use with your class. Check it out.

You may want to acquaint yourself with resources in the selection of reading materials for children. Each year The Association for Childhood Education International (3615 Wisconsin Ave., NW, Wash., DC 20016) publishes a *Bibliography of Books for Children*. It includes hundreds of new titles covering fiction, non-fiction, all-time favorites and classics, and it also includes many titles about aging, changing sex roles and topics which reflect current social patterns. Check your library for a copy or send for a personal copy (about $4). ACE also offers titles such as *Guide to Children's Magazines, Newspapers, Reference Books* (50 cents) which would be helpful in preparing for a new school year.

The publication *Sexism in Education* offers good bibliographies on children's books, and literature on sexism in textbooks. This book can be obtained by writing The Emma Willard Task Force on Education, Box 14229, Minneapolis, MN 55414. It costs $4 (including postage) and makes enlightening reading.

A Final Anecdote

After delivering a lecture on the solar system, philosopher-psychologist William James was approached by an elderly lady who claimed she had a theory superior to the one described by him.

"We don't live on a ball rotating around the sun," she said. "We live on a crust of earth on the back of a giant turtle."

Not wishing to demolish this absurd argument with the massive scientific evidence at his command, James decided to dissuade his opponent gently.

"If your theory is correct, madam, what does this turtle stand on?"

"You're a very clever man, Mr. James, and that's a good question, but I can answer that. The first turtle stands on the back of a second, far larger, turtle."

"But what does this second turtle stand on?" James asked patiently.

The old lady crowed triumphantly, "It's no use, Mr. James—it's turtles all the way down."

Appendix:
Recipes

Classroom Cookery:

During their Social Studies reading, the children may learn of unusual or interesting foods prepared in other countries or areas. As these foods are mentioned, the teacher could prepare some for the students to taste. This allows the children an opportunity to see the food in a raw form as well as in its cooked state. Tortillas, succotash, poi and maple sugar are a few possibilities.

Seven of the following recipes require no cooking. Twenty-four of the recipes require no oven. The few utensils necessary can be kept in a classroom cupboard: wooden spoons, plastic or metal measuring cups, measuring spoons (which have been separated one from another), a plastic wash basin for mixing ingredients (preferable to glass bowls which are awkward for children to handle and can accommodate only one child at a time), cooky sheets and wax paper. A sponge and a 2-lb. coffee can of warm water will facilitate quick clean-ups. Several men's shirts, worn buttoned down the back, will make excellent aprons.

Each recipe can be organized so as to involve each student (in each reading group) in some aspect of the preparation. This preparation of food in the classroom will give the children experience with volumetric measures and will impress upon them (as nothing else may) the importance of careful reading. After clean-up, children may be asked questions based on the set of directions which a recipe represents.

Classroom cooking also offers a chance to break down the stereotyped idea that many children have that it is only *women* who belong in (or more subtly, can function in) the kitchen.

If a hot plate is available for classroom use, many other creative cooking experiences, including the making of art supplies, are possible. With the addition of a double-boiler and a candy thermometer to the store of cooking utensils, the children will be able to prepare any of the recipes that follow.

Culinary Etymologies

For many centuries Latin words have poured into our language. One of hundreds which we have adopted without even a spelling change is "recipe."

It is from *dactylus*, the Latin word for "finger," that we get our word "date," as that fruit was once thought to resemble a human finger.

In 496 B.C. a terrible drought afflicted the Roman countryside. The priests brought forth a new goddess, Ceres, and the people were told that if they immediately made sacrifices to her, rain would fall. Because Ceres was successful in ending the drought, she became "the protector of the crops." The Latin word *cerealis* meant "of Ceres," and gave us our word "cereal."

"Currants" were named for the corrupt city of ancient Greece, Corinth.

In the first century before Christ, the Roman legions were in Germany. Whenever anything was sold to the semi-savage tribes found living there, the Latin name for the object went with it. In this way many Latin words found their way into German. Some centuries later, German invaders brought nearly a hundred Latin derivatives into Britain—and into English; "butter" was one of these.

"Walnuts" means "foreign nuts." The Anglo-Saxons called them *wealhhnutu (wealh*="foreigner" and *hnutu*="nuts"), as these nuts were unknown to England before the arrival of invading armies.

"Yolk" is a derivative of a Middle English word *yolke* or *yelke*, through an Old English word *geolea*, from *geolu*; all of these words mean "yellow."

Sometime in the year 850 A.D. a goatherd named Kaldi became puzzled by the strange actions of his goats. He noticed that they were nibbling at the berries of a certain bush. When Kaldi tried some of these berries himself he was amazed at the feeling of exhilaration he experienced. He rushed off and told the other goatherds of his discovery. The Arabs learned to boil the berries of these bushes, calling the brew "gahve." The Turks introduced it to the French who called it "cafe," and in this way, we got our English word, "coffee."

"Vinegar" is actually *vyn egre* meaning "sour wine," and comes from Old French.

The Latin word *gelo* means "to freeze" or "to congeal," and it led to the French word *gelee*, "a jelly," and in English this became "gelatine."

Under William the Conqueror, in 1066, the Normans (Northmen) conquered the Germanic tribes who, in turn, became their servants. The vocabulary of these conquered peoples was of the field and kitchen and from it we get such words as "house," "hearth," "oven," "pot," "stone," "wheat" and "milk."

The Mexican Indians called the tree from which the cacao seed comes, "caucauatl." The invading Spanish had difficulty pronouncing this Indian word and shortened it to "cacao." In English it became "cocoa." Another Mexican Indian word, "chocolatl," meaning "bitter water," gave us "chocolate."

The word "*coconut*" (also spelled "cocoanut," thanks to an error by Dr. Samuel Johnson in his dictionary), comes from the Spanish and Portuguese word *coco* which means "a grimace." The three holes in the bottom of the coconut were thought to resemble a grimacing face and so "coconut" actually means "funnyface nut."

In ancient Polynesia, farmers cultivated a native grass and developed it into sugar cane. Moorish traders brought it to Palestine and soon were harvesting huge crops of cane, refining it in crude sugar mills. Boiled in open pots, the cane produced a sweet liquid that was made into flat cakes. European crusaders invading the Holy Land became acquainted with the sweet flat cakes made by their enemies. In Arabic the term "gand" meant a broken piece of sugar cake. English fighting men modified this term to "candy." It wasn't until 1420 that any reference to candy was even made in an English document. Much later, huge cane plantations would be developed in the New World and only then would large quantities of candy be available around the world.

You may want to notify your students' parents about the plans you have for cooking in the classroom. Here is a sample letter to parents which you can have duplicated.

Dear Parents:

As your child may have told you: each Friday our class "cooks." As of this week, we have prepared _____ and _____ . The children have decided to make _____ this Friday.

We begin cooking lessons only when we have learned the (35 Dolch sight) words assigned that week. Each recipe prepared by the children incorporates these Dolch words. The cooking experience helps to re-enforce math (and metric) skills and emphasizes how essential it is that we read instructions carefully.

Thank you for any ingredients you may donate and for helping us learn our weekly word list. We would really enjoy having you visit our class *any* time.

Sincerely,

Some things to remember when you cook:

1. Wash your hands.
2. Push up your sleeves; put on an apron or a man's shirt turned backwards.
3. Get the utensils and ingredients all together.
4. Have a sponge handy in case of spills.
5. Read the directions. Do you understand them all?
6. If a hot pan is used, keep its handle to the *back* of the stove and use a pot holder to pick it up.
7. When you're finished cooking:
   • turn off the hot plate or electric skillet and
   • clean up everything: wash, dry, and wipe off the tabletop
   • put everything back where it belongs

Presentation of Weekly Recipe

Using two thumb tacks or punch pins, tack the recipe (which is printed by hand on large newsprint sheets) onto the front board area. Present and review the 3-4 totally new words that appear in this recipe. Each new word appears in a different color of felt-tip pen on the newsprint recipe sheets.

When first cooking, go over the recipe orally with students *prior* to preparation of food. After 1-2 cooking experiences, let 2-3 kids read the new recipe aloud to the entire class. Eventually, after the students know the cooking and clean-up routines, have them read the big recipe sheet silently and prepare food to that point, at which time you dramatically pull off the top recipe sheet to reveal the sheet beneath and the *next* steps in the recipe.

Marshmallow Treats

[sample recipe for classroom presentation to young kids]

1/2 cup butter	4 tsp. vanilla
80 big marshmallows	10 cups Rice Krispies

You are going to cook! We will help to make the Marshmallow Treats.

Here is how. Have fun!
But first: Are your hands clean?
Are both hands clean?
Do you have *clean* hands?

Now the cooks are ready. Let's begin:

1. Put a little butter in the 2 pans. Get it all over the insides of the 2 pans.
2. Put the Rice Krispies into the cup. Then put them into the big bowl. Do this 10 times, back and forth.
3. Put the butter into the big pot.
4. Put the vanilla into the teaspoon. Now put it in the pot, too.
5. Do this 4 times.
6. Turn on the stove. Melt the butter in the pot.
7. Put the marshmallows into the pot with the butter.
8. Get some spoons. Stir the butter and marshmallows.
   Stir and stir and stir.
   Stir until it all melts.
9. Turn off the stove.
10. Put the Rice Krispies into the the big pot too.
    Stir it all around in the big pan. Stir *fast!*
11. Now put it all into the two pans. Put a little butter on your hands. Press down on the Rice Krispies.
12. Soon we will eat!

See if you like it. Is it good? Was it fun to make these Marshamallow Treats?

- *September Recipes*

*Apple Balls

1/2 cup melted butter	1 tsp. nutmeg
1 cup honey	2 cups grated apple
3 cups oatmeal	1 cup finely chopped nuts
1 tsp. cinnamon	

Boil honey, butter and apple one minute. Mix oats with spices. Pour into apple mixture. Add nuts. Mix well. Roll into small balls. Let stand a bit before eating.

Bread Baked in a Bowl

This recipe was used in colonial times when the bowl was placed by an open fire. Because it is a soft, light bread it has become known as "spoonbread."

2-1/2 cups boiling water	2 egg yolks, beaten
2 cups corn meal	1-3/4 cups milk
1-1/2 tsp. salt	3 Tbsp. melted shortening
1 Tbsp. sugar	2 egg whites, beaten
2 tsp. baking powder	

Add boiling water slowly to corn meal, stirring constantly. Then let stand until cool.

Mix salt, sugar and baking powder with beaten egg yolks; add milk.

Add milk mixture to corn meal. Beat well.

Add melted shortening and blend; then fold in beaten egg whites.

Pour into 2-quart greased baking dish.

---

*Asterisk in *front* of recipe title indicates *no-bake* recipes, no oven required.

Bake in preheated oven at 375°-400° for about 40 minutes until it is good and crusty. Serve immediately by heaping spoonfuls (this bread is eaten warm with butter and honey or maple syrup).

*Peanut Butter Logs
(30 pieces)

1-1/2 cups peanut butter

1-1/2 cups raisins

6 Tbsp. honey

7-1/2 Tbsp. dry milk (10-1/2 Tbsp. instant dry milk): more as needed

Blend peanut butter and honey. Work in powdered milk until dough is stiff. Knead in raisins. Roll into 1″ × 10″ long logs. Chill, and slice.

*Navajo Fry Bread:
(traditional bread of Navajo Indians)

2 cups all-purpose flour	1 Tbsp. lard
1/4 cup instant nonfat dry milk powder	3/4 cup warm water
2 tsp. baking powder	Cooking oil for deep-fat
1 tsp. salt	frying

Stir together flour, nonfat dry milk powder, baking powder, and salt.

Cut in lard until mixture resembles coarse crumbs. Stir in water.

Turn out onto floured surface; knead to form a smooth ball, 10-12 strokes. Divide dough into eight balls.

Cover; let rest 10 minutes.

On floured surface, roll each ball to a 6-inch circle. (With finger, make a hole in center of each.)

Teacher fries, one at a time, in deep hot fat (400°) till golden brown, about 1-1/2 minutes, turning once.

Watch children around hot oil.

Drain bread on paper toweling.

(Divide bread into pieces as recipe makes 8.) Serve with honey.

• *October Recipes*

Stina's Apple Cake
(an eggless recipe)

2 apples, peeled and sliced	3/4 cup honey
2 tsp. cinnamon	1/2 cup buttermilk
2 cups whole wheat pastry flour or	2 tsp. vanilla
unbleached flour	(sugar)
1 tsp. baking soda	(whipped cream)
1/2 cup butter	

Mix apples with cinnamon. Mix flour, baking soda. Then cut butter into flour until butter is reduced to small, evenly mixed pieces.

Make a well in the center and put in honey, buttermilk and vanilla.

Stir into flour mixture. Stir a bit.

Butter a 9-inch pan. Pour in some batter. Layer apples, add more batter. Continue in this way, ending with batter on top.

Bake at 350° for 35-40 minutes: until center is firm. The cake is especially good with whipped cream frosting.

*Jessica's Specialty

Shredded coconut	sunflower seeds
carob chips	granola
mixed nuts: e.g. cashews,	currants
pecans, walnuts	sesame seeds

Mix together. Good "on the trail" or sprinkled on frozen yogurt.

*Potato Chips

Invented in the 1920s by George Crum, an American Indian and chef at a hotel in Saratoga Springs, New York.

vegetable peeler	4 big potatoes*
paper towels	oil
slotted spoon	salt
big pot	
paper bag	

Peel, rinse, and *dry* potatoes. Slice (with a sharp vegetable peeler.) Make wide THIN slices and place on paper towels. *Dry.*

Put 1 inch of oil in a wide pot. Put over medium heat.

When oil is hot, put potato slices, into the pot one at a time until the surface of oil is almost covered. *Watch children carefully.*

In 30-45 seconds, remove slices using a slotted spoon. Place chips on paper towels. Cool.

Put chips in a paper bag and shake salt over them. Shake bag.

*Quick Caramel Popcorn Balls

120 Kraft caramels

8 Tbsp. water

8 quarts popped corn, salted

Melt caramels with water in a double boiler or in a pan over low heat. Stir until sauce is smooth.

Pour over popcorn. Toss until corn is well-coated.

With slightly moistened hands form mixture into balls (makes 24).

---

*increase number according to size of group

• *November Recipes*

Beef Jerky

3 lbs. flank steak (frozen: for easier slicing)
Pepper
Salt
(1/2 tsp. Liquid Smoke)

Slice the meat very thin across the grain. Remove all fat. Salt meat generously, adding just a dab of Liquid Smoke to one side before salting. Place strips layer upon layer in a large crock and pepper each layer as you complete it. Place a plate and a weight on top of meat. Let stand overnight or at least for six hours.

Stretch strips of meat across oven racks (pieces of meat touch, but don't overlap). Upper rack should be at least 4 inches from top of oven, and lower rack at least 4 inches from bottom of oven.

Set oven at 150° and dry meat for 11 hours, overnight.

Apple Pandowdy

The pioneer homemaker would have passed rich, thick cream around with the following recipe, as it was considered a very special company dessert.

5 cups apples, peeled, cored and sliced
1/2 cup firmly packed brown sugar
1/4 tsp. cinnamon
1/4 tsp. nutmeg

Place apples in a greased 2-quart baking dish. Mix brown sugar with spices and sprinkle on top of apples. Toss lightly and bake uncovered at 350° for 30 minutes, stirring once or twice.

1-1/4 cups flour	2/3 cup butter
1-1/2 tsp. baking powder	1/3 cup sugar
1/4 tsp. salt	1 egg
pinch nutmeg	1/2 cup milk

About 10 minutes before apples are done, cream butter and sugar until fluffy, then beat in egg.

Sift flour with dry ingredients and add alternately with milk to creamed mixture; continue mixing until well blended.

Spread batter evenly over the apples and continue baking uncovered for about 40 minutes, or until topping is nicely browned and begins to pull away from the sides of the dish.

Serve in bowls with whipped cream.

Cranberry Leather

2 pounds fresh cranberries   1 tsp. cinnamon

1/4 tsp. cloves   4 tsp. finely grated orange peel

1 small can frozen orange juice, undiluted

1/2 to 1-1/2 cup sugar (honey) depending on tartness desired

Wash cranberries and cook on low heat with orange juice till cranberries pop, about 20 minutes. Add sugar and spices and puree in blender.

Pour onto 2 large cookie sheets lined with plastic wrap. Spread very thin.

Dry in 150° oven on two racks. Takes about 8 hours.

[NOTE: Sheets may also be left in broiler tray of gas stove, beneath pilot light and leather will form overnight. Then Cranberry Leather may be rolled in plastic wrap and stored in refrigerator (over a weekend or longer).]

Makes four rolls or 20 pieces.

Strawberry Leather

10 cups halved strawberries

1/2 cup sugar or honey

Place strawberries, one cup at a time, in blender. Puree strawberries until smooth. Stir in sugar or honey.

Line two 15-1/2" × 10-1/2" × 1" jelly roll pans with plastic wrap. Secure edges with tape. Spread fruit puree evenly in pans.

Place in 150° oven to dry. Leave oven door ajar approximately four inches. Place candy thermometer in back of oven. Check temperature periodically to be sure it is correct. If necessary, turn oven off for a while to reduce temperature. Rotate pans every two hours or so. The leather is dry when the surface is no longer sticky. (Drying time is 6-12 hours.)

When dry, remove from oven. Let cool completely.

Leathers can be stored at room temperature for 1 month, in the refrigerator for 3 months, and in a freezer for 1 year.

Apricot, Plum, Peach, or Nectarine Leather

Wash and cut up 6 pounds fresh fruit. Remove pits. (No need to peel fruit.) Proceed as above.

- *December Recipes*

*Egg Nog

12 eggs	12 cups COLD milk
1 cup honey	1 Tbsp. vanilla
3/4 tsp. salt	grated nutmeg

Beat eggs thoroughly. Then beat milk into eggs. Add honey and salt. Beat again. Add vanilla. Sprinkle with (freshly) grated nutmeg. Adjust flavoring to taste. Serves up to 30 children.

*White Christmas Pretzels

8 oz. white chocolate (breakaway kind sold in candy stores)

2 Tbsp. vegetable shortening or butter

36 big twisted pretzels

red and green sugar or finely chopped nuts (for decoration)

Put chocolate and shortening in double boiler over very hot water. Stir until smooth.

Children dip pretzels into chocolate and remove with a fork, draining off excess chocolate. Then pretzels are put on unoiled cooky sheet and sprinkled with nuts or red and green sugar.

Let pretzels stand until coating is firm.

Fruitarian Plum Pudding

An extravagant recipe with an extraordinary flavor.

1 cup figs, chopped	1/2 cup shelled Brazil nuts
1 cup bread crumbs	2 lemons: juice and grated rind
1/2 cup seedless raisins	3 eggs
1/2 cup currants	1/2 cup brown sugar
1/2 cup candied fruit peel	1/2 cup honey
1 cup blanched almonds	3 tart apples
1/2 cup pine nuts	pinch of salt
1/2 cup butter	
1 tsp. allspice (freshly ground in mortar)	

Core, peel, and chop apples. Chop nuts and fruit peel. Combine all ingredients *except* eggs.

Beat eggs and fold into mixture. Fill a mold (round stainless steel bowl) two-thirds with pudding. Cover with oiled cloth.

Set on wire rack in big pot with boiling water halfway up mold. Boil 3 hours.

Unmold and serve with vanilla ice cream, whipped cream or plain cream.

[NOTE: (It may be best to serve very small pieces initially as many children will not be familiar with flavor of plum pudding.)]

Mrs. Andrés Martinez' Recipe for Biscochitos*
(a traditional Christmas cookie from New Mexico)

6 cups sifted flour	1/2 cup sugar
3 tsp. baking powder	2 eggs
1 tsp. salt	

2 cups pure lard (obtain, if possible, from organic meat market)

3 tsp. anise seed, bruised in a mortar

1/4 cup orange juice (sweet wine, traditionally)

---

*pronounced: bees-ko-chee-tos

Sift flour, baking powder, and salt together.

In separate bowl, cream lard and sugar. Add flour mixture to lard mixture.

Mix anise seed and eggs until fluffy. Then add to flour and lard mixture.

Add orange juice (or sweet wine) until dough holds together.

Dough should be as firm as biscuit dough.

Preheat oven to 400°. Roll out dough 1/4 inch thick. Cut into shapes. Sprinkle with mixture of 1/2 cup sugar and 1 Tbsp cinnamon.

Bake 10-15 minutes.

- *January Recipes*

Fortune Cookies

This is a unique treat that can be made for or with children who can invent some wonderful, original fortunes.

1/4 cup flour	2 Tbsp. cooking oil
2 Tbsp. brown sugar	1 egg white, beaten until stiff
1 Tbsp. cornstarch	1/4 tsp. vanilla or lemon flavoring
a dash of salt	3 Tbsp. water

8-10 paper "fortune" strips, either typed out, hand-printed or assembled from magazine letters

Combine flour, sugar, cornstarch and salt. Stir in oil and fold in egg white until mixture is smooth. Add flavoring and water and mix well.

In a small skillet, an electric fry pan (medium heat) or on a lightly greased griddle, pour one tablespoon of batter, spreading it to a 3-inch circle. Cook for four minutes or till lightly browned, turn with a spatula and cook for one more minute. Batter will turn from beige to brown. Remove from griddle and quickly place "fortune" paper in the center of the circle. Fold in half over the edge of a glass, and then in half again. Hold for a few seconds until cool, then place in an empty egg carton to help cookie keep its shape. You will improve with practice.

This recipe makes 8-10 fortune cookies. If they do not seem crisp enough for you, toast them in the oven at 300° for 10 minutes, or just let them "sit around" a few days.

Triple recipe for classroom use.

[NOTE: This recipe is from *The Taming of the C.A.N.D.Y. Monster (Continuously Advertised Nutritionally Deficient Yummies)* by Vicki Lansky which is available for $5.00 from Ms. Lansky, 16648 Meadowbrook Lane, Wayzata, MN 55391. Also available is her other equally good cookbook, *Feed Me, I'm Yours*, $4.50.]

*Won-Tons
(about 60)

Buy a package of Won-Ton skins, wrappers. A pound of skins (about 60) costs about a dollar.

3/4 pound ground meat	5 tsp. soy sauce
3 white scallions, minced	3 tsp. orange juice*
1-1/2 tsp. cornstarch	3 Tbsp. parsley, minced
1 carrot, finely grated	

Mix all ingredients and knead well. Make into penny-sized balls. Place just off center in won ton square. Moisten edges of dough with water. Fold skin over into triangular shape and seal edges.

Deep fry in an electric frying pan or a wok. *Watch children around hot oil.* Drain won tons on paper towels. Serve hot with catsup or mustard.

*Early American Catsup

8 ripe tomatoes	allspice, cinnamon, celery
2 small onions, peeled	salt, paprika, dry mustard
2/3 cup sugar (honey)	several sterilized long neck bottles
1 red or green bell pepper	olive oil
juice of 1 lemon	ribbon
1/2 tsp. each: salt, cloves,	plastic wrap

Carefully drop tomatoes into pot of boiling water. Turn off heat. In three minutes remove tomatoes (this procedure may be done prior

---

*wine is the classic ingredient

to class). Peel and core. Chop onions and pepper and tomatoes. Put these vegetables into a blender. Run at medium speed for 15 seconds.

Add all ingredients *except* lemon juice. Taste and adjust flavors if necessary.

Cook over low heat, uncovered. Stir every quarter hour. Cook for 2-3 hours until sauce is the correct thickness.

Now stir in lemon juice and cook four minutes longer.

Cool. Pour into sterilized jars. Olive oil poured into neck of bottle will prevent fermentation. Cover jar mouth with plastic wrap and secure with ribbon. Refrigerate. Good with tiny meat balls, won tons and French fries.

*No-Bake Chocolate Dream Cookies

4 Tbsp. cocoa	1 tsp. vanilla
2 cups sugar (sifted unrefined)	1/2 cup milk
1 stick margarine	1 cup shredded coconut
1/2 tsp. salt	3 cups oatmeal

Stir cocoa, sugar, margarine, salt, and milk together in a saucepan until it reaches a rolling boil.

Remove from heat and add vanilla, oatmeal and coconut. Stir. Drop on waxed paper by teaspoonful.

● *February Recipes*

*Make Believe Fudge

1 cup powdered milk

1 cup shredded coconut

1 cup carob powder*

1/2 cup water (enough to make it all stick together)

1/2 cup chopped walnuts or pecans

---

*Carob is the bean of an evergreen tree of the Mediterranean area. As it is powdered, it takes on its sweet flavor, that's why this candy does not have to be sweetened. Carob powder can be bought in a health food store.

Mix together the powdered milk, coconut, and carob powder.

Add the water, a little at a time, and mix together until it is a consistency that can be easily worked.

Roll into balls with the palms of the hands.

Some balls can be rolled in additional coconut or finely chopped nuts.

*Fried Tofu Balls

1 pound tofu, drained	1 egg
2 Tbsp. grated carrot	2 tsp. shoyu
1 tsp. grated ginger root	2 Tbsp. finely chopped onion
3 Tbsp. cornstarch	

Wrap tofu in clean, dry cloth and pat to remove excess water.

Put all ingredients into a mixing bowl and beat with rotary beater at medium speed for 3 minutes.

1/2 cup flour	cooking oil
1/2 cup cornstarch	

Mix flour and cornstarch together.

Put flour-cornstarch mixture on a plate. Drop one teaspoon of tofu mixture into the flour-cornstarch mixture and roll once or twice. Try not to get too much flour around the ball.

Deep fry in hot cooking oil (375°) for 5 minutes or until golden brown. *Watch children around hot oil.* Makes 30 balls.

Serve with shoyu and (hot) mustard.

*Homemade Peanut Butter
(2 cups)

4 cups dry-roasted peanuts	2 tsp. salt
2 Tbsp. vegetable oil	soda crackers

Remove shells and skins from enough roasted peanuts to make 4 cups.

Preheat oven to 350°. Bake peanuts 15 minutes. Stir every 5 minutes.

Put nuts, one cup at a time, into blender. Run at medium speed for 10 seconds, then scrape sides of blender and run again for 5 seconds.

Add vegetable oil if blender seems to be working too hard.

Continue to scrape blender sides and run blender for 5-second periods until peanut butter is formed.

Add salt to taste. Serve with soda crackers.

*Junket Pudding

A pudding with no artificial flavors or colors

candy thermometer	2 tsp. vanilla
4 cups milk	2 Junket rennet tablets
1-1/3 cup powdered milk	(sold in grocery and drug stores)
1/2 cup brown sugar	

Put milk, powdered milk and sugar in a pan. Use candy thermometer: heat mixture to 110° F.

Dissolve rennet tablets in 2 Tbsp. of water. Stir into warm milk for about 5 seconds (no longer than 10 seconds).

Pour into plastic cups. *Do not move* cups for 10 minutes, until pudding is set up.

Refrigerate if you like. Eat plain or with whipped cream.

[VARIATION: For chocolate pudding, add 1/3 cup sifted cocoa or carob to powdered milk before adding to milk. Use a wire whisk to achieve smooth mixture.]

● *March Recipes*

*Grape Finger-Gelatin

3 envelopes unflavored gelatin

1 can (12 oz.) frozen grape (apple) juice concentrate, thawed

1-1/2 cups water

Soften gelatin in grape juice. In saucepan, bring the water to boiling, add the grape juice-gelatin mixture and stir until gelatin dissolves.

Remove from heat, pour liquid into a lightly oiled, 9 x 13-inch pan and chill.

Cut into squares when firm. Refrigerate in a covered container.

This is a good field trip snack. It can go unrefrigerated for four hours under normal conditions.

[VARIATION: Jello Fingers. Dissolve 4 envelopes of unflavored gelatin in 2 cups of boiling water. Stir in 1-16 oz. can of frozen unsweetened pear-apple juice, thawed, and 1 cup of beaten yogurt. Refrigerate until firm. Cut into long rectangles.]

Hot Cross Buns
(An Easter tradition in Great Britain)

[NOTE: This is an all day project]

1-1/2 cups milk	4 eggs
2/3 cup sugar	2-1/2 tsp. ground cinnamon
1 tsp. salt	2 egg yolks
1/2 cup (1 stick) butter	4 Tbsp. cold water
1/2 cup warm water (105° - 115°)	confectioner's sugar frosting
2 pkg. or cakes yeast, active dry or compressed	1-1/2 cups raisins
7-1/2 cups unsifted all-purpose flour (app.)	

Scald milk; stir in sugar, salt and butter. Cool to lukewarm.

Measure warm water into a large, warm bowl. Sprinkle or crumble in yeast; stir until dissolved.

Stir in lukewarm milk mixture, eggs, cinnamon, and 5 cups flour. Beat until smooth. Add enough additional flour to form a soft dough.

Turn out onto lightly floured board and knead until smooth and elastic, about 10 minutes. Place in greased bowl and turn once to grease top. Cover and let rise in warm place, free from draft, until doubled in bulk (about one hour).

Punch down dough and turn out onto lightly floured board; knead in raisins. Divide dough into 36 equal pieces. Form each piece into a ball; arrange in four greased 8-inch cake pans.

Combine egg yolks and water and brush over tops of buns. Cover; let rise in a warm place, free from draft, until doubled in bulk (about one hour).

Snip a shallow cross in the top of each bun with sharp scissors, or slash with a paring knife. Bake in a moderate oven (375°) for 20-25 minutes or until lightly browned.

Set buns on rack to cool slightly. Fill in crosses with frosting, made by adding enough cream to one cup sifted confectioner's sugar to make it of spreading consistency. Add a drop or two of vanilla or lemon extract.

Serve buns while still warm and fragrant.

*Fried Cornmeal Mush

An early American favorite.

1 tsp. salt	flour
6 cups water	(maple-flavored syrup or jelly)
1 cup yellow cornmeal	(butter)
bacon fat	

Bring water and salt to a boil in top of double boiler. Gradually add cornmeal, stirring constantly. Cook until thick. Continue to cook, covered, over boiling water for one-half hour.

Pour into buttered bread pan and refrigerate.

Carefully slice, lightly coat with flour, and fry in bacon fat or butter until brown on both sides. Serve with butter, syrup or jam.

Bagels (or Pretzels)
(by Howard Craig)

You may want to have the class involved with just the shaping, boiling and baking parts of this recipe.

3 Tbsp. sugar   1 Tbsp. baking soda

4 tsp. salt   1 Tbsp. salt

3-1/2 quarts boiling water

1 pkg. active dry (1 Tbsp.) or compressed yeast

2 cups warm water (lukewarm for compressed yeast)

6-1/2 cups regular all-purpose flour (unsifted)

1/2 cup instant toasted onions (optional)

1/4 cup poppy seed or caraway seed (mm good!)

In a large bowl, dissolve yeast in the 2 cups water. Use a wooden spoon to stir in sugar and the 4 teaspoons salt. Gradually stir in 5 cups of the flour; add onion and seeds if used.

Stir in 1 more cup flour to make a soft dough.

Turn out dough onto a board spread with part of remaining 1/2 cup flour and knead dough for about 10 minutes or until it is firm and non-sticky; add more flour if necessary.

Let dough rise in a greased bowl with a moist towel over it until doubled, about 1-1/2 hours.

Punch down dough and knead on a lightly floured board until smooth. To make ring-shaped bagels, cut off 1-1/2-inch lumps of dough. Roll dough between palms to make ropes about 6 inches long. Wrap each rope around three fingers to form a ring; moisten ends and squeeze to seal. Let rise 15 minutes.

Dissolve the 1 tablespoon salt in the boiling water. Drop in about four rolls at a time and boil for three minutes, turning rolls often. With a slotted spoon, remove rolls and arrange on a greased baking sheet.

Bake in a 425° oven for about 25 minutes or until crust is browned. Serve warm or reheat. Makes 12 bagels. Children may each have a half.

To make pretzels, roll out long thin rope of dough. Bend and twist to form this shape:

Moisten ends and press on dough beneath to seal pretzel into shape. Place in a large pot of boiling water to which 1 Tbsp. baking soda has been added. When pretzels rise to top of water, remove with slotted spoon. Place on oiled cookie sheet. Brush with beaten egg yolk and sprinkle with coarse salt. Bake in 400° oven for 15 minutes or until browned.

● *April Recipes*

Granola Crunch

Makes 12 cups. Requires lots of ingredients; ask for some volunteers to bring in some of the ingredients.

1/2 cup honey	1 pkg dried fruits, cut up
1/3 cup brown sugar	1 cup wheat germ
1/2 cup instant dry milk	1/2 cup vegetable oil
4-1/2 cups Quaker Oats	1/2 tsp. salt

1 pkg dried dates, snipped into small bits

1/2 cup peanut butter (with no preservatives)

(1-1/2 cups dry-roast peanuts, chopped cashews or almonds)

Heat honey, oil, sugar and peanut butter to a simmer. Heat oven to 300°.

Combine rest of the ingredients. Pour honey mixture over dry ingredients. Mix well.

Spoon onto cooky sheet. Bake for one hour at very low heat.

Stir every 20 minutes. Remove from oven. Transfer granola to cake pans and pack down by placing weight on top of granola. Cool. (Thanks, Dixie.)

*Mother's Scandinavian Hot Iron Cookies

These waffle/patty irons are sold in specialty kitchen shops. Makes 60 cookies.

1 cup pastry flour	1/2 cup water
1/2 cup Pet Milk	powdered sugar

1 tsp. sugar	(2 pounds shortening for frying)
1 tsp. salt	(paper towels)
1 egg, unbeaten	(electric frying pan)

Mix milk, water, sugar, salt and egg together. Stir slowly into flour, then beat smooth. Batter should be thick as cream.

Heat iron by dipping for about 10 seconds into 365° heated oil. *Watch children carefully around hot oil.* Remove iron from oil and dip into batter evenly *just up to top* of iron. Dip iron into hot oil.

[CAUTION: Don't get batter over top of iron.]

As soon as batter begins to expand away from iron, use fork to lift cookie off iron and back into oil. When cookie is brown on one side, turn it over and brown it on the other. Lift out cookie and drain on paper towel. Sprinkle with sifted powdered sugar.

*Homemade Cheese

Makes two pounds (4 cups).

candy thermometer	salt, parsley
4 quarts whole(RAW) milk	Fines Herbes
1 quart cultured buttermilk	wheat crackers
1 tsp. salt	

In heavy 8-quart pan combine milk and buttermilk. Attach candy thermometer to side of pan. Place over medium heat. Stir occasionally. Once temperature reaches 170°, reduce heat to low. *Keep temperature between 170° and 175°.*

Line colander with four thicknesses of cheesecloth, previously wrung out in cold water. Set colander inside a bowl and place beside pan of milk. As white curds separate from whey, use slotted spoon to scoop curds into colander.

Once all floating curds are removed, place colander in sink. Pour in any curds left in pan. Discard whey left in bowl or better yet, here the children each sample a bit of the whey. Let curd drain 2-3 hours.

Place cheese in a bowl. Use fork to mix in salt. (Finely chopped parsley or Fines Herbes may also be mixed in.) Refrigerate until served. Serve with wheat crackers.

*Berry Ices

A milk-free treat.

8 cups berries, fresh or frozen   3 cups water

3 cups honey (or sugar)   1 cup orange or lemon juice

Puree fruit in blender. Heat water and honey to form a clear syrup and pour into blender.

Carefully mix fruit, juice, and syrup completely. This may take several blender batches.

Freeze in small paper cups as popsicles.

● *May Recipes*

*Keep-On-Hand Snow Cones

Freeze orange juice (or any other fruit juice) in ice-cube trays. Pop frozen juice cubes into a plastic bag to store.

Put three to six of these cubes at a time in blender. Turn blender on and off until cubes reach snowy consistency. Pile into a paper cup to serve.

The whole batch can be blended at once and stored in the freezer and it will keep its consistency.

Adding a little water makes it a "slush." Even those who don't usually care for orange juice will like it this way.

*Puffed Brown Rice
(Makes 3 quarts)

1-1/2 quarts soy or vegetable oil

6 cups cooked brown rice

Cook rice so grains are separate and dry. Spread out rice on cookie sheets, let dry 3 days. Turn kernels once in a while.

Heat oil to 360° in deep fryer/cooker.

Put 1/4 cup rice at a time into a sieve and lower into hot oil. *Keep children well back from the hot oil.*

Fry rice for 20 seconds, or until lightly golden. Drain on paper toweling.

Cheddar Cheese Sticks

3 sticks of butter, softened and heated with

2 pounds of sharp cheddar cheese, grated

Mix until doughy, thick. Add:

1/2 tsp. salt	2 cups whole wheat flour
1 tsp. cayenne (optional)	sesame seeds

Put mixture in a cookie press. Squeeze out into 3″ strips or press out into thin twisted shapes or sticks. Sprinkle with sesame seeds. Bake at 300° for 15 minutes or until golden brown. Shapes or sticks should be crispy.

Granola Dream Bars
(Makes 24 bars)

2 eggs	1/4 tsp. salt
3/4 cup Granola (cereal)	1 cup flaked coconut
1 tsp. baking powder	1/4 cup raisins

1 cup plus 3 tablespoons unbleached flour

1-1/2 cups packed brown sugar (honey doesn't work in this recipe)

1/2 cup butter or margarine, softened

1 tsp. frozen orange-juice concentrate, thawed

In bowl combine 1 cup flour and 1/2 cup brown sugar. Work in butter with fork. Press mixture into 13×9×2-inch baking pan and bake in preheated 350° oven for 10 minutes. Cool on rack.

Beat eggs until light; beat in remaining one cup sugar until well blended. Stir in juice concentrate. Stir in Granola and remaining three tablespoons flour, the baking powder and salt until well blended. Stir in coconut and raisins and spread over crust.

Return to oven and bake 25 minutes. Cool slightly before cutting into bars.

- ## *June Recipes*

*Yogi Tea

4 3-inch long cinammon sticks	5 allspice berries
10 whole cloves	10 cardamom seeds
1 small fresh ginger root (peeled)	1 gallon water

Simmer over low heat for one hour (or more). May be mixed with milk, honey, apple, orange, or lemon juice.

*Peanutty Pops
(Makes 24 pops)

4 envelopes Knox Unflavored Gelatine	4 cups boiling water
	4 cups peanut butter
2 cups sugar (honey)	4 cups chocolate milk

In medium bowl, mix Knox Unflavored Gelatine and sugar; add boiling water and stir until gelatine is completely dissolved.

With wire whip or rotary beater, blend in peanut butter; stir in milk.

Pour into 5-ounce paper cups and place in freezer until partially frozen. Insert wooden ice cream sticks or plastic spoons and freeze until firm.

[VARIATIONS: Stir in small carob chips or finely chopped banana just before inserting stick.]

*Uncooked Berry Jam

Mix 4 cups berries and 2 cups sugar in an electric mixer until juices run and berries are a pulp.

Berries absorb sugar, which becomes a preservative. Pack jam in sterilized jars.

*Sun-Cooked Berry Preserves

You'll need *lots* of sunshine to make this recipe which is over 150 years old.

2 Tbsp. lemon juice

4 cups sugar

1 quart strawberries (hulled)

Combine all ingredients. Heat slowly to boiling point and cook rapidly for 8 minutes, slowly stirring.

Pour berry mixture into shallow container, cover with cheesecloth. (You can use plastic wrap instead, propping up one side of wrap to permit some evaporation.)

Place trays in sunshine. Occasionally stir the mixture gently. Bring inside at night. At the end of 2 to 3 days, preserves will be thickened. Pack in sterilized jars. Makes about 4-1/2 pints.

Krazy Kake

A wonderful way to wrap up the year!

1 cup sugar (unrefined)   **6 Tbsp. vegetable oil**

3 Tbsp. unsweetened cocoa   **1 Tbsp. vinegar**

1 tsp. baking soda   **1Tbsp. pure vanilla extract**

1 tsp. baking powder   **1 cup cold water**

1/2 tsp. salt

4 1/4 ounce pure milk-chocolate candy bars

1-1/3 cups unsifted all-purpose flour

Preheat oven to 375° F. Lightly grease a 9x9x2-inch square pan.

In sifter, combine flour, sugar, cocoa, baking soda, baking powder and salt. Sift dry ingredients directly into prepared pan.

Make 3 evenly spaced holes in dry ingredients. Into the first, pour vegetable oil; into the second, pour vinegar; into the third, vanilla.

Pour cold water over all. Stir thoroughly with fork or wire whisk until completely blended. Don't forget the corners of the pan!

Bake 35-45 minutes, or until a cake tester poked in the center comes out clean.

Set cake pan on rack. Immediately place chocolate bars on hot cake. Allow to soften for one minute, then spread with spatula to frost top of cake. Let cool completely, then cut into squares.

RECIPES FOR ART SUPPLIES

Modeling Materials

Baked Dough Ornaments

Makes 30 small inedible objects. This recipe cannot be halved or doubled.

4 cups flour

1 cup salt

1 cup water (or more as needed)

Preheat oven to 350°. Mix 4 cups flour with 1 cup salt. Make a hole in center of flour-salt mixture and pour in 1 cup water. Mix thoroughly with hands or fork, adding more water if necessary (dough should be smooth and satiny and neither crumbly nor sticky). Form into balls and store in plastic bags to prevent dough from drying out.

On surface covered with waxed paper, roll out one ball at a time to 1/2" thickness. Cut out shapes. Put away excess dough, knead into ball and roll out again. (Make a hole centered at top of each ornament and insert a piece of copper wire for hanger.)

Bake ornaments in 350° oven 45 minutes to 1-1/2 hours or until pin inserted in dough comes out clean. Remove from oven and cool on rack.

Use a small brush to paint details or designs with thinned acrylic paints. (Raised trim can be made by squeezing paint onto ornament through the art tip on the end of special acrylic paint tubes.) Allow paint to dry. Brush on two or three coats of polyurethane or varnish for a protective finish and let dry.

Natural Clay

Dig up some natural clay. Leave it in the open, in dry weather, until clay is dried. Then break it up and take out impurities. Mix remaining clay with a lot of water and put through a sturdy wire sieve to eliminate any unwanted materials. Let mixture stand. Once clear water rises to the top, carefully pour it off. Let the pure clay dry sufficiently for children to handle and shape.

Cooked Salt

Mix two parts of salt to one part of cornstarch and one part of water. Cook over low heat, *stirring* vigorously, until material is stiff. Ready to mold when cool. Dries in 36 hours if small in size. Eight boxes of salt and proportionate amounts of cornstarch and water make enough material for 32 small objects.

Favorite Play Dough

#1

2 cups flour	2 cups water
1 cup salt	2 Tbsp. salad oil
4 tsp. cream of tartar	food coloring

Cook over medium heat until soft, lumpy ball forms. It happens quickly!

Knead for a few minutes until dough is smooth.

Store in airtight container. Dough can be frozen and refrozen several times, and it lasts for weeks when kept in a plastic bag.

#2

The following recipe will make six good-sized balls. Stir together and knead:

4 cups flour	8 Tbsp. salad oil
1 cup salt	7-8 Tbsp. water

Add food coloring if desired. Keep covered when not in use.

Colored Beeswax (excellent for modeling tiny things), as well as beeswax crayons, is available from:

St. George Book Service
P.O. Box 226
Spring Valley, NY 10977

Sawdust Modeling Mixture

Mix 1 cup sawdust (*not* redwood) with 1/2 cup wallpaper paste. Add just enough water to make a soft putty. Squeeze and pat modeling mixture onto wire construction.

Another modeling mixture can also be made by mixing 1 cup sawdust (*not* redwood) and 1 cup plaster of Paris with very thin glue.

Snow Paint or Clay

2 cups Ivory *Flakes* (*not* Ivory Soap, which is granular)

water to moisten

(food coloring)

Whip soap*flakes*, water (and food coloring) until it's the right consistency to mold. This "clay" dries slowly. Children can mold objects° or they may apply it to a sheet of dark blue, purple or black construction paper and form a 3-D painting, or use it to frost window panes or bulletin board letters.

Finger Paint

Mix together 1 cup cornstarch and 3/4 cups cold water. Soak 1 envelope unflavored gelatine in 1/4 cup of cold water. Stir 2 cups hot

---

°Igloos, snowmen, mountains (with ski-runs) or polar bears, ermine, rabbits, owls, seals, weasels: all in their winter coats

water into the cornstarch. Cook and stir until mixture is clear and boiling. Remove from heat. Blend in gelatine. Then add 1/2 cup of Ivory *Flakes*. Stir until flakes are dissolved. Cool.

Divide into small covered containers. Add food coloring or dry tempera.

Glue Paint

Mix Elmer's Glue-all® with diluted tempera for shiny paint. (Sprinkle sawdust, fine sand or glitter on some areas of the painting.)

Egg Yolk Paint

Crack egg and separate the yolk from the white. Then grasp yolk between index finger and thumb, and let the yolk run into a small dish, discarding the thin yolk membrane sac that you are left holding. Mix powdered tempera (and a bit of water) with the yolk. Use this mixture to paint salt beads, dough ornaments, and Easter eggs. This paint gives vibrant, lovely colors.

Window Paint

Mix equal parts of Bon-Ami®, Alabastine (whiting) and dry tempera. Add water to form a creamy paste. Apply to window with small soft cloths. Washes off with water and a sponge.

Missionary Glue

1/2 cup flour	1/2 cup sugar
1-1/2 Tbsp. powdered alum	1/2 cup cold water

Stir ingredients in the top of a double boiler. When they are well-mixed, add 1-1/2 cups boiling water. Cook over boiling water, stirring constantly until mixture is clear. Add 15 drops of oil of cloves (sold at drug stores). Beat mixture with an electric beater until cooled.

Casein or "Milk" Glue

Pour a pint of skim milk into an enamel sauce pan and add 1 cup vinegar. Heat and stir until lumps are formed. Pour coagulated milk into a bowl. Cool. Discard excess water that forms, add 1/4 cup water and 1 teaspoon baking soda. This type of glue was used by the Egyptians thousands of years ago. Objects on which this glue was used have been found in tombs today, and the glue is still holding. Furniture makers of the Middle Ages also used it.

Crayon Scratch Board

tagboard	knitting needle
wax crayons	pin
India ink or poster paint	nail
brush	

Divide the tagboard into several irregular areas. Use crayons and color in each area with a solid heavy coat of any bright color. Don't leave any uncolored areas.

Cover the whole scratch board with a thick layer of a dark color of poster paint or India ink. Let dry. If any crayon shows through, use another coat of paint or ink.

Design is made by scraping off small parts of painted area. Children should experiment to achieve distinctive types of lines. Some areas of the board are left painted. (Final design would not follow underlying crayon areas.)

Fixative

At least three weeks before needed, mix 1/2 pint white shellac and 2 qts. denatured alcohol. Keep tightly covered. Shake well before using. Use as a spray to fix chalk or charcoal drawings.

[VARIATIONS: Substitute gum arabic (thinned in water to the consistency of thin mucilage) in place of denatured alcohol or mix two parts denatured alcohol to one part white shellac.]

Art Aids

• Collect empty roll-on deodorant bottles. Wash thoroughly and fill with poster paint. Let little kids have fun on big sheets of butcher paper, using large arm-swings as they apply paint.

- Cut down plastic starch bottles and wedge them into the paintholder on each easel. Plastic paint containers are, you will find, preferable to all others, as they do not weaken with time.

- Using a funnel, pour mixed poster paints into large plastic bleach bottles. This will greatly simplify storage and will reduce time spent in weekly preparation of paints.

- Tie a pencil by heavy yarn to each easel so that the children will be reminded to sign their paintings.

- Need classroom easels? Cut heavy cardboard boxes in half.

- Place a brick on table and put box easel over brick to ensure stability. Tape or thumbtack newsprint to slanting face of easel.

- Try to keep a bottle of ink eradicator and a tube of spot remover in your desk for classroom emergencies.

and now for....
An Afterword

    I do hope you'll write me about your impressions of The <u>New</u> Teacher's Almanack'— your ideas about teaching, your classroom successes- and frustrations. I really appreciate your letters and I've answered every one I've received. They've been enlightening and warming and very helpful to me.

    I want to say a special thanks to Gene and Alba for all the support and understanding they've shown through the months it took to finish this new edition!

    THANK YOU to MaryLou Denning for her fine learning Center ideas, to Carrie Vogel for many little-known facts and Yiddish proverbs, to Arlee Craig for the unbeatable bagel recipe and to Jack Gill for his dandy bird-feeder plans! And my thanks to Bev Graham for the Geologic Time chart and for his unfailing optimism about the value of good teaching!

    Please do drop me a line if you'd like*. I love hearing of and from you.

Warmest regards,
Dana Newmann

*(in care of the publisher)

Index of Activities